Saint John Chrysostom, Thomas William Allies, Mary Helen Allies

Leaves from St. John Chrysostom

Saint John Chrysostom, Thomas William Allies, Mary Helen Allies

Leaves from St. John Chrysostom

ISBN/EAN: 9783743329621

Manufactured in Europe, USA, Canada, Australia, Japa

Cover: Foto ©ninafisch / pixelio.de

Manufactured and distributed by brebook publishing software (www.brebook.com)

Saint John Chrysostom, Thomas William Allies, Mary Helen Allies

Leaves from St. John Chrysostom

CONTENTS.

PREFACE.—ST. JOHN CHRYSOSTOM.

	PAGE
Birth and Parentage,	1
Named Preacher at Antioch,	3
Archbishop of Constantinople,	5
State of Constantinople,	7
Enmity of Eudoxia,	9
Synod of the Oak,	10
Exile at Kucusus,	11
Judgment of Pope Innocent I.,	12
Comana,	13
His Death,	14
Translation of his Body,	15
Final Burial at St. Peter's,	16
Summary of his Works,	17

PART I.

THE KING'S HIGHWAY.

1. The Way, the Truth, and the Life,	23
2. Who is the Greater?	26
3. The First are Last and the Last First,	29
4. Variety of Human Lot,	34
5. Whence the Rich?	38

		PAGE
6. The Rich Young Man,	. . . . . .	41
7. Different Kinds of Friendship,	. . . .	46
8. The Buyers and Sellers in the Temple,	. .	49
9. The Voice of Good Deeds,	. . . . .	51
10. The Best Controversy,	. . . . .	55
11. The Tongue a Royal Power,	. . . .	63
12. Golden Vessels and Golden Hearts,	. . .	66
13. True Almsgiving,	. . . . . .	70
14. I was hungry and you gave Me to eat,	. .	73
15. The Archetype and the Type,	. . . .	77
16. The Weak Things of God,	. . . . .	83
17. The Secret of our Faith,	. . . . .	94
18. The Victory of our Faith,	. . . . .	100
19. Marriages as they were and as they are,	. .	105
20. 'Use a little Wine,'	. . . . . .	109
21. Possessing the Land,	. . . . . .	118
22. The Word of Praise,	. . . . . .	125
23. Sufferings of the Just,	. . . . .	130
24. The Folly of the Cross,	. . . . .	141
25. The Abode of the Humble,	. . . . .	148
26. The Prisoner of Jesus Christ,	. . . .	152
27. The Seed not vivified unless it dies,	. .	157
28. The Resurrection in Creation,	. . . .	163
29. Resurrection confirmed by Signs which followed,	.	169

PART II.

THE KING'S HOUSE.

1. 'Thou art Peter,'	. . . . . .	183
2. 'Peter rose up,'	. . . . . .	188
3. Built upon the Rock,	. . . . . .	189
4. The Priest a Man, not an Angel,	. . .	193
5. The Authority of the Priest,	. . . .	198
6. The Priest a Shepherd of Souls,	. . .	204
7. One Sacrifice,	. . . .	212
8. The New Pasch,	. . . . . .	217

		PAGE
9. The 'Eyes of Rome,'	. . . . . .	221
10. 'This is My Body,'	. . . . . .	228
11. The Union of the Holy Eucharist,	. . .	237
12. Bone of our Bone, Flesh of our Flesh,	. .	241
13. Remembrance of the Dead,	. . . .	248
14. The Departed at the Sacred Mysteries,	. .	252
15. The Tombs of the Martyrs,	. . . .	256
16. The Bodies of the Martyrs,	. . . .	259
17. The Tombs of the Servants,	. . .	266

PART III.

PERSONAL.

1. Letter to Pope Innocent, A.D. 404, ...	272
2. Letter to some Imprisoned Bishops and Priests (404),	282
3. To the Priests and Monks Nicholas, Theodotus, &c. (405), ...	283
4. To some Priests and Monks in Phœnicia (405), .	284
5. To Studius the Prefect of the City, on the Death of his Brother (404), ...	286
6. To Malchus on the Death of his Daughter, .	288
7. To Olympias. The Virginal Life, . . .	288
8. To Olympias. The Blessedness of Suffering, .	290
9. To Olympias (406), ...	293
10. To Pœanius. 'Glory be to God in all things,' .	295
11. Vanity of Vanities, ...	296

ERRATA.

Page 16, *for* "surrounded" *read* surrounds.
Page 21, *for* "Nirockl" *read* Nirschl.

ST. JOHN CHRYSOSTOM.

JOHN OF ANTIOCH was born about the year 347, of a noble family. His father, Secundus, held a high rank in the imperial army; he died early, and left a very young widow, in the bloom of age and beauty, and amply endowed with wealth. Many suitors sought to obtain the hand of St. Anthusa. She remained faithful to the memory of her husband, and devoted to the education of her only son. She brought him up in all the knowledge of the age and in strict piety, which she enforced by her example. St. Anthusa, amid all the perils of Antioch, guarded her son John with the same care which her contemporary, St. Monica, bestowed in the small circle of an African town on her Augustine. She was happier in one thing. The heathen charms of Antioch exerted no such power over her son John as the like seductive beauty of Carthage exerted over the young Augustine. The prayers and the care of St. Monica and St. Anthusa were equally zealous. In the one case, after the most terrible fall, lasting over a period of at least fourteen years, the African mother had the unspeakable joy of seeing her son's mind delivered from the most dangerous heresy of the day, and was allowed to die in the arms of the new-born Christian, who could share all her hopes of eternal life, which are recorded in the beautiful dialogue between mother and son preserved for us by that son, who was to be the greatest doctor of the Church. In the other case, the Antiochene parent to whom was applied that expression of the admiring heathen, 'See what mothers these Christians have,' had the still rarer gift of rearing a son who never fell, who pursued from beginning to end a holy life, who was crowned with a confessorship exceeding the glory of many martyrs, and whose least merit is that he was the greatest preacher of the Eastern Church, and gave to the language of Plato, eight hundred years after him, in its decline, a glory equal to that which the Athenian gave to it in its prime.

Two men—I know not if there be any others in all history—have had their personal name merged by posterity in the name which expressed their special qualities. As the son of Pepin is for ever Charlemagne, so John, the son of St. Anthusa, is for ever Chrysostom, the Golden Mouth. It is thus the world calls the one great and the other eloquent.

To return to the facts of John of Antioch's life. As he grew up he had lessons from the renowned heathen rhetorician Libanius. He studied philosophy, and distinguished himself, at twenty years of age, in preparation for the bar. Libanius considered him the best scholar he had, and even wished to be succeeded by him in his office.

But John speedily renounced this and all worldly renown. He practised a most strictly ascetic life, and gave himself up to the study of the Christian religion. He was a pupil of that Diodorus, afterwards bishop of Tarsus, who was then held in high repute as a Scripture commentator. He was also under St. Meletius, patriarch of Antioch. From him he received baptism in 369, at the age, therefore, of twenty-two years; and the minor order of Lector three years later. The bishops who met at Antioch in 373 designated him, with his friend Basil, for the episcopal dignity. In his humility he took flight to the anchorets who dwelt in the mountains near Antioch. With them he spent four years, and two years after that in a cavern, until his health failed, and he was obliged to return to Antioch. Here the patriarch Meletius made him a deacon in 380; and his successor Flavian gave him the priesthood in 386, in his fortieth year, and named him to be preacher in the cathedral.

Then during ten years the great see of the East wondered at the eloquence, the teaching, and the zeal of the greatest preacher it had known. In her sorest time of need he was at hand to comfort and support the city of his birth. When a great riot broke out, and led the citzens in their haste and anger to insult the statues of the emperor Theodosius and his wife, the most pious Flaccilla, and Antioch trembled lest this act of treason should be followed by summary destruction; when her patriarch Flavian hurried across the five hundred miles to Constantinople, that if possible he might soften the wrath of the emperor before the bolt was launched, St. Chrysostom preached some of his most famous sermons, those entitled, 'On the Statues'. He kept up the courage of the fainting people, and when Flavian returned with a pardon which left untouched the privileges of the city, the preacher shared with the patriarch the gratitude of those who were saved.

After ten years of incessant labours by the preacher, which form a large part of the writings preserved to us, the see of Constantinople fell vacant by the death of the patriarch Nectarius. Theodosius had died in 395, leaving the great eastern empire in the hands of his elder son Arcadius, scarcely out of his boyhood. The young emperor was unwilling to trust the see of his capital to any one of his clergy, and he listened to the advice given to him to call from Antioch the man whose genius was as great as his character was stainless. The great officer who carried out the imperial invitation, or command, at Antioch, was obliged to use artifice for the purpose of securing the preacher. His people would not knowingly have suffered him to leave them. He was taken out of the city under a plausible pretence. 'Asterius, count of the East, had orders to send for him and ask his company to a church without the city. Having got him into his carriage, he drove off with him to the first station on the high road to Constantinople, where imperial officers were in readiness to convey him thither.'[1] Thus he was carried across Asia with all possible speed. Upon his arrival at Constantinople he was chosen bishop with one voice, and consecrated on the 26th February, 398. His consecrator was Theophilus, patriarch of Alexandria, who very unwillingly performed this office. He had striven to get a certain priest who was devoted to himself appointed. His subsequent enmity to St. Chrysostom was a main cause of the banishment and death which befel the man whom he had consecrated.

Thus, at fifty years of age, St. Chrysostom was placed, not only without seeking for it, but against his wishes, upon that see which, through the residence of the emperor, was already become the most conspicuous of episcopal thrones in the East. From the moment that Constantine, sixty-seven years before, had made Byzantium Nova Roma, and founded, in fact, a new empire, all the ambitious spirits among the prelates of the East sought to seat themselves on that perilous height. This new centre of temporal power was from that time forth the centre of trouble, heresy, and disaster to the Church. Eusebius left his former see, Nicomedia,

[1] Card. Newman.

to possess it, and to be the emperor's bishop. One after another Arian heretics succeeded. In 379, when the small number of Catholics remaining in the new capital invited St. Gregory Nazienzen to come to their aid, he could only open in a private room a small church, which he called by the significant name of Anastasia, the Resurrection. In that year Theodosius was promoted by the young Grotian to share his throne, upon the destruction of his uncle Valens by the Goths. Valens had all but destroyed both empire and Church in the East. It was the great effort of Theodosius to restore both. In fifteen years of unexampled energy, terrible trials, and almost miraculous success, he did what valour, piety, and prudence could do. These years were all that the Divine Providence had allowed him for a work almost transcending human power; and when he died, not yet fifty years old, in 395, the great empire of Rome, both in East and West, may be said to have fallen into orphanage. His two sons, Arcadius and Honorius, one a youth of nineteen and the other a boy of eleven, proved to be utterly incompetent. Even Theodosius had failed to overcome the deep degeneracy and rooted party spirit to which the Arian heresy had reduced the eastern episcopate when St. Athanasius and St. Basil had been freshly laid in their tombs. The council called by Theodosius at Constantinople in 381 suffered St. Gregory to give up the see, which was surrounded by envious rivals. For when Meletius, the patriarch of Antioch, died, in presiding over that council, instead of extinguishing the Antiochene schism by the election of Paulinus, the bishop who was already in communion with Rome and Alexandria, according to an actual agreement, they suffered the schism to be prolonged by the election of Flavian. Nectarius took the place which St. Gregory had vacated, and St. Chrysostom was called after about fifteen years to succeed to his patriarchate.

Such was the state of things when, in 398, he began the charge of a city which, in corruption, party spirit, and unquenched enmities of long-standing, surpassed, if it were possible, his own native Antioch. It is true, that instead of the small remnant who listened to St. Gregory eighteen years before in the Church of the Resurrection, the whole city was, in name at least, Catholic. Its bishop was seated in a magnificent church, with a clergy more numerous, perhaps, than in any episcopal see in the world: with vast revenues, and a position second only to that of the emperor. But the court of the East was the focus of endless rivalries: of eunuchs who were ministers of state exercising the terrible autocratic powers of an emperor scarcely of age, and dominated by an imperious empress, whose splendid beauty held him in thraldom, while her lust of power was endless and her vanity excessive. And then there were foreign and barbarian generals, whose struggle with each other for mastery was always keeping the empire in disquietude. And lastly, the rivalry of the

Gallic Rufinus, whom Theodosius had left to advise his son in the East with the semi-barbarian Stilicho, to whom he had given both his favourite niece Serena for wife, and his younger son Honorius for pupil in the West, was preparing the ruin of Constantine's empire by its own hands.

In such an atmosphere the preacher and the saint was placed to struggle as he might against court intrigues, and to correct and purify a clergy whose conduct left much to be desired. He showed himself throughout an admirable bishop. Pursuing himself the most simple and ascetic life, he bestowed his whole great income as patriarch on the poor. He founded hospitals and homes. He celebrated the divine service with the utmost care and splendour. He watched over discipline among his clergy. He was unwearied in preaching. Nor did his vigilance end with the limits of his own see. He sent missionaries to Phœnicia and Palestine; to the Scythians, also, and the Goths. For the latter he established a special service of their own—he did all he could to deliver them from the fatal error which the deceit of the emperor Valens had infected them with, in presenting them with Arianism instead of the Christian faith. He exerted also the very questionable claim of his see—which the council of 381 had attempted to exalt to the utmost—by judging the case of the Exarch of Ephesus, and removing several faulty bishops from their seats in that exarchate.

But the 'Court's stern martyr-guest,' who was also 'the glorious preacher with soul of zeal and lips of flame,' could not go on long practising the life of a saint with the power of a patriarch under such sovereigns as the weak Arcadius and the imperious Eudoxia. His virtues offended many in a city of intense worldliness. His censures, delivered with his wonted eloquence from the pulpit of the cathedral, roused great enmities. In Theophilus, patriarch of Alexandria, he had a watchful enemy, eager to punish, in the person of Chrysostom, the new rank which his see arrogated of being the second in the Church, as the see of Nova Roma. By that arrogation, the see of St. Mark at Alexandria was degraded from a rank which it had held since the beginning of the Christian hierarchy. Not only among the magnates of the court, but among his brother bishops, Chrysostom found much opposition: and at last the empress set herself at the head of his opponents. While he was absent in Asia Minor, restoring to order the exarchate of Ephesus, Severian, bishop of Gabala in Syria, sought, by sermons delivered in the cathedral itself, to take from him the favour of the people. But it received him with acclamation on his return, and drove Severian out of the city.

But certain disturbances about the doctrine of Origen which had broken out among the monks in Egypt involved him in unfortunate difficulties. Among many monks who fled to Constantinople from the desert of Nitria in Egypt, under excommunication from Theophilus, were the 'four tall brothers'. They came to accuse their patriarch before the emperor and Chrysostom. He took them up, showing kindness and sympathy, though he did not admit them to communion. Theophilus was summoned to Constantinople by the emperor, to answer for his conduct before a synod. To escape this humiliation he used every effort to ruin Chrysostom, whom he took to be his own opponent. He accused Chrysostom himself of Origenism. This scheme of the Egyptian patriarch brought over to his side all the opponents of Chrysostom at the court. Theophilus even ventured to appear as the accuser and judge of the patriarch in the capital itself. He was able to draw together a synod of thirty-six bishops at the Oak, a country-house near Chalcedon, and to summon the bishop of Constantinople to appear before it. Chrysostom, on the double ground of his own rank and his innocence, refused to appear. The unlawful synod 'of the Oak' condemned him, supported by the influence of the empress. Forty bishops around him in Constantinople attested his innocence, and objected to a proceeding utterly unlawful and, until then, unknown. Chrysostom was willing to obey a command of the emperor that he should cross the Bosphorus and attend; but the people threatened insurrection if the command were not withdrawn. Chrysostom had to return, and was reseated in his church with the joyful acclamation of his people.

Not long did the peace last. A statue of the empress had been inaugurated before the cathedral. The crowd indulged in most intemperate rejoicings, and paid almost idolatrous homage to the statue. This Chrysostom, in preaching, censured. The empress took the blame to herself: it kindled her wrath afresh. It was whispered to her that the great preacher had alluded to her under the name of Herodias. A new synod of the patriarch's opponents was convoked. It issued, in the year 404, a second sentence of deposition against him. It alleged that Chrysostom, after being deposed by a synod, had, contrary to the law of the Church, resumed his see without being restored by another synod. The emperor Arcadius confirmed the decision, and subscribed a decree of banishment. This time Chrysostom waited for force to be used. Soldiers were sent into the church: they pushed aside the people who were protecting their bishop. Blood flowed, and the church was desecrated.

Chrysostom was carried away to Nicæa in Bithynia, and was ordered, in the midst of the summer heats, to go thence on foot, amid the greatest privations and hardships, to Kukusus in Armenia. The journey brought on him a grievous illness. Thus he was detained for some time at Cæsarea in Cappadocia. He was scarcely recovered when he was driven further on. In 406, he reached Kukusus.

But he kept up intercourse by letter with his friends in the capital. Arsacius, in the meantime, had been intruded by the emperor's power into his see; and a grievous persecution was instituted against those who would not recognise the intruder. Chrysostom consoled them in many letters. Banished as he was, he concerned himself for the spread of the faith among Persians and Goths. His sufferings, and the magnanimity with which he bore them, won for him sympathy far and wide. But his enemies remained unmoved. He besought the intercession of Pope Innocent I., describing to him, in a letter which is translated in this volume, the utter illegality of the violence which he was suffering. The Pope applied to the emperor Honorius for succour, and was supported by him in sending a solemn deputation to the emperor Arcadius; but he was under the dominion of the offended Eudoxia, and refused to listen either to his brother emperor or the Pope.

The Pope withdrew his communion from the intruder Arsacius, who had been put unlawfully in the see of Chrysostom, and from his successor Atticus; and for many years this mark of reprobation was all that the Pope could do in the difficult circumstances of the times. It lasted until the name of Chrysostom was replaced in the diptychs of the Church at Constantinople.

But Arcadius went further, and condemned Chrysostom to a more-distant and ruder exile at Pityus, a seaport on the most desolate eastern coast of the Euxine. In the utmost summer heat, with exhausted strength, the deposed patriarch had to undertake this journey. He never reached the end. His merciless guards pressed his weakness to the utmost. When at Comana he thought his end was near; but the guards urged him on. For an hour he could drag himself along; then his strength utterly failed. He was taken into the small church of the Martyr Basiliscus, which was near. His friend and biographer, the Bishop Palladius, thus describes the last scene :

'In that very night (that is, at Comana) the martyr of the place stood before him, Basiliscus by name, who had been bishop of Comana, and died by martyrdom in Nicomedia in the reign of Maximinus, together with Lucian of Bithynia, who had been a priest of Antioch. And he said, " Be of good heart, brother John, for to-morrow we shall be together ". It is said that the martyr had already made the same announcement to the priest of the place : " Prepare the place for brother John, for he is coming ". And John, believing the divine oracle, upon the morrow besought his guards to remain there until the fifth hour. They refused, and set forward; but, when they had proceeded about thirty stadia, he was so ill that they returned back to the martyr's shrine whence they had started.

'When he got there, he asked for white vestments suitable to the tenor of his past life; and taking off his clothes of travel, he clad himself in them from head to foot, being still fasting, and then gave away his old ones to them about him. Then, having communicated in the symbols of the Lord, he made the closing prayer " on present needs ". He said his customary words, " Glory be to God for all things," and having concluded it with his last Amen, he stretched forth those feet of his which had been so beautiful in their running, whether to convey salvation to the penitent or reproof to the hardened in sin. And being gathered to his fathers, and shaking off this mortal dust, he passed to Christ, as it is written, " Thou shalt come to thy burial like full wheat that is harvested in season, but the souls of transgressors shall die prematurely ". But so great a crowd of virgins, ascetics, and those who had the witness of sanctity in their life were present from Syria, Cilicia, Pontus, and Armenia, that many thought they had come by agreement. With these solemn rites, like a victorious athlete, he was buried in the same shrine with Basiliscus.'[1]

In the meantime, the empress Eudoxia had passed away in child-bed before her victim. In the undimmed lustre of her beauty, and the undiminished power of her will over her husband, she had been called to her account. Her husband, the emperor Arcadius, died not long after. He finished an utterly inglorious reign of twelve years at the age of thirty-one. His miserable government had gone

[1] Palladius, *Life of St. Chrysostom*, in his works, vol. xiii., pp. 39, 40.

near to destroy the empire which his father saved, and had actually thrown Alaric with his Goths upon Rome and Italy. He was succeeded by Theodosius II., a boy eight years old.

Thirty years after, a disciple and friend of Chrysostom sat in the see of Nova Roma, the orthodox Proclus, who was a theologian and a saint. He moved the emperor Theodosius II. to bring back the body of Chrysostom to its place among the bishops in the Church of the Apostles, where only the bishops and the emperors were buried—the former in the church, the latter in the vestibule. Theodoret, bishop of Cyrus at the time, says: 'A great multitude of the faithful crowded the sea in vessels, and lighted up a part of the Bosphorus near the mouth of the Propontis with torches. These sacred treasures were brought to the city by the present emperor. He laid his face upon the coffin, and entreated that his parents might be forgiven for having so unadvisedly persecuted the bishop.'

Those remains now rest in a fitter place. St. Chrysostom, in words quoted further on, when dilating as a fervent lover of St. Paul upon his praise, cried out: 'Rome, for this do I love, although having reason otherwise to praise her, both for her size, and her antiquity, and her beauty, and her multitude, and her power, and her wealth, and her victories in war. But passing by all these things, for this I count her blessed: because, when alive, Paul wrote to them, and loved them so much, and went and conversed with them, and there finished his life. Wherefore the city is on that account more remarkable than for all other things together, and like a great and strong body, it has two shining eyes—the bodies of these saints. Not so bright is the heaven when the sun sends forth his beams, as is the city of the Romans sending forth everywhere over the world these two lights. Thence shall Paul, thence shall Peter, be caught up. Think, and tremble, what a sight shall Rome behold, when Paul suddenly rises from that resting-place with Peter, and is carried up to meet the Lord. What a rose doth Rome offer to Christ! with what two garlands is that city crowned! with what golden fetters is she girdled! what fountains does she possess! Therefore do I admire that city, not for the multitude of its gold, nor for its columns, nor for its other splendours, but for these, the pillars of the Church.'

The body, therefore, of him who spoke these words, while a preacher at Antioch, rests more fitly than in any other place amid that matchless group of apostles, saints, and martyrs which surrounded the body of the Fisherman, in the central shrine of Christendom. There he awaits the sight which he anticipated with so much joy.

I must notice one more fact of the eight great brethren, the chief doctors of the East and West. St. Ambrose, St. Jerome, St. Augustine, St. Gregory the Great, St. Athanasius, St. Basil, St. Gregory

Nazianzen, and himself, all suffered persecution; the life of St. Athanasius was for years in danger from the bitter hatred of the emperor Constantius, and the emperor Valens would have destroyed St. Basil, had he dared. But to Chrysostom alone was given actually to lay down his life itself for justice' sake, and to follow St. John the Baptist not only in sanctity of life and preaching the cross of Christ, but in his death through the persecution of a woman, and the blinded tyranny of a king devoted to her will.

It may be well to give here a summary of St. Chrysostom's works. Very much of his labour he spent in commenting upon Scripture. This took the form of homilies, of which the larger part was delivered before the people in Antioch. He belongs to the Antiochene school of literal explanation. He was a fellow-pupil under Diodorus of Tarsus, with that Theodorus, afterwards bishop of Mopsuestia, whose writings were the fountain-head of what was afterwards called Nestorianism. They were composed exactly at the same time as those of St. Augustine, and were as prolific for evil as those of St. Augustine for good. But the piety and accurate doctrine of St. Chrysostom preserved him from the errors of his early comrade and friend. His homilies in their structure may be divided into the careful expounding of the text, even to its particles, and then the moral application, both in popular yet scientific form, finished with such skill that the art of eloquence seems blended with that of exposition in the fairest union.

He thus expounded the whole of Genesis in sixty-seven homilies; the Psalms in sixty homilies; the prophet Isaias, but only to the middle of the 8th chapter, according to both the historical and the mystical sense. There are five discourses on St. Anne, the mother of Samuel; three on David and Saul; two on the obscurity of the prophets; six upon the seraphim, in which he speaks on the incomprehensibility of the Divine Being. To the gospel of St. Matthew he has given ninety homilies, so skilfully interweaving Christian doctrine with literal exposition that, in Montfaucon's opinion, no such work exists elsewhere; and St. Thomas Aquinas is reported to have said that he would rather have it than the city of Paris. He has given seven homilies to the history of Lazarus and Dives in St. Luke; and eighty-eight homilies to the gospel of St. John, shorter, however, than those on St. Matthew. To the Acts of the Apostles he has given fifty-five homilies, delivered at Constantinople, and written down by shorthand. To the epistles of St. Paul he has given two hundred and forty-six homilies; which make up the number of four hundred and eighty-six on the whole New Testament.

All these are counted among his best works: but the best of all, those on the Pauline epistles, particularly that to the Romans. St. Isidore of Pelusium says: 'I believe if Paul had interpreted himself in

Attic phrase, he would have done it no otherwise than this distinguished holy teacher. So admirable is his exposition in meaning, elegance, and choice of words.'

Besides biblical exposition, St. Chrysostom has left a great number of other discourses on various occasions.

Such are eight homilies against the Jews; twelve against the Anomœans, the worst branch of the Arians. Discourses on the great festivals; panegyrics on saints, among them on bishops of Antioch, Ignatius, Babylas, Philogonius, Eustathius, and Meletius. Seven on the Apostle Paul, held at Antioch, whom he seems to have chosen for his model: to have read perpetually, and, as it were, to have seen at his side.

Of occasional discourses, there are twenty-one 'On the Statues' held at Antioch in the Lent of 387, full of tenderness and the most stirring eloquence. Of moral discourses, there are two to 'those about to be illuminated,' that is, baptised: nine upon penance. Eleven at Constantinople in 398 and 399, one of these in praise of the empress Eudoxia when she came at night to Sancta Sophia to venerate the relics of the martyrs; nine others on various subjects.

Among his dogmatic works are the demonstration against the Jews that Christ is God, proving the divine dignity of the Messias from the fulfilment of Old Testament prophecies, from the wonderful spread

of the Christian faith, from the fulfilment of the
prophecies of Christ, especially on the temple and
the Jewish people : the writing on St. Babylas,
and against Julian and the heathen. He points out
how the miracles worked at Antioch in Julian's
attack on Daphne were a warning to the restorer of
heathenism, disregarding which, he was punished by
an early death. A treatise on two books to Theodorus, when he lapsed, the Theodorus mentioned
above : on compunction, two books : on Providence, three books, to a friend grievously troubled.
To the opposers of the monastic life, three books :
the comparison between a monk and a king : on
the priesthood, six books, written in solitude, in 376.
It dwells on the holiness and exalted character of
the New Testament priesthood : on its divine
powers in offering the sacrifice and forgiving sins ;
on the difficulty and the dangers of preaching ; on
the great qualities required by a priest and a bishop.
So he excuses himself to his friend Basil for
recommending him to an office which he fled from
himself. A treatise on the virginal life, which he
gives only as a counsel, not as a precept, recognising
the honour due to marriage. Two books to a young
widow, advising her not to remarry. Against the
prohibited dwelling of unmarried women in the
same house with priests, and a most beautiful
treatise upon 'No one can be hurt except by
himself,' written in the last moments of his own
banishment, of which his own life and death is the

best assurance; and a like one 'on those who are scandalised at misfortunes'.

Lastly, we possess 238 letters, all but one called forth by the incidents of his own banishment. These show the holy confessor in the whole beauty of his magnanimous life. They are instinct throughout with trust in the Divine Providence, like the last words which he uttered when he lay down to die.

Out of this vast mass of works, the largest left to us by any Greek Father, the Translator has ventured to make a small selection, which, together with the translation itself, is entirely her own; and for which her excuse is the desire to bring in the easiest form specimens of so great a writer, and of one greater yet in deed than in writing, greatest of all in his death, before some who know him rather by the reputation he has left in the Church than by his actual words.[1]

THOS. W. ALLIES.

11*th July*, 1888.

[1] In writing the above sketch, Nirockl's *Lehrbuch der Patrologie und Patristik* has been used, and Cardinal Newman's notice of the Saint quoted once or twice, and everywhere borne in mind.

PART I.

THE KING'S HIGHWAY.

The Way, the Truth, and the Life.

(*Homilies on St. Matthew*,[1] lxxvi., vol. ii., p. 395.)

. . . .

Is not it with justice, then, that He turns away from us and chastises us, since in everything He is offering us Himself, and we are resisting Him? This is clear to all. 'For,' He says, 'if you wish to adorn yourself you have My adornment, or to arm yourself you have My arms, or to dress yourself you have My clothing, or to eat you have My table, or to walk you have My road, or to inherit you have My inheritance, or to go into your own country you have that city of which I am the Builder and the Architect, or to build a house you have My tents. I do not demand of you a reward for the things which I give, but I owe interest to you besides for that reward if you are willing to make use of all that is Mine.' What could equal this munificence? 'I

---

[1] Translated from the Greek Oxford and Cambridge Edition.

am father, I am brother, I am bridegroom, I am dwelling-place; I am food, I am clothing, I am root and foundation; I am all things whatsoever you desire: stand in need of no man. I will also be a slave, for I came to minister, not to be ministered to. I am a friend too; I am member and head, and brother, and sister, and mother; I am all things; only hold Me for your own. I am poor for you, and a wanderer for you; I was on the cross for you, and in the tomb for you; I intercede with the Father for you up above, and I came down to earth as a messenger to you from the Father. You are all things to Me—brother and co-heir, and friend and member.' What more do you ask? Why do you turn away from Him, your Lover? Why do you labour for the world? Why do you pour water into a broken pitcher? For this is to toil for the life which now is. Why do you spin a web for burning? Why beat the air? Why run at random? Has not every art an object? This is clear to everyone. Show me, then, you also, the object of your labour in life. You have none.

Vanity of vanities, and all is vanity. Let us go into a churchyard; show me now your father, show me your wife. Where is he who was clothed in gold? Where is he who rode in his chariot? Where is he who had an army at his command, he who had a treasury, and he who held a public office? Where is he who killed some and cast others into prison, who slew whom he pleased and acquitted whom he pleased? I see nothing except bones, and the moth and the cobweb; all those things were dust and fable, and dream and shadow, and idle talk and an epitaph—indeed, not even an epitaph, for we see an epitaph on a figure, but in this place not even a figure. And would that evils ended here! Now, that which pertains to honour and feasting and great name is like a shadow and idle talk, but that which they produce is by no means a shadow or idle talk. Their effects remain, and will abide with us there and be evident to all—rapacity and selfishness, fornication, adultery, and a thousand vices of the same kind. These are not in the image nor in the ashes, but both words and deeds are written above. With what eyes, then, shall we look upon Christ? For if a man would not venture to see his father if he were conscious in his own mind of sinning against him, how shall we in that hour confront Him Who is infinitely gentler than a father? How shall we bear Him? For we shall stand before the tribunal of Christ, and there will be a strict scrutiny of all things. But if anyone disbelieve in that future judgment, let him consider things as they are on earth—those in prisons, for instance, those in mines and on dung-hills, possessed men, madmen, those who are fighting with incurable disease, those who are pinched by persistent poverty, those who are mated with hunger, those who are given over to unhealable sorrow, those who are in captivity. Men, indeed, would not now suffer these things if He did not ordain that reward and punishment should await all those who have been guilty of the like transgressions. And if these men incur no penalty in this world, you must take this to yourself as a sign that there is to be something in the next after our departure hence. For He Who is the Lord of all would not chastise some and leave others, who had been guilty of the same or of worse things, unchastised, if He did not reserve a punishment for them in the next world.

. . . .

Who is the Greater?

(Homilies on St. Matthew, lviii., vol. ii., p. 167.)

. . . .

At that time the disciples came to Jesus, saying: Who, then, is the greater in the kingdom of heaven? The disciples had a human feeling, this is why the Evangelist lays special stress upon it, saying, *at that time*—that is, when He had singled out Peter for special honour. For in the case of James and John one was the first-born, but He did nothing of the kind for them. As, then, they are ashamed to own to their annoyance, they do not say openly: 'Why hast Thou honoured Peter more than us?' or, 'Is he greater than we?' they would not say this, but ask indefinitely: *Who is the greater?* When they saw the three singled out for special honour, they had felt nothing of the kind; they *were* grieved, however, when so great a distinction was conferred upon one. This was not all, for their feeling was intensified by putting many other favours together. For Our Lord said to him: *I will give thee the keys*, and, *Blessed art thou, Simon Bar Jona*, and again, *Give it to them for Me and thee;* and, seeing Peter's great fearlessness, they were irritated. And if Mark says that they did not put their question, but thought it in their own minds, this is not in any way contrary to Matthew's account. For it is probable that they did both one and the other, both that they felt this at one time, and that at another they spoke out, and also had their own thoughts about it. Now, do not look merely at the accusation, but consider further, first, that they are not seeking earthly things, and secondly, that they afterwards overcame this feeling, and ceded the first places to each other. We, on the contrary, are neither able to reach their defects, nor do we seek who is the greater in the kingdom of heaven, but who is the greater in the kingdom of the world, who is the richer and the more powerful.

Now, what does Christ say? He reveals their conscience to them, and answers this feeling rather than their mere words. *Calling unto Him a little child, He said: Unless you be converted and become as little children, you shall not enter into the kingdom of heaven.* 'You, indeed, enquire who is the greater, and dispute about the first places; *I* tell you that he who has not become meeker than all the rest is not worthy even to enter into that kingdom.' And He brings the example before them in a beautiful way; and not only does He bring it before them, but He sets the child in the midst of them, admonishing them by the sight, and urging them to be both humble and unaffected. For a child is free from envy and from vainglory, and from the love of the first places, and he possesses the greatest virtue—simplicity, and unaffectedness and humility. It is not sufficient to have courage and prudence, but this virtue also: I mean humility and simplicity. For with the greatest, our salvation will be at fault, if we have not these. Contempt, blows, honour, or praise cause a child neither annoyance nor envy, nor is he thereby inflated. Do you see again how He excites us to natural qualities, showing us that these may be rightly directed by a free choice, and how He thus condemns the wretched fury of the Manicheans? For if nature be bad, why does He take from nature illustrations in favour of asceticism? The child seems to me most truly a child standing in the midst of them, free from all these passions. Such a child, indeed, is without folly, and the love of reputation, without jealousy and envy, and every affection of the kind; and having many virtues—simplicity, humility, unmeddlesomeness—he is not puffed up by any one of them; it is doubly wise to possess these things and not to be vain of them.

This is why Our Lord called the child and set him in the midst of them; nor did He close His argument here, but He adds this further exhortation, saying: *He who shall receive one of these children in My name receives Me.* 'Not only if you have become like to them shall you have a great reward, but also if you honour those like them for My sake, I will give you a kingdom as a reward for your honour of them.' He says, indeed, more than this in the words *receives Me*. Thus, ardently am I to desire meekness and unaffectedness. Hence He calls men who are thus simple and humble, and cast off by the multitude, and despised, children.

. . . .

———

The First are Last and the Last First.

(*Homilies on St. Matthew*, lxvii., vol. ii., p. 285.)

. . . .

Let no sinner despair: let no just man give way to sloth. Neither let the just be presumptuous, for it often happens that the harlot outstrips him; nor let the sinner be downcast, for he may overtake those who are first.

Listen to what God says to Jerusalem: *I said all these things after her adultery, Turn to Me, and she did not turn.* As often as we return to the burning charity of God, He no longer remembers our former sins. God is not as man: He does not reproach those who come to Him, or say, if we be really changed, 'Why hast thou wasted so much time?' but He loves us whenever we go to Him. Let us only go to Him in the right way. Let us cling fast to Him, and nail our hearts to His fear. These things have taken place not only recently, but they happened also of old. What was worse than Manasses? Yet he was able to appease God. Who was more blessed than Solomon? But torpor made him fall. Indeed, I can show the two things happening in one man; in Solomon's father, for he himself was just and became wicked. Who was more blessed than Judas? Yet Judas became a traitor. What could be more miserable than Matthew? But he became an evangelist. What was worse than Paul? Still, Paul became an apostle. Who was more zealous than Simon? And yet Simon himself became the most wretched of all. How many more of the same vicissitudes would you contemplate — those both of the past and those which are taking place every day? So I say, neither let the man who is on the stage despair, nor let the man who is in the Church make too bold. To the latter it was said: *He who seems to stand, let him be careful lest he fall*, and to the former: *Does the fallen man not rise up again?* and, *Restore languid hands and disabled knees*. Again, to the just it was said: *Watch*, but to sinners: *Arise, thou who sleepest, and rise from the dead*. The former have need to watch over what they possess, and the latter to become that which they are not as yet: the just to preserve their health, sinners to put off their sickness. For they *are* sick, but many of the sick are sound, and some of the sound, by their carelessness, become sick. For it was to these that Our Lord said, *Go, thou art sound: sin no more, lest something worse should befal thee;* but to sinners, *Wilt thou be made sound? Take up thy bed and walk, and go into thy house.* Sin is indeed a dire paralysis, or, rather, it is not only a paralysis, but something more fearful. For a paralysed man is not only lacking good things, but is also a prey to bad ones. Still, if you are even in this state, and are willing to make a small effort to rise, all sins are remitted. Even if your sickness has lasted thirty-eight years, yet you strive to become sound: there is no one to prevent you. Christ is at hand now as then, and He says, *Take up thy bed.* Only be willing to rise; do not lose heart. Have you no man? You have God. Have you no one to put you into the pool? But you have One Who will not allow you to require the pool in vain. Have you no one to hold you in it? You have One Who commands you to take up your bed. You have not to say, *When I come, another gets down before me.* For if you wish to go down to the fountain no man hinders you. Charity is not spent nor consumed: it is a source which is always flowing upwards: out of His fulness we are all cured as to our soul and as to our body. Now, therefore, also, let us approach Him. Rahab was a harlot, yet she was saved; and the thief was a murderer, but he became a citizen of paradise; and Judas, being in the society of the Master, was lost, whilst the thief on the cross became a disciple. These are God's paradoxes. Thus it was that the Magi found favour, that a publican became an evangelist, and a blasphemer an apostle.

Consider these things, and never despair, but be of good heart always, and raise yourself up. Keep to that path alone which leads above, and you will make rapid progress. Close not the doors nor block up the entrance. This time is short and the labour small. And if it were heavy, even then we should not refuse it. For if you are not weary with this most delicious weariness of wisdom and virtue, you will be weary with the weariness of the world, and will be worn out in another way. But if there be weariness here too, why do we not choose for ourselves that other which is so productive of fruit and has so great a reward? And yet this last weariness is not as the former. For in worldly things there are always risks and continuous penalties: hope is uncertain, much slavery of spirit is required, and there is expenditure of money, and of strength of body and of mind, and even then the compensation of results is far below the expectation, if there be any results at all. The sweat and toil of worldly business do not, indeed, in all cases produce fruit. Even in those instances in which they are not fruitless, but rich in results, these are short-lived. For it is when you grow old, and have no longer an acute sense of enjoyment that your labour yields its fruit. The hard work falls to the lot of the body at its prime, whereas the fruit and its enjoyment come when it is worn and aged, and time has dulled its perceptions, or, if it has not dulled them, the prospect of an approaching end forbids enjoyment. It is not so in the other case, but labour is the part of a mortal and corruptible body, and the crown belongs to a glorified and immortal one which is eternal. The labour comes first and is slight, but the reward comes last and is infinite, so that you may rest with security and be untroubled as to the future. There is no fear of change or of misfortune as there is here on earth. What goods, then, are these—insecure, slight, and earthly, which disappear before they appear, and are possessed with so much toil? How are they equal to those immutable, undecaying good things which are free from all hardships, and crown you in the time of warfare? The man who despises money receives his reward even on earth : he is free from care and envy, slander, treachery, and heart-burnings. The wise man, he who lives decorously, is crowned and in luxury before his flight hence, in his freedom from unseemliness and senseless laughter, and dangers and accusations, and all evils. In the same way, virtue, of whatever other kind, puts us already in possession of our reward. Let us then, fly from evil and choose the good, so that we may arrive at both present and future rewards. Thus we shall both enjoy our lives here and possess our crowns in heaven, which may it be given to us all to do through the love and mercy of Our Lord Jesus Christ, to Whom be glory and power for ever and ever. Amen.

Variety of Human Lot.

(*Homilies on the First Epistle to the Corinthians,*[1] xxix., vol. ii., p. 359.)

. . . .

One and the same Spirit worketh all things, distributing to each his own gifts according to His pleasure. Therefore he says, let us not be troubled or grieved, thinking to ourselves, 'Why have I received this and not received that?' Neither must we scrutinise the doings of the Holy Spirit. For if you know that He has shown you favour out of kindness, considering that out of the same kindness He has also put a limit to His gift, acquiesce and rejoice in what you have received, and be not down-hearted about what you have not received, but rather give thanks that your gift is not beyond your power. If it behoves us not to be over-eager in spiritual things, how much less in those of the flesh; but we should be at ease, and not be disturbed because one man is rich and another

[1] Translated from the Greek Oxford Edition.

poor. In the first place, not every rich man gets his wealth from God, but many become rich through injustice and avarice and graspingness. For how could He, Who commands us not to lay up riches, have given that which He prohibited our taking? Now, in order that I may silence those who differ from us in this with the more authority, let us go deeper into the argument. Tell me why were riches given by God? Why was it that Abraham was rich, and that Jacob even wanted bread? Were not both righteous men? Had not God said equally of the three, *I am the God of Abraham, and of Isaac, and of Jacob?* Why then was the one rich and the other in poverty? Or, rather, why was Esau, the unjust and fratricidal man, rich, and Jacob in servitude for so long? Again, why did Isaac pass his whole life in ease, and Jacob in toils and hardships, so that he said, *My days are short and miserable?* Why did David, too, being both prophet and king, as he was, live his life in labour, whilst his son Solomon was, during forty years, the richest of men, in the enjoyment of enduring peace, glory, and honour, and every possible luxury? Why, in short, amongst the prophets was one tried more and another less? Because thus it was profitable to each. Therefore, every man should say, *Thy judgments are a deep abyss.* For if God exercised those great and admirable men in different ways—one through poverty, another through riches; one by a life of ease, another by tribulation—it behoves us all the more to take the same lesson now to heart. Together with these considerations, we must admit that many things happen to us, which are not according to His judgment, but the result of our own wickedness. Say not, then, 'Why is it that a man is rich, being bad, and another man is poor, being just?' We may easily explain this, and say that neither does the just man suffer any harm from his poverty, which is a source of greater merit to him, and that the unjust man, unless he be converted, possesses in his riches a store of wrath, and that, in place of chastisement, the riches of many men have often been the cause of evil to them, and led them into a thousand abysses. But God leaves them these riches, showing everywhere the free action of divine choice, everywhere teaching other men not to fight nor to strive for money. 'What, then,' you say, 'if a bad man becomes rich, and suffers no harm? If a righteous man were to become rich, it would be just, but what are we to say when a bad man does?' That on this account he is to be pitied. For wealth added to wickedness increases the intensity of passions. But a man is just, and he is starving. Well, it does him no harm. But he is bad, and starving. Well, he has his just deserts, or, rather, what is for his good. 'But so and so,' you say, 'received his wealth from ancestors, and has squandered it on bad women and parasites, and he is none the worse.' How is this? Will you call him a dissolute man, and say he is none the worse? He is a drunkard, and do you call it enjoyment?

He wastes for no good purpose, and do you look upon him as enviable? What could a man do worse than to be making his soul an ignominy? If a body were to be distorted or maimed, you would think it the saddest matter in the world; yet, contemplating that man's soul wholly maimed, do you consider him a happy man? 'But,' you say, 'he does not feel it.' And for this very reason he is the more to be pitied, just as men who lose their wits are. For he who knows that he is ill will seek the physician honestly and apply remedies; whereas he who does not know it will be beyond cure. Tell me, then, is this the man you consider happy? But this is not astonishing, for the majority of men are devoid of a right estimate of things. So it is that, when chastised, we pay the extreme penalty, and are not freed from wrath; hence come desires and despondencies and perpetual anxieties, since, when God shows us a painless life, that of goodness, by removing ourselves from it, we choose another road, the way of riches and money, which is productive of a thousand evils. We act as a man would act, who, not being able to judge of physical beauty, but, ascribing everything to clothes and adornment, should pass over a young woman, possessing comeliness of body, and take to himself an ugly one, deformed and crippled, merely for her fine dress. The great mass of men now do something of this kind in the matter of goodness and badness, by following their bad nature on account of its outward attraction, and by turning away from the good nature, which is blooming and beautiful, on account of its unadorned comeliness, the very reason why they should have chosen it.

. . . .

Whence the Rich?

(*Homilies on First Epistle to Corinthians*, xxxiv., vol. ii., p. 430.)

. . . .

You ask, 'Whence come the rich?' for it is written, *Riches and poverty are from the Lord.* Now let us ask those who urge this upon us, 'Then is all wealth and all poverty from the Lord?' Who would say as much? For we see many laying up riches for themselves through rapacity, through the spoliation of tombs, through sorcery, and other means of the same kind, and that those who possess these riches are unworthy even of living. Now, tell me, is this the wealth we recognise as from God? No, far from it. Whence, then, does it come? From sin. For a bad woman grows rich by misusing her body, and the handsome youth often bartering the flower of his years possesses his money in ignominy, and the invader of graves who unearths tombs amasses the wealth of unrighteousness, just as the thief does by breaking down walls. Therefore not all wealth is from God. How then, you ask, shall we answer this argument? In the first place, understand that poverty was not made by God either, and then we will examine our argument. When a licentious youth either spends his riches upon bad women, or upon magical arts, or upon any other lusts of the same nature, and thus becomes poor, is it not evident that it is brought about not by God, but by his own riotousness? Again, if a man were to become poor through sloth, or to fall into poverty because of his want of sense, or to engage in perilous and unlawful pursuits, is it not evident once more that no one of these or those like them would be thrust into this want by God? Then, is the Scripture false? God forbid, but those who lay down the law on all the Scripture with insufficient discernment are wanting in sense. For if it be asserted that the Scripture is trustworthy, and it be proved that not all wealth is from God, then the difficulty lies in the weakness of those who put an inconsiderate construction upon such things. I ought indeed to have let you alone on this point, having first cleared the Scripture of blame, in order to make you pay a penalty for your carelessness concerning it; yet since I have great pity on you, and cannot bear to see you more troubled and confounded, let me add the explanation, considering in the first place who said it, then when it was said, and to whom.

For God does not speak in the same way to all, just as we ourselves do not use children as we use men. Now, when is it said, and by whom, and to whom? By Solomon of old to the Jews, who were familiar with sensible things only, and measured God's power by these. It is they who say, *Is He not able to give us bread?* and, *What sign dost Thou show us? Our fathers ate manna in the desert, whose belly is their God.* Since they estimated Him by these things, he tells them that God is also able to make men rich and poor, not that He Himself does it altogether, but that He can do it if He choose, as when He says, *He rebuketh the sea, and drieth it up, and bringeth all the rivers to be a desert,* although this never happened at all. How, then, does the prophet say that it did? Not as really taking place, but implying His power to do it. Now, what sort of poverty does He give and what sort of wealth? Call to mind the patriarch, and you will see what the riches are which God bestows. For it was He Who made Abraham rich, and Job after him, as Job admitted in the words: *If we have received good things from the Lord, shall we not endure the bad things as well?* And later on their twofold increase was His gift. And Jacob's riches began from the same source. There is a poverty which is praised by Him, that which He proposed to that rich young man, saying, *If thou wilt be perfect, go sell what thou hast, and give to the poor, and come and follow Me;* and again, when legislating for the disciples, He said, *Ye shall not possess gold nor silver nor two cloaks.* Therefore, do not say that He gives wealth to all without exception, for I have shown you that it is put together by murders and covetousness and a thousand other like causes.

. . . .

THE RICH YOUNG MAN.

(*Homilies on St. Matthew*, lxiii., vol. ii., p. 227.)

And behold one came and said to Him: Good Master, what shall I do that I may inherit eternal life? Some reject this young man as insidious and bad. I, however, would not deny that he was a lover of money, and unable to resist it, since Christ convicted him of this; but I should not admit that he was insidious, because it is not safe to make a venture upon what is unknown, especially in accusations, and because St. Mark has removed this doubt. For he says *that running up and kneeling before* Him, he asked Him a question, and again, that *Jesus, looking upon him, loved him.* But great is the tyranny of money as we gather from this; for even if we be quite faultless as to other things, it alone spoils everything else. St. Paul too justly called it the root of all evils. *The love of money*, he says, *is the root of all evils.* Now, why did Our Lord answer him by saying, *No man is good.* Because the youth approached Him as a mere man, as one of many, and a Jewish teacher: on this account Our Lord spoke as man to man with him. For He frequently answers according to the secret mind of those who come to Him, as, for instance, when He says, *We adore what we know*, and, *If I bear witness to Myself, My witness is not true.* When, then, He says, *No man is good*, He does not say it to repudiate His own goodness—far from it; for He does not say, 'Why do you call *Me* good? I am not good,' but, *No man is good*, that is, no man at all.

When He speaks in this way, He is not defrauding men of all goodness, but making a distinction as to God's goodness. So He added: *Only God is good.* And He did not say, 'Only my Father,' that you may know that He did not disclose Himself to the youth. Thus, higher up, He called all men bad, saying, *But if you who are bad know how to give good gifts to your children.* And if He called them wicked in this place, He did not condemn human nature as altogether bad (for He says *you*, not 'you, the human race'). He so called them, because He was putting the goodness of man by the side of the goodness of God, and therefore He added, *How much more will your Father give good gifts to those who ask Him.* And, you may say, what necessity or advantage was there that He should answer the young man in this way? He leads him up by degrees, teaches him to put off all deception, withdraws him from the things of earth, nailing him to God, inducing him to seek the things to come, to know the good, the root and foundation of all things, and to refer honour back to Him. And thus when He says, *You shall call no man master upon earth*, He said it to make a distinction as to Himself, that they might learn Who was the first Beginning of all things. For, so far, the young man had shown no slight willingness by rushing eagerly to embrace this love; and whilst others had come, some to tempt, others for the curing of disease, whether it was their own or their neighbours', he had come and had spoken for the sake of eternal life. The soil indeed was rich and moist, but the brambles overpowered and stifled the seed. For consider how far up to this point he is disposed to obey commands. *What shall I do*, he says, *that I may inherit eternal life?* Thus ready was he to accomplish what he should be told. But if he had come to Our Lord to tempt Him, the Evangelist would have told us so, as he does in other instances, and in that of the advocate. But if the young man was silent, Christ would not have allowed him to escape unknown, but would have convicted him wisely, or have hinted at his meaning, so that the youth should not think he had deceived and escaped without recognition, and so have been misled. If he had come to tempt, he would not have gone away sad, because of what he heard. This, at least, was not what any one of the Pharisees of the day did; but when they were silenced, they were angry. It was not so with the young man: *he* went away cast-down, which was no small proof that he had come with a weak rather than a bad intention, with the desire of life, but weighed down by another and a stronger passion.

Therefore, when Our Lord said, *If thou wilt enter into life, keep the commandments,* he asks, *Which commandments?* This was not said tempting—far from it—but thinking that he was to know of other commandments besides those of the Law, which would help him to life. This showed a great desire on his part. Then, when Jesus enumerated those of the Law, he said, *All these have I kept from my youth.* And he did not stop his enquiry here, but asked further, *What is yet wanting to me?* which in itself was a proof of his eagerness. His thinking himself to be still wanting in something, and his deeming that the things already specified were not sufficient, was no small step towards gaining what he desired. What does Christ say? As He was about to accomplish a great work, He put the prize before the youth and said, *If thou wouldst be perfect, go, sell what thou hast and give to the poor, and thou shalt have a treasure in heaven, and come and follow Me.* Do you see what rewards and crowns He sets for this career? If the young man had been tempting, he would not have spoken these things to Him. But now He does speak, and, as it were, draws him to Himself, shows him the reward to be exceedingly great, and unfolds the whole before his mind, hiding throughout the semblance of irksomeness in the advice. Therefore, before speaking of the combat and the labour, He shows him the reward, saying, *If thou wilt be perfect;* then He adds, *Go, sell what thou hast and give to the poor, and,* again returning to the rewards, *thou shalt have a treasure in heaven, and come and follow Me.* For the following Him is a great compensation. *And thou shalt have a treasure in heaven.* Hence, as the matter turned on money, and He was exhorting the young man to strip himself of everything, He points out that He does not take away possessions, but adds to them, and that He gives more things than those of which He commanded the sacrifice; and not merely are they more, but they are as much greater as heaven is than earth, and even more. He spoke of a treasure which is double the thing given, showing it to be abiding and secure, intimating thus through human things what His listener was to understand. Indeed, it is not enough to despise money, but a man must also feed the poor and follow Christ above all things; that is, he must carry out all His commandments, hold himself in readiness to be slaughtered and to suffer death any day. *If any man wish to come after Me, let him deny himself and take up his cross and follow Me.* As this command was a much higher one than the giving up of money—even the shedding of blood—so the giving up of money is no slight help towards its fulfilment. And when the young man had heard this word, *he went away sad.* Then, as if to show that he had felt nothing unreasonable, the Evangelist said, *for he was very rich.* Those who possess a little and those who are steeped in abundance are not equally restrained; then it is that love becomes more tyrannical. So I will not cease to say that the addition of superfluities is fuel to the fire, that it makes their possessors poorer, that it increases, indeed, their desires, and makes them conscious of greater needs. See how, in this case, passion showed its strength. For when Our Lord commanded the man, who came to him with joyful readiness, to renounce his money, he was so cast down and perturbed as to go away without giving any answer at all; and having become silent and sad and gloomy, he thus departed.

. . . .

Different Kinds of Friendship.

(*Homilies on St. Matthew*, lx., vol. ii., p. 199.)

. . .

Let us now consider the various forms which friendship takes with the majority of men. One man loves because he is loved; another because he has been honoured; another shows a liking for a man who has been of use to him in some practical matter or other; another, again, for some such similar reason; but it is difficult, indeed, to find a man who loves his neighbour thoroughly and as he ought for Christ's sake. For in most cases it is temporal business which brings men together. St. Paul did not love in this way: he loved for Christ's sake, so that he loved others whether he was loved by them or not, and did not break charity, since he had laid a strong foundation for his love-charm. It is not so now; indeed, if we search diligently, we shall find in most men a fictitious friendship rather than this. And if anyone gave me power to enquire into the matter in so great a multitude, I could show that the majority are bound to each other for worldly reasons. This is apparent from the causes which produce enmity. Since, then, men are bound to each other for motives so paltry, there is neither warmth nor fidelity in their mutual dealings; but contempt, and money losses, and jealousy, the love of honour, or any similar thing showing itself, destroys the love-charm. It rests not upon a spiritual foundation. If it were so, worldly things would never break up spiritual things. The love, indeed, which is born of Christ is strong and enduring and invincible, and nothing has power to dissolve it—neither calumnies, nor dangers, nor death, nor any other of these things whatsoever. If a man who thus loves should suffer in a thousand ways, contemplating that on which love rests, he stands unmoved. But the man who loves because he is loved, if he should suffer some foolish thing or other, breaks up his friendship, whilst the former is firm to the end. This is why St. Paul said, *Charity never falleth away.* What answer would you make? That the man whom you have honoured is a reviler? or that the one whom you have benefited would wish to put you to death?

But if you love for Our Lord's sake, this encourages you to love all the more. For those things which are destructive to love in other cases become productive of it in this particular one. How so? In the first place, because the man so loved is the cause of your reward; secondly, because one thus situated requires special help and much care. On this account a man who loves for Our Lord's sake does not enquire about family, or country, or riches, or demand love in return: he concerns himself about none of these things, but even if he be hated, or despised, or destroyed, he still loves, because his affection is built on a strong foundation—Christ. Hence he stands firm, steadfast, immutable, with his eyes on Our Lord. So it was that Christ loved His enemies—harsh men, scoffers, blasphemers, haters, those who wished not even to see Him, those who preferred stones and wood to His love, and He loved them with the charity from above, in comparison with which there is no other charity to be found. *For*, He says, *no man hath greater charity than this, that he giveth his life for his friends.* See how loving He ceases not to be towards the very men who crucified Him and reviled Him. He even spoke for them to His Father, saying, *Forgive them, for they know not what they do.* And, later on, He charged His disciples with those same men. Let us, then, be zealous for this same charity, and strive to possess it, that, being made the imitators of Christ, we may enjoy both present and future good things by the grace and tenderness of Our Lord Jesus Christ, to Whom be honour and glory for ever and ever. Amen.

The Buyers and Sellers in the Temple.

(*Homilies on St. Matthew*, lxvii., vol. ii., p. 277.)

And Jesus went into the temple of God, and cast out all them that sold and bought in the temple, and overthrew the tables of the money-changers, and the chairs of them that sold doves. And He saith to them: It is written, My house shall be called the house of prayer; but you have made it a den of thieves. John says the same thing, but he says it in the beginning of his gospel, whereas Matthew says it towards the end. Hence it is evident that the thing recounted took place twice and at different times. This is clear from the time and from the answer. In St. Matthew it happened at the very time of the Pasch; in St. John a good deal before it. In the latter the Jews say, *What sign dost Thou show us?* but in the former they are silent as if rebuked, because He was an object of wonder to all men. His doing the same action twice, and this in an authoritative way, strengthens the charge against the Jews, for they remained at their traffic, and called Him God's enemy, when they should have learnt from this His action how much He honoured His Father and what His own power was. For He was working wonders, and they saw a correspondence between His words and His deeds. Still they were unmoved and discontented, and this in the face of the loud testimony of the Prophet and of children witnessing to Him, with a wisdom beyond their years. This is why He Himself uses as an arm against them the accusing words of Isaias: *My house shall be called the house of prayer.* He shows His power not only in this way, but in the curing of many kinds of diseases; for the lame and the blind came to Him and He cured them, and He shows forth His power and His authority. They, however, were not persuaded in this way; but after seeing these wonders, and listening to children bearing witness to Him, they say, *Dost Thou not hear what these say?* This was what Christ might have said to *them:* 'Do you not hear what these say?' for they sang to Him as to God. What does He do? Since they spoke against visible signs, He makes use of a stronger correction, saying, *Have you never read, Out of the mouths of infants and of sucklings Thou hast perfected praise?* He said well, *out of the mouths.* For that which they said did not come from themselves, but from that power of His which controlled the words of their tongues. This indeed was a type amongst the nations of those who faltered and cried out confusedly, speaking great things with discernment and faith. Hence it was no small encouragement to the Apostles also. In order that they should not be perplexed as to how they, being unlearned, are to announce the Gospel tidings, these children by anticipation have cast out their fear, because He who has caused the children to sing will give them also reasoning powers. This was not all that the wonder made manifest: it showed Him to be the Lord of creation. These children of unripe age, on the one hand, gave voice to words of good omen which were in harmony with the things above; but men, on the contrary, to outbursts of folly and madness. Such was their badness. Whilst then, they had many incitements to anger, the attitude of the crowd, the throwing over of the tables of the buyers, the voice of His wonders, that of the children, He again leaves them, allowing their passion to cool, and not wishing to begin His teaching lest, boiling over with jealousy, they should be still more angered at what had been said.

. . . .

The Voice of Good Deeds.

(*Homilies on St. Matthew*, xlvi., vol. ii., p. 14.)

. . . .

If twelve men leavened the whole world, consider what *our* wickedness must be, inasmuch as we, being so many, are unable to convert the remainder, when we ought to suffice for the leavening of a thousand worlds. 'But,' some one says, 'they were apostles.'

What does this matter? Had not they the same surroundings as you? Were they not reared in cities? Did they not lead the same sort of life? Did they not follow a trade? Were they angels? Did they come down from heaven? 'But,' you say, 'they worked wonders.' It was not the wonders which made them famous. How long shall we use our own softness as a pretext for not considering those wonders? For many who cast out devils, since they afterwards worked iniquity, did not become renowned, but were even chastised. And what is it, you ask, which pointed them out as great? The despising of money and of reputation, and the withdrawal from worldly business. If they had been without these things, and had been slaves to their passions, even if they had raised up a thousand dead men, not only they would have done no good, but they would have been looked upon as deceivers. Thus, it is the life in every case which is resplendent, and which draws upon itself the unction of the Spirit. Did not John work a sign when he made so many cities hang upon his words? Yet listen to the Evangelist saying that he worked no wonder: *John did no wonder.* How did Elias become renowned? Was it not by his outspokenness with the king—by his zeal for God's service—by his possessing nothing —by his sheep-skin, and his cavern, and his mountains? For he worked his wonders after all these things. What sign did the devil see Job doing when he was struck with amazement? Not any at all, but he found him leading a resplendent life, which showed forth an endurance firmer than adamant. What sign had David accomplished for God to say of him, when still a youth, *I have found David, the son of Jesse, a man after My own heart?* What dead man did Abraham, Isaac, and Jacob raise to life? What leper did they cleanse? Do you not know that, if we are not watchful, wonder-working is often harmful? Thus it was that many of the Corinthians fell into schism and many Romans lost their right mind. Thus, too, that Simon was cast out, and that the man who desired to follow Christ refused the call when he heard that *foxes have holes, and birds of the air have nests.* Each of these, the one seeking money, and the other glory from the working of signs, fell away and were lost. But purity of life and the love of goodness not only do not produce this desire, but they take it away where it exists. And what did He Himself say when He was laying down the law to His disciples? Did He say, 'You shall do signs in order that men may see'? Not at all, but, rather, *Let your light shine before men, that they may see your good works, and glorify your Father Who is in heaven.* Nor did He say to Peter, 'If thou lovest Me, work wonders,' but, *Feed My sheep.* And, honouring Peter, with James and John, in every instance more than the rest, how does He show this honour, tell me? Is it in the doing of wonders? No; for they all cleansed lepers, and raised the dead to life, and to all He gave authority in equal measure. How then were those three distinguished? By interior virtue. Do you see that, everywhere, life is the need, and the manifestation of works? *By their fruits*, He said, *you shall know them*. What is it which approves our life? Is it the manifestation of wonders or an irreproachable conduct? Clearly it is the latter; for the reason which calls forth signs belongs to this world, and they cease in the next. The man who gives an example of a good life draws this charity upon himself; and he who shines by charity shines in this way, in order that he may correct the life of others. Since Christ also worked those wonders in order that He might appear worthy of confidence in this world, and, drawing men to Himself, might introduce virtue into life; therefore, more stress is laid upon this point. For He is not contented with signs alone, but He threatens hell, and He preaches the kingdom, and He enacts those marvellous laws, and everything is done with a view to His making men like to angels. But why do I say that Christ does everything unto this end? Tell me, if anyone gave *you* your choice either to raise up the dead in His name or to die for His name's sake, which would you choose? The latter surely; for the one is a sign and the other is a deed. Again, if anyone offered you the power of turning grass into gold, or that of looking down upon all gold as if it were grass, would you not rather choose the latter, and with good reason? It would be this which would attract men. For if they were to see food turned into gold, and were even desirous of taking the same power into their own hands, as Simon was, the love of money would be increased in them; but if they were to see all men looking down upon money as upon grass, and making little of it, they would be cured of this disease.

. . . .

The Best Controversy.

Homilies on St. Matthew, xv., vol. i., p. 201.)

. . . .

Then He goes on to a higher example—*You are the light of the world.* It is again *of the world;* not of one people, nor of twenty cities, but of the whole world; and it is a reasonable light, far superior to this physical light, just as spiritual salt is to material salt. And first they are salt, and afterwards light, in order that you may learn the force of strong words and the advantage of this holy teaching. For it is urgent and will not be diverted from its aim, and, leading us by the hand, makes us look towards goodness. *A city seated on a mountain cannot be hidden. Neither do men light a candle and put it under a bushel.* He leads them once more through these things to purity of life, teaching them to be soldiers, as if before the eyes of all men and wrestling in the midst of the arena of the whole world. 'Look not,' He said, 'to rest now whilst you are in a small corner; for you are to be visible to all men, like a city seated on a mountain, and like a candle shining upon all those in the house.' Where, now, are they who have distrusted the power of Christ? Let them listen to these things, and, being frightened by the might of the prophecy, let them fall down and adore His almightiness. Think what great things He promised to those who were not known even in their native place: that they are to go over land and sea, and to lift up their voice against the temptations of the world, or rather not their voice, but the force of their goodness. For it was not their universal fame which made them conspicuous: it was the manifestation of works. As if they had had wings, they spread over the whole earth quicker than light, sowing the light of piety. Hence, it seems to me that He stimulates them unto fearlessness, for His saying, *A city seated on the mountain cannot be hidden,* was the manifestation of His own power; for, if it were useless to hide that, so neither could the Gospel tidings be hushed or concealed. And to prevent them from thinking that persecutions, and accusations, and plots, and wars, since He spoke of these things, would have power to check them, He encourages them by saying that not only these persecutions will not pass unnoticed, but that they will shine forth to the whole world, and that through this very fact they themselves were to be renowned and famous. In this, then, His own power is manifested; but He furthermore requires fortitude from each one of them, saying, *Men do not light a candle and put it under a bushel, but upon a candlestick, and it gives light to all in the house. So may your light shine before men, that they may see your good works and glorify your Father Who is in heaven.* 'For it is I Who have enkindled the light,' He says. Whether, however, it remains lighted or not must depend upon your zeal, not on your own account alone, but for the sake of those who are to enjoy this beacon, and whom it is to lead to the truth. For the slanderings of men will not be able to veil your brightness if you yourselves are leading strict lives, and thus are preparing to convert the whole world. Show forth, therefore, a life worthy of grace, that, as the truth is preached everywhere, so your life may harmonise with it. And, again, He holds out another advantage besides the salvation of men, which is capable of firing them with courage and making all zealous. Not only will you reform the world, He says, by living upright lives, but you will also prepare the glory of God; just as by the contrary course you destroy men, and cause the name of God to be blasphemed. 'And how,' you ask, 'is God to be glorified through us if men are to slander us?' Not all men are to do this; but those who do so hypocritically will wonder and admire you in secret, just as outward flatterers of those who are living in wickedness despise them in their own minds. 'How, then, would you have us live for show and vainglory? No, indeed, I said nothing of the kind. I did not say, Make haste to bring forth your good deeds before men; nor did I say, Point them out; but, *Let your light shine;* that is, let your virtue be solid, and the fire plentiful, and the light undimmed.' Whenever virtue is thus great, it cannot possibly be hidden, even if he who pursues it conceal it in a thousand ways. Show forth a spotless life and let them have no real ground of accusation, and then, even if accusers be numbered by hundreds, no man shall have power to overcloud you. And His expression, *the light*, was pertinent. For nothing distinguishes a man so much, even if he wish to be hidden a thousand times over, as an example of goodness. Just as physical light envelops a man, so does he shine forth with greater brightness, not letting his rays sink into the earth, but directing them beyond heaven itself. So He encourages them the more. 'If,' He says, 'you are grieved at being reviled, many men through you will be in admiration of God.' He lays both wages to your account—God's glorification through you, and your being blasphemed for God's sake. In order, therefore, that we should not give heed to evil speaking, knowing that it procures us a reward, He did not simply mention the thing itself, but made two distinctions—that of calumny and that of calumny for God's sake; and He shows, moreover, that patience under it bears much fruit, by referring the glory back to God; and He holds out pleasant hopes to them. The accusation of the wicked, He says, is in nothing so powerful as in helping others to see your light. When you act foolishly, then only it is that they will trample you down, not when, doing what is right, you are cast aside. Then many will be in astonishment, not at you alone, but, through you, at our common Father. He said the Father, not God, laying already the seeds of the spiritual birth which He was to give them. Then, showing His equality with the Father, He said higher up, 'Grieve not for evil report; for it is sufficient for you that it is on My account'. Thereupon He speaks of the Father, manifesting their equality everywhere.

Recognising, therefore, our gain from this zeal and the danger of our negligence (for it is much worse that our Master should be blasphemed because of us than that we should be lost), *Let us not give offence to the Jews, or to heathens, or to the Church of God;* and, showing forth a life more shining than the sun, even if anyone should wish to accuse us, not grieving at evil report, but at hearing a just report unworthily. For if we are living in wickedness and there be no accuser, we are the most miserable of men, but if we are practising virtue, even if the whole world should speak ill of us, we shall be the most enviable of all, and we shall draw all those who are called to be saved to ourselves; for it is not by the accusation of the wicked but by a good life that they will cleave to us. And a good example speaks louder than any trumpet, and a pure life is more resplendent than the very light, even if there be a thousand adversaries. If we are all that I have specified—if we are meek and humble and merciful, and clean of heart and lovers of peace, and when we are slandered do not repine but rejoice— we shall draw those who look upon us to ourselves no less than by signs, and every man will deal kindly with us, whether he be a wild beast or a demon, or anything else whatsoever. Still, if there should be calumniators, do not be troubled at this, nor at seeing yourself publicly accused, but examine their inmost heart, and you will find that they applaud and admire you, and are loud in your praises. Just consider how Nabuchodonosor praised the children in the furnace, although he was their declared enemy; and when he saw their brave endurance, he acclaimed and acknowledged them for nothing else whatever than for turning away from his commands to listen to those of God. For when the devil sees that he is accomplishing nothing, he desists, fearing lest he should be the means of increasing our crowns; and when he is gone, however bad and depraved a man may be, he recognises virtue, that mist being removed from before his eyes. And if men should form a wrong judgment, you will have greater praise and admiration from God. Therefore, be not sorrowful or wavering, since the Apostles themselves were an odour of death to some and of life to others. If you have offered no offence to any man, and have kept free from all reproach, you are blessed indeed. Shine, then, by your life, and make no account of slandering words. For it is quite impossible that a man who cultivates goodness should not have many enemies; but this is nothing to him, for through these very enemies his life will shine the more. Taking these things to heart, let us seek for one thing—to order our own life with purity, for in this way we shall lead those who sit in darkness to that future life. Such, indeed, is the power of this light, that it not only shines here, but it escorts those who follow it to that heavenly country. Whenever men see you looking down upon all present things, and holding yourselves in readiness for eternal ones, your works will convince them better than any argument. Who so foolish as not to deduce a clear proof of the future life when he sees a man, thinking yesterday only of luxury and money-making, giving up everything, freeing himself from all cares, and stretching out his hand towards hunger, and poverty, and hardship, and dangers, and blood-shedding, and a violent death, towards everything which seems an evil? But if we are wholly engrossed with present things, and plunge into them deeper and deeper, how are men to be persuaded that we are looking for another home? What excuse shall we have if the fear of God cannot do among us that which human fame did amongst Greek philosophers?

Some of them also gave up money and despised death, in order to be a spectacle to men, and so their hopes were vain. What can be said for us with these things before us, and so great a philosophy being unfolded, that we cannot do even what they did, but are destroying ourselves and others too? For a heathen who acts against his conscience does not do the same harm as a Christian who thus acts, and most justly. Their reputation is corrupt, whereas ours, through God's goodness, is sacred and manifest even amongst impious men. Consequently, whenever they want particularly to reproach us, and to make their accusation more telling, they bring this additional charge against us: 'So and so is a Christian,' which they would not do if they had not a great opinion of Christian teaching. Have you not heard how many and what great things Christ enjoined? Now, how can you observe one of those commandments when, forgetting the rest, you go about investing your money, looking greedily after interest, involving yourself in lawsuits, buying herds of slaves, preparing silver plate, laying up stores of fields and houses, and quantities of furniture? And would that this were all! When you add iniquity to these inopportune pursuits — encroaching upon the land of others, pulling down houses, aggravating poverty, increasing hunger—how will you be able to mount up to those gates? But supposing that you *are* merciful to the poor, I know what this means, and it again will call for a great expiation hereafter.

For if you are merciful through conceit or vainglory, so that you gain no merit even from good works, what could be more wretched than to be shipwrecked in harbour? In order to prevent this from happening, seek not a reward from me when you have done a good action, so that God may be your debtor. *Lend*, He says, *to him from whom you expect no return.*

The Tongue a Royal Power.

(*Homilies on St. Matthew*, li., p. 76.)

Let us understand what those things are which sully a man, and when we have understood let us shun them. In the church we see a certain habit prevailing amongst the majority of men—how they are eager to come in with spotless clothes and clean hands, whilst they do not trouble themselves about how they are to offer up a pure heart to God. I say this, not forbidding men to wash their hands or their mouths; my wish, however, is that they should wash them in the right way, not with water alone, but rather with virtues. For slandering, blasphemy, foul language, bad words, laughter at low jokes, are the mouth's defilement. If, then, you perceive that you are not dwelling on any of these things, nor guilty of this uncleanness, approach with good heart; if, on the contrary, you have laid yourself open to these numerous stains, why are you so foolish as to rinse your tongue with water whilst you carry in it this pernicious and destructive impurity? Tell me, now, if you had dirt or dung in your hands, would you dare to utter a prayer? Certainly not. Yet one is not at all harmful, and the other is perdition. How comes it that you are particular in things of no consequence, and negligent about the prohibited ones? 'What, then,' you ask, 'are we not to go on praying?' Certainly you are, but not in this filthy condition, nor with this dirt upon you. 'What am I to do,' you ask, 'if I fall by accident?' Then, purify yourself. How, and in what manner? Be in mourning and groaning, give alms, apologise to the man you have insulted, and reconcile him to yourself by these things; purify your tongue in order that you may incite the less the anger of God. For if anyone with his hands full of mud were to grasp your feet in supplication, not only would you not listen to him, but you would kick him away; how, then, are you so bold as to approach God in this way? The tongue of those who pray is a hand, and through it we touch the knees of God.[1] Therefore do not defile that tongue, lest He should say to you, *And when you multiply your prayer I will not hear.*

[1] Compare ἀλλ' ἤτοι μὲν ταῦτα Θεῶν ἐν γούνασι κεῖται ('Ιλιαδος p. 514).

For, *in the hand of the tongue are life and death;* and, again, *By thy words thou shall be justified, and by thy words thou shalt be condemned.* Therefore guard the tongue more carefully than the pupil of the eye. The tongue is the horse of a king. If you put a bridle upon him and teach him to walk at a measured pace, the king will rest and lean upon him; but if you allow him to be at large unbridled, and to be unmanageable, he becomes the vehicle of the devil and his angels. . . . Dishonour not the tongue, for how will it pray for you when it has lost its proper confidence? Adorn it rather with mildness and humility; make it worthy of the God Whom you are invoking; fill it with words of kindness and much almsgiving. For there is an alms which is to be given by words: *The good word is better than the gift;* and, again, *Answer the poor man in mildness and gentleness.* And make the rest of your time profitable by dwelling on the divine laws. *Let all thy conversation be on the law of the Most High.* Thus adorning ourselves, let us go forth to the King and fall at His feet, not with the body only, but with our mind. Let us consider Whom we go to, for what purpose, and what it is we wish to accomplish. We go to that God from Whom the seraphim turned away their gaze, unable to bear His splendour, on Whom the earth trembles to look. We go to God, Who is in the region of light inaccessible. And we are going to Him in order to escape hell, for the remission of our sins, to deliver ourselves from those overwhelming penalties, for the winning of heaven and the goods which are there.

. . . .

Golden Vessels and Golden Hearts.

(*Homilies on St. Matthew*, l., p. 62.)

. . . .

Let us then, too, touch the hem of His garment, or rather, if we please, we have Himself whole and entire. For His body too is now put before us, not His garment only, but His very body, not to be merely touched, but to be eaten and taken away. Let us therefore approach with faith, each one with his own infirmity. For if those who touched the hem of His garment drew forth so much strength, how much more those who possess the whole of Him? Approaching with faith is not only taking what is there before us, but touching with a pure heart, and being so disposed as if we were going to meet Christ Himself. What matters it if you hear no voice? You see Him before you, or rather you *do* hear a voice, that of Himself speaking through the Evangelists. Believe, therefore, that even now there is that banquet at which He Himself sat. Nor is this banquet different from that; nor is ours the work of a man, and that the work of God, but God is the worker now as He was then. When, then, you see the priest offering it to you, think that it is not the priest who is doing this, but that it is the hand of Christ which is presenting it. Just as, when he baptises, it is not he who is baptising you, but it is God Who is holding your head with an invisible power, and neither angel nor archangel nor anyone else whatsoever presumes to approach and touch you; so it is now. For whenever God generates, it is His gift alone. Do you not know how those who adopt sons in this world do not entrust their adoption to servants, but appear themselves in the court? In like manner God has not entrusted His gift to angels, but He is Himself present, commanding, and saying, *You shall call no man your father upon earth*, not wishing you to dishonour your natural parents, but that before all the rest you may prefer Him Who created you, and Who wrote your name amongst His children. For He Who gives more, that is, Who gives Himself, will all the more certainly not disdain to make over His body to you. Let us then, both priests and laity, consider what that is of which we have been made worthy; let us consider and be in awe. He gave us to be filled with His sacred flesh, and placed before us Himself offered up in sacrifice. Now, what will our excuse be, if feeding on such food we commit such sins; when we eat the Lamb and are become wolves; when we eat the sheep and ravage like lions? For this mystery obliges us to purify ourselves not only from robbery but from the merest enmity. This mystery is indeed a mystery of peace; it cannot be conciliated with a struggle for money. For if He did not spare Himself for our sakes, what should we deserve for hoarding up money and neglecting our soul, on which account He did not spare *Himself?* God indeed bound the Jews to a remembrance of their domestic blessings every year at the feasts, but you He has bound to a daily remembrance, so to say, through these mysteries. Be not, then, ashamed of the cross, for these are our august things, these are *our* mysteries, we are adorned with this gift, and it is our beauty. Even when I say that He stretched the firmament overhead, and unfolded earth and sea, that He sent forth prophets and angels, I speak of nothing equal to this. This is the fountain-head of all good, that He did not spare His only Son in order to save alienated servants. Therefore, let neither Judas nor Simon approach this table, for avarice destroyed both one and the other. Let us avoid this abyss, and think not that it is sufficient for our salvation, if, after stripping widows and orphans, we offer a cup of gold and precious stones for this table. If you wish to show honour to the sacrifice, offer your soul for whose sake it was sacrificed. Make this golden, for if *it* should be inferior to lead and potsherd, what is the gain of the vessel being of gold? Then, do not let us be concerned only about how we are to offer a vessel of gold, but let it be also a vessel of honest labours, for that which is without avarice is more precious than gold. The church is neither a gold nor a silver-smith's shop, but an assembly of angels, therefore souls are what we want, and these things are acceptable to God through souls. The table which He then used was not of silver, nor was the chalice a golden one out of which Christ gave His own blood to His disciples; but all those things were sacred and terrible, since He filled them with the Spirit. Would you honour the body of Christ? Leave Him not naked, nor honour Him *there* with silk coverings, passing Him by outside in cold and nakedness. He who said, *This is My body*, ratifying the deed by His word, said likewise, *You saw Me in want and did not feed Me*, and, again, *Inasmuch as you did not do it for one of the least of these, you did it not for Me*. For the former does not require the giving of garments but a pure heart, whereas the latter demands great attention. Let us, then, learn to be wise and to honour Christ as He Himself wishes, for to Him Who is honoured, that honour is the sweetest which He chooses for Himself, not that which may be according to our judgment. Since Peter, too, thought to honour Him by forbidding Him to wash his feet, he was not showing honour, but the reverse. So in your case do you honour Him with the honour which He Himself laid down, by giving your riches to the poor. God has no need of golden vessels, but of golden hearts.

True Almsgiving.

(Homilies on St. Paul's Second Epistle to the Corinthians, xvi., vol. iii., p. 182.)

. . . .

Charity is, indeed, a great thing, and a gift of God, and when it is rightly ordered, likens us to God Himself as far as that is possible; for it is charity which makes the man. Some one, at least, wishing to characterise man, did it in these words: *Man is great, and the merciful man is honourable.* Kindness is better than raising up the dead. For it is a much greater thing to feed Christ in His hunger than to raise the dead in the name of Jesus. By feeding Christ you confer a benefit upon Him; in the other case He is benefiting you. And the reward is for doing, not for receiving. As to the signs, you are under an obligation to God, but with regard to the almsgiving, you put God under an obligation to you. It is an alms when you give willingly, generously, thinking that you are rather taking than giving; when you give as if you were receiving something, as gaining rather than losing, otherwise there would be no thanks in it. He who helps his neighbour should be in gladness, not in gloom. In truth, is it not foolish that in removing the despondency of another you yourself should be despondent. You will not suffer it to be a real alms. If you are sad because you are taking away another man's sadness, you are giving a proof of extreme unkindness and inhumanity; it is better to leave it undone than to do it in this way. Why are you sad at all? Is it for fear of diminishing your money? If this is your motive, then do not give; if you are not encouraged by the thought that it will be made up to you over and above in heaven, do not put out your hand in alms-giving. Perhaps you look for a compensation in this world. What is the good of this? Let your alms be alms and not traffic. Now, many have received their due here on earth, yet not so that they will be on this account much better than those who have not; these have been a few of the weaker, since they did not go vigorously after the things above. And like greedy and common people, slaves of their belly, who, called to a royal table, and not waiting for the right time, do as children do, spoil their own mirth by snatching up and satiating themselves with inferior food: so, indeed, is it that they who seek and receive temporal good things lessen the reward above. Again, in lending your money, you become desirous of securing the capital after a time, or, perhaps, of not spending it, so that you may lay up more for the future, whereas in this case you demand it at once, although you are not always to be here, but for ever there. Nor are you to be judged here, but to give an account there. Supposing that a man prepared houses for you where you did not mean to stay, you would view his act as a penalty; and would you wish to grow rich in a place from which you may be called away before the evening? Know you not that we are spending our time in a foreign land, like sojourners and strangers, and that sojourners may be cast out when they are not thinking of it or expecting it. And this is our case. So it is that we leave behind us whatever we may have busied ourselves with on earth. Our Master does not allow us to take our labours with us, whether it is that we build houses, or buy estates, or slaves, or furniture, or anything else of the kind. Not only He does not allow us to go away with them, but He refuses you a reward for them. He told you beforehand that you should not build or spend with the property of others, but with your own. Why, then, leaving your own, do you labour with what is not yours, and squander it so that you will lose both your labour and your reward, and endure the extremity of punishment? Do not so act, I beseech you; but, as we are sojourners by nature, let us become so by choice, so that we may not be aliens there, rejected without honour. If we wish to be citizens in this world we shall be so neither here nor there, but if we remain sojourners, and spend our time after the fashion of sojourners, we shall receive the assurance of being citizens both here and there. For the just man, even with nothing, will be as free on earth with the common property of all as if it were his own, and when he departs hence to heaven he will look upon the eternal dwelling-places; he will neither suffer any unpleasantness in this world, nor will any man be able to make him a sojourner, who has the whole world for his city; and in taking possession of his country, he will, moreover, receive true riches. In order, then, that we may gain both the things of time and the things of eternity, let us use present goods in the right way. Thus we shall become citizens of heaven, and enjoy much consolation. May this be the portion of us all, through the love and mercy of our Lord Jesus Christ, to Whom, with the Father and the Holy Ghost, be glory and power for ever. Amen.

I WAS HUNGRY AND YOU GAVE ME TO EAT.

(*Homilies on St. Matthew*, xlv., vol. ii., p. 5.)

. . . .

Are you unable to practise the virginal life? Then make a prudent marriage. Are you unable to do without possessions? Give, then, of what you possess. Is such a burden too heavy for you? Divide your goods with Christ. Are you not willing to cede Him everything? Make over to Him at least the half or the third part. He is your brother and co-heir; make Him your co-heir even on earth. How much soever you give to Him you give that to yourself. Do you not listen to the Prophet's words, *Despise not thy own flesh?* But if we may not despise relations, how much less the Master, Who, besides

His superiority, has the rights of relationship on His side, and many other stronger claims? He has made you a partaker of His own possessions, taking nothing from you, but being the first to give to you out of His unspeakable mercy. Then, is not it extreme folly neither to grow kind by this gift, nor to return a reward for a favour, and to give less instead of more? For He has made you heir to the kingdom of heaven, but you have not even given Him a share of the things of earth. You He reconciled without any merit of your own, when you were even His enemy; will you not make any return to your lover and benefactor, although, over and above the kingdom and all His other gifts, it was just that you should feel grateful to Him for the giving itself? Servants, indeed, when they call their masters to dinner, deem not that they are offering, but receiving; here, however, it was just the contrary. It was not the servant who first called the Lord, but the Lord Who first called the servant to His own table; and will you not call Him even after this? He was the first to bring you under His own roof; can you not even follow His example? He covered you in your nakedness, and in the face of this do you refuse to bring in a stranger? It was He Who first gave you to drink of His own cup, and will you not offer Him even cold water? He gave you the Holy Spirit to drink, and will you not relieve bodily thirst? He gave you the Spirit to drink, who were worthy of chastisement, but do you disregard a thirsty man whilst you are about to do all this out of what is His? Do you not consider it a great honour to hold the cup out of which Christ is about to drink, and to approach it to His mouth? Do you not see that the priest alone may give the chalice with the Blood? 'I go into none of these particulars.' Our Lord says: 'If you yourself give it I receive it; even if you are a layman I do not refuse it. I do not require what I have given, for I seek not blood but cold water.' Consider, then, *Whose* thirst you are relieving, and be in awe. Consider that *you* have become Christ's priest, giving with your own hands not flesh but bread, not blood but a drink of cold water. He has put on you the robe of salvation, and has clothed you through Himself; do you also clothe *Him* in the person of a child. He has made you a name in heaven; do you drive away cold, and nakedness, and unseemliness. He has made you a citizen of the angels; if you can bear it, give Him a portion only, give Him house-room as you would your servant. He says, 'I will not turn away from this refuge, and that when I have opened all heaven to you. I have delivered you,' He says, 'from the bitterest captivity: *I* do not require this, nor do I say, Deliver Me; but if you only see Me in chains, this is sufficient to console Me. I raised you from the dead: this I do not require from you; but I say, only visit Me when I am sick.' Since, then, the gifts given to us are thus great, and the things demanded of us so very small, and we do not offer even these, what sort of hell should we not deserve? It is just that we should go down into the fire which was prepared for the devil and his angels, since we are harder than a rock. For, tell me, what insensibility is this, receiving gifts so great with the prospect of the same hereafter, to be the slaves of money, which in a little while we shall have to give up, and to give up unwillingly? Others have laid down their lives and shed their blood, but you have not hazarded the smallest thing for heaven or for those unfading crowns. What sort of excuse or pardon would you deserve for enjoying all things with the fat of the earth, neglecting nothing for putting your money out to interest, and yet being cruel and inhuman in feeding your Lord in the person of the indigent? Pondering all this in our minds, and considering what we have received, and what we are going to receive, and what we are asking for, let us show forth all our zeal in spiritual things. Let us, then, become gentle and kind, so that we may escape the weight of that tremendous judgment. What is there which is not sufficient to condemn us?—the enjoyment of things so wonderful, the being asked for nothing great, the fact that we shall have to give up what we are asked for in spite of ourselves when we leave this world, the ostentation of great ambition in worldly things. Each one of these is by itself sufficient to condemn us, but when they are all combined, what hope will there be of salvation? In order, then, that we may escape this great condemnation, let us show ourselves kind towards the poor.

. . . .

THE ARCHETYPE AND THE TYPE.

(*Homilies on the Epistle to the Philippians*, xiii., vol. v., p. 136.)

. . . . . .

The Apostles presented a type, maintaining in their own persons a certain archetype. Consider how austere their life was, as if offering an archetype, and example, and living laws. For they set forth to all, through their deeds, that which the Scripture said. This is the best teaching, which has power to lead the disciple. You may talk and use fine words, but if your actions do the contrary you are no teacher. The disciple thinks very little of fine words; they should be accompanied by the teaching and leading of works: this makes both the master venerable, and disposes the disciple to agree with him. How so? When he hears a man making a display of words, he says that he has enjoined what is impossible, and that he who is not a doer is the first to prove their impracticability. Now, if he saw a man practising goodness in deed, he would not be able to say this. Moreover, supposing the master's life be careless, let us rouse ourselves, and listen to the Prophet, saying, *All shall be taught by God*, and again, *They shall teach no more every man his brother, saying: Know the Lord; for all shall know Me, from the least of them even to the greatest.* Have you no righteous teacher? You have the real Master, Him Whom alone you may call Master, learn of Him. *He said, Learn of Me, for I am meek.* Cleave, then, to no teacher, but to Him and to His teaching. Take your model from Him; you have a most excellent one; fashion yourself after it. The Scripture offers us numberless examples of a holy life; choose which you will, and follow the Master with His disciples. One shone by poverty, another through riches; for instance, Elias by poverty, Abraham by his wealth; choose whichever you think the easier and securer. Again, the one was holy through marriage, the other through virginity, as Abraham and Elias: choose your road, for each leads to heaven. John was holy by fasting, and Job without it. Job, moreover, was what he was by despising wife, and sons, and daughters, and house, having great wealth, whilst John possessed nothing except his sheep-skin. And why do I speak of house and abundance and money, since a king has it in his power to win goodness for himself. A royal palace would be found to be far more troublesome than any private house. David, then, shone in his royalty, and his purple and his crown impeded him in nothing: another was entrusted with the leadership of a whole people—I mean Moses—which is a more difficult thing. In the latter, power was greater, therefore the difficulty was greater. Do you see men who gained a good name both in riches and in poverty, in marriage and in continency? Now look, on the other hand, at those who were lost both in marriage and in continency, in riches and in poverty. For instance, many men, living in the married state, have been lost, like Samson, not because of marriage, but through their own will; in virginity, too, as the five virgins; in abundance, as the rich man who despised Lazarus; in poverty, for thousands of poor are lost every day. I can show you many men lost in monarchy, many in leading the people. Would you like to know of some in armies who have been saved? There is Cornelius. And of some in stewardships? There is the eunuch of the Ethiopian. Thus, if everywhere we use wealth as we should, it does us no harm; if we do not, everything harms us—royalty and poverty and riches. Nothing can hurt the man who is watching. Tell me, has captivity ever harmed anyone? No, never. Think of Joseph in servitude, bearing goodness in his mind; think of Daniel and the three children taken captive, how they shone the more. Everywhere goodness is resplendent and invulnerable, and nothing can master it. Why do I speak of poverty and captivity and slavery? I may add hunger and ulceration and a painful illness, for this is worse than slavery. Lazarus suffered this, and Job, and Timothy with his frequent infirmities. Do you see how nothing can overcome goodness? Neither wealth, nor poverty, nor power, nor leadership, nor being at the head of affairs, nor illness, nor being unknown, nor cast aside: disregarding all these things on the earth, it makes its way to heaven. Only have a brave spirit, and there is no obstacle against goodness. When the labourer is strong, no external thing hinders him. And so, in the case of handicrafts, when a mechanic is experienced and steadfast, and possesses all his art, even if illness should come, he has it still; or if he should be in poverty, he has it; and whether he has the instrument in his hands or not, whether he works or not, it is not diminished, because the science is in himself. So is it with God's servant: even if you throw him into riches, his art is shown forth; or into poverty, or disease, or health, or contempt, or fame, it is all the same. Did not the Apostles work through everything? *Through honour and dishonour, and evil report and good report.* This shows the soldier, the being invulnerable against everything. For this is the nature of virtue. If you say, 'I am unable to be set over many, I do best alone,' you insult virtue, for it can benefit all, and show itself, let it only be in the mind. Has hunger to be endured? or is there abundance? Virtue, again, shows its own strength; as Paul said: *I know both how to be brought low, and I know how to abound.* Was it necessary to work? He was not ashamed, but laboured for two years. Was hunger to be borne? He neither pined nor doubted. Had he to die? He did not lose heart, but showed in all things a brave soul and his skill. Now let us emulate him, and we shall have no cause for sorrow. For, tell me, what is capable of grieving such a man? Nothing. As long as no one robs us of virtue, the man who possesses it is the happiest of creatures even here—not only there. Supposing there is a holy man, with wife and children, and money, and a great name, and he still remains holy in spite of them: take them away, and he will still be holy: neither dejected by tribulation, nor elated by his righteousness, but like a rock which stands immovable whether the sea rages or whether it is calm, not troubled by the waves nor affected by the calm, so does the steadfast soul stand bravely both with calm, and with foaming waves. And, as children sailing on the sea are frightened whilst the pilot sits still and laughs at them, sees their trouble and is of good cheer, so does the mortified soul recline as if on some land or oasis of contentment, whilst all men are troubled, and laughing in an untimely way at the vicissitudes of things. For what can disturb the soul of a peaceful man? Death? But this is the beginning of a better life. Or poverty? This helps that soul on to virtue. Or illness? It accounts both refreshment and suffering as nothing, for it punished itself beforehand. Or being defamed? But the world is crucified to it. Or the loss of children? It had no fear if fully convinced of the resurrection. What, then, can make it miserable? Nothing whatever. If this man be rich, is he puffed up? By no means, for he knows that money is nothing. What of fame, then? He has been taught that *all human glory is like the flower of the field.* Or luxury, again? He has listened to Paul's words: *She that liveth in pleasure is dead while she is living.* Now, since this soul is neither lifted up nor dejected, what could come up to this well-being? Not all souls are so disposed, but they are more changeable than wind or weather, so that it is most ludicrous to see the same man now laughing, now weeping, now buried in thought, now loquacious beyond measure. Therefore he said: *Be not conformed to this world:* our citizenship is in heaven, where there is no change. Immutable rewards are offered to us: let us show forth that citizenship whence we have already received good things. But what if we cast ourselves into uncertainty and a surging sea, into a storm or a hurricane? Let us be at peace. The point lies not in riches or poverty, or glory or dishonour, or sickness or health, or weakness, but in our own soul. If this be steadfast and well-grounded in goodness, all things will be easy to it, and even here it will behold its rest, and the peaceful harbour, and departing hence it will gain endless goods. May it be granted to us all through the love and kindness of Our Lord Jesus Christ, to Whom, with the Father and the Holy Spirit, be glory, power, and praise now and for ever. Amen.

The Weak Things of God.

(*Homilies on First Epistle to Corinthians*, vi., vol. ii., p. 59.)

. . . .

And I was with you in weakness, and in fear, and in much trembling. Here, again, is another point. Not only are those who believe illiterate, not only is the teacher illiterate, not only is the mode of teaching replete with illiterateness, not only is the teaching itself qualified to terrify — for it was the Cross and death — but together with these there were other obstacles: dangers and plottings, and daily anguish, and harassing pursuit. For he often calls persecution weakness, as he does in another place: *Ye have not spurned the weakness in my flesh;* and again: *If it behoves me to glory, I will glory in my weakness.* What weaknesses are these? *The governor of king Aretu was keeping the city of Damascus, wishing to take me.* And again: *Therefore I rejoice in my infirmities.* Then, going on to distinguish what infirmities, he added: *In contumely, in want, in persecutions.* So here he speaks in the same way; for, saying, *And I was in weakness*, he added, *and I was with you in fear and in much trembling.* What is this? Did Paul himself fear dangers? He did indeed, and greatly too; for, if he was Paul, he was also a man. This is no accusation against Paul, but a weakness of nature, and an encomium of his choice, that whereas he *did* fear stripes and death, this fear did not lead him to do any unworthy action; so that those who say he did *not* fear stripes not only do not exalt him, but take much away from his praises. If, indeed, he did *not* fear, where is the fortitude and where is the merit of braving dangers? For my own part, this is what I admire in him, that, fearful as he was, and not only fearful, but trembling at dangers, he came out victorious through everything, and in no case surrendered, cleansing the world, and sowing the Gospel all over the earth and sea. *And my speech and my preaching was not in the persuasive words of human wisdom*—that is, it has not outward wisdom. If, therefore, his preaching had no subtlety about it, and those who were called were uncultured as well as the preacher, and there was, besides, persecution, and fear, and trembling, tell me, how did they gain the mastery without divine power? So, in saying, *That which I say and preach does not consist in the persuasive words of wisdom*, he added, *but in the manifestation of the Spirit and of power*. Do you see how the folly of God is wiser than man, and how the weakness is stronger? Illiterate as they were who preached these things, in chains and imprisoned, they overcame those who bound them. How? Was it not through showing the faith which is of the Spirit? This, indeed, was an irrefutable argument. For, tell me, what man, seeing the dead arise and devils put forth, would not have received their teaching? Since, however, there are powers of deception, such as those of magicians, he removed this ambiguity. He did not speak of power only, but first of the Spirit and then of power, thus showing that what had taken place was spiritual. Consequently, there having been no learning about the preaching of the Gospel is no lessening of its value, but its greatest glory. This, at least, shows it to be divine, and to have had its root above, in heaven. On this account he continued: *That your faith may not be in the wisdom of man, but in the power of God*. Do you see how clearly in everything he pointed out the gain of illiterateness and the harm of culture? While human wisdom made the Cross vain, ignorance proclaimed the power of God: the one disposed men not to find the necessaries of life, and so to glory in themselves; the other, to receive the truth and to glory in God. Again, wisdom persuaded many men to regard dogma suspiciously as human; ignorance pointed it out clearly as divine, and coming down from heaven. Now, whenever a proof is arrived at by word-wisdom, it is very often the bad men who get the better of the more moderate, being the more skilful in their arguments, and falsehood outwits the truth. It is not so here: for neither does the Holy Spirit take possession of an unclean soul, nor when He has taken possession can He be ever lessened, even if all the clever words in the world be used. A manifestation through works and signs is much clearer than that of words.

But some one might reasonably say that, if the

Gospel is bound to conquer, and the Cross needs no eloquence, that it may not be proved vain, why is it that miracles have now ceased? Why is it? Do you speak as an unbeliever, and not receive those which took place in the case of the Apostles, or do you honestly seek to learn? If as an unbeliever, then I will first direct myself to this. Now, if miracles did *not* take place then, how did they make themselves heard, standing up against whole peoples and speaking such things, driven about as they were, pursued, in fear, in chains; one and all an object of hatred to the world; at the mercy of everyone's ill-treatment; having nothing attractive of their own—neither eloquence, nor fame, nor riches, nor city, nor nationality, nor family, nor career, nor reputation, nor any one of these things, but just the reverse of them all, an illiterate and sorry condition, poverty, hatred, and enmity? Their injunctions also entailed much hardship and their teaching many dangers, and the hearers too who were to be persuaded were given up to much feasting and drunkenness and vice. Now, tell me, whence their power of persuasion, whence their titles of credence? As I was saying, if they *did* gain men without miracles, the wonder appears very much greater. Therefore do not conclude that because there are no miracles now there were none then. It was to the point, both that they took place then and that they do not take place now. Persuasion by word alone now is no security that the Gospel lies in the possession of wisdom. For they who in the beginning were sowers of the Word were uncultured and ignorant, and they spoke nothing of themselves, but they gave to the world that which they had received from God; now, we also spread abroad not our own inventions, but we speak to all what we have received from them. We do not persuade by arguments now but by Holy Scripture, and the signs which then took place inspire us with confidence in what we say. Neither did they persuade by signs alone, but also by discoursing, whilst the signs made their words appear the more powerful together with the testimony of the Old Testament, not the cleverness of what was said. 'Why,' you ask, 'were miracles good then and not now?' Let us suppose a case, for so far my contest has been directed against a heathen, and therefore I will suppose something that must undoubtedly happen; let us then suppose a case, and let the unbeliever submit to believe, for instance, that Christ will come, even if he take my word for it; well, then, when Christ shall come and all the angels with Him, and He is shown to be God, and all things are under His dominion, will not the heathen too believe? It is evident that he will fall down in adoration and confess Him to be God, however stubborn he may be. Who, indeed, seeing the heavens opened and Christ Himself seated on the clouds, with all the heavenly host surrounding Him, the rivers running fire, all men standing by in great fear, would not worship Him and acknowledge Him as God? Tell me now, shall that worship and knowledge be accounted to the heathen as faith? By no means. For it is *not* faith; sheer force produces it, and the manifestation of visible things. It is not a matter of choice, but reason is constrained by the greatness of the vision. Therefore, the more evident and undeniable that which happens is, by so much is faith diminished, and this is why miracles are not worked now. And that it is so, listen to Our Lord's words to St. Thomas: *Blessed are they who have not seen yet have believed.* Therefore the reward of faith is diminished just in proportion to the greater evidence of the sign, so that if signs took place now the same would follow. In the words, *Now we walk through faith, not through sight,* Paul made it clear that then we shall no longer know Him by faith. Thus, if you believe then, you will not be convinced by the wonder of the thing, so neither would you be now if the same signs took place as of old. Whenever we receive things which are in no sort of way discoverable to anyone by reasoning, that is faith. On this account, too, hell is threatened, but is not apparent, for if it were, the same would be the case here also. Still, if you seek for miracles, you will see them even now, though they are not the same kind of miracles. You will see a thousand prophecies concerning a thousand things, the conversion of the world, the holy life of barbarians, the change of cruel habits, the increase of piety.

'What prophecies are these?' you ask. 'For all that was foretold was written down after the event.' Tell me when, and where, and by whom, and how long ago? Shall we say it was fifty years ago or a hundred? Therefore a hundred years ago there was nothing at all written down. Then how did the world receive the teaching and all other things, as memory did not suffice? How did they know that Peter was crucified? How after this did it occur to men to foretell such things, for instance, as that the Gospel should be preached in the whole world, that the Jewish dispensation should stop and not come back again? How would those who had staked their lives for the Gospel have borne to see it counterfeited? How were the writers trusted when there were no more miracles? How did those writings penetrate into uncivilised lands, and into India, and even unto the farthest extremities of the ocean, if the speakers were not worthy of faith? Now, who were the writers? When and where did they write? Why did they write? Was it to make themselves famous? Why did they ascribe the Scriptures to others? Were they desirous of embodying a system of doctrine? Then was it true or false? For if they looked upon it as false, there was no pretext for their coming forward at all; but if as true, there was no need of counterfeits, as you truly say. Moreover, the prophecies are such that up to the present day what has been said cannot be restricted by time. If, on the one hand, the destruction of Jerusalem took place many years ago, there are other prophecies dating from the same time which reach up to His coming. Examine these, if you like—as, for instance, *I am with you always, even unto the consummation of time*, and, *Upon this rock I will build My Church, and the gates of hell shall not prevail against it*; again, *This Gospel shall be preached to all nations*, and the deed of the woman who was a sinner, and many more than these. Now, whence comes the truth of this prophecy if it was an invention? How have the gates of hell not prevailed against the Church? How is Christ always with us? If He were not with us, the Church would not have conquered. How has the Gospel been spread about the whole world? Our adversaries are able to bear witness to the antiquity of our Scriptures—I mean Celsus and his party, and the man of Batavia after him—for they did not contradict what those who came after them put together; moreover, the whole world with one voice has received it. For if it was not the grace of the Spirit, there could not have been so great an unity from end to end of the earth, but the inventors would speedily have been convicted, nor would successes so great have been produced by forgeries and falsehood. Do you not see the whole world coming to meet it, and error extinguished?—the mortification of monks shining brighter than the sun? Do you not see bands of virgins, the piety of barbarians, men all serving under one yoke? Nor are these things foretold by us alone, but first by the prophets. You must not overlook those prophecies of theirs either, for our Scriptures are present to our enemies, and Greeks have set themselves eagerly to translate them into the language of Greece. These prophecies foretell many things, and show that He Who was to come is God.

Now, why do not all men now believe? Because things have been going to the bad, and it is we who are the cause of it. The rest of my discourse is for your benefit. It was not, indeed, through signs only that they then believed, but many were led on by an example of life. *Let your light shine before men*, Our Lord says, *that they may see your good works and glorify your Father Who is in heaven*. And, again, *They all had one heart and one mind, and no man among them called anything his own, but they had all things in common, and to each man was given according to his need*, and their life was an angelical one. And if this were to take place now, we should convert the whole world even without wonder-working. In the meantime, let those who wish to be saved follow the Scriptures: there they will find both these successes and many more besides. For the teachers themselves surpassed those deeds, living their lives in hunger and thirst and nakedness; we, on the contrary, wish to enjoy much feasting, and refreshment, and security. Not so those men who cried out: *Up to the present hour we are in hunger and thirst and nakedness, and are homeless and beaten about.*

Some went out from Jerusalem as far as Illyria, one to the Indies, one to the Moors, another to all parts of the earth; we, on the other hand, have not courage to leave even our own country, but seek for luxury, and splendid households, and abundance of every kind. Which of us ever suffered hunger for God's Word, or went into the desert, or took a long journey for it? What teacher living by his hands has come to the help of others? Who has encountered death day after day? Hence our people are growing softer. For if anyone were to see soldiers and generals wrestling with hunger and thirst, and death, and every possible evil, and bearing cold and dangers with the fortitude of lions, and conquering; and if, after this, he were to see them giving up their life of heroism, becoming fainthearted, loving money, absorbed in their own affairs and business, and then defeated by their enemies, it would be extreme folly to seek for the reason. Let us apply this to ourselves and our forefathers, for we have grown weaker than anyone else, and we are nailed to this present life. Even if a man be found with a trace of the old mortification, who leaves the city and the market-place, and the thick of the fray, and the ordering of others, and flies to the mountain, and if anyone ask why he retires, he will discover no sound reason for it. He says: 'I withdraw that I may not perish, and that I may not become weak in goodness'. How much better it would be that you *should* grow weaker and gain others, than remain on the heights and see your brethren perishing. Now, when some neglect goodness, and others who *do* care for it are withdrawn from their rank in the fight, how shall we gain our enemies? If signs took place now, who would be convinced? Or who of those without would attach himself to us whilst vice is so apparent? An upright life on our part seems to the multitude more convincing. For signs from shameless and bad men arouse a suspicion of evil, but a pure life is able to shut the devil's mouth with great force. These things I say both to rulers and ruled, and to myself, before all, in order that we may show forth an admirable life, and, forming ourselves into battle array, may disregard all present things. Let us despise money, and not despise hell; think little of fame, but not little of our salvation; let us endure struggles and labours here, that there we may not encounter chastisement. Thus let us fight the heathen, thus let us take them prisoners in a captivity which is better than freedom. But we talk persistently and often about these things, and scarcely ever do them. However, whether we do them or not, it is right always to insist upon them. For if some cheat through fine words, how much more should those who are leading others to the truth not weary of speaking what is due. For if cheaters make use of these tactics—for they lay up money, and bring arguments to bear, and encounter dangers, and make their power felt—how much more should we, who lead men away from deceit, endure dangers, and death, and all things, so that, gaining ourselves and others, and standing invincibly against our adversaries, we may arrive at the promised goods in Christ Jesus our Lord, to Whom be glory and power for ever and ever. Amen.

THE SECRET OF OUR FAITH.

(*Homilies on First Epistle to Corinthians*, iii., vol. ii., p. 27.)

Show me, if you can, whether Peter and Paul were scholars. But you cannot; for they were ordinary men and unlettered.[1] Just as Christ, when He sent His disciples out into the world, showed His power first to them in Palestine, saying, *When I sent you without purse, and scrip, and shoes, did you want anything?* Afterwards He charged them to have a scrip and a purse, and so He did in this case. For that which was aimed at was to show the power of Christ, not that the lack of external accomplishments should cause those who approached to be rejected from the faith. Now, whenever heathens accuse the disciples of being unlearned, let us be even louder than they in our accusations. Let no one say that Paul was skilful, but praising great men amongst them for their skill, and those re-

---

[1] St. Chrysostom here refers from memory to the *Acts*, where Peter and *John* are spoken of as "illiterate and ignorant men" (c. iv., v. 13).

markable for their clever speeches, let us say that all of ours are unlearned. We shall not a little overthrow them on this side too, so brilliant will be the victory. I have said these things because I once heard a Christian making himself ridiculous in discussion with a heathen, and each in their fight against the other destroying his own side. That which the Christian should have said the heathen said, and that which it would have been natural for the heathen to say the Christian put forward. For, Paul and Plato forming the subject of dispute, the heathen, on the one hand, tried to show that Paul was uneducated and unlearned, and, on the other, the Christian, out of simplicity, was all eager to prove that Paul was a better reasoner than Plato. Thus the heathen gained the victory, as this consideration prevailed. For, if Paul *had* been a better dialectician than Plato, many would naturally have used the argument that he succeeded through his skilful speech rather than by grace. So the Christian's argument told for the heathen, and the heathen's for the Christian. For if Paul was untaught and still conquered Plato, as I have said, it was a triumphant victory. The unlearned Paul, taking Plato's disciples, convinced them and drew them to himself. Hence, it is evident that the Gospel was not preached by human wisdom, but by the grace of God. In order, then, that we may not encounter the same defeat, nor make ourselves ridiculous when we are thus in discussion with heathens, let us condemn the Apostles as unlearned: this very condemnation is praise. And when they tell us that the Apostles were rustic, let us admit and confess that they were untaught, and unlearned, and poor, and needy, and unintelligent, and obscure. This is no blasphemy of the Apostles, but their glory, that, being what they were, they appeared more famous than the whole world. Those very unlearned, rustic, untaught men beat down men wise in their conceits, powerful men, tyrants, men who were enjoying riches and glory and all outward goods, as if they had not been men at all. Whence it is clear that the power of the Cross was great, and that it was not through human strength that these things took place. They do not, indeed, come from nature at all, but that which was accomplished was above nature. Whenever something takes place which is above nature, and very much above it, and is also opportune and good, it is evident that it happens by a certain divine power and co-operation. For, consider—a fisherman, a tent-maker, a publican, an unlearned man, and an untaught man, coming from their outlandish province of Palestine, drove out from their own stronghold philosophers, and orators, and rhetoricians, and overcame them in a short time in the midst of many dangers, peoples and kings resisting them, nature itself being adverse: inveterate custom, force of habit, fighting them to the teeth: evil spirits armed against them: the devil in agitation setting all things in motion—monarchies, and rulers, and democracies, and nations, and cities, barbarians, heathens, philosophers, orators, sophists, lawmakers, laws, tribunals, every sort of chastisement, and manifold deaths. And yet all these things were overcome, and gave way at the voice of fishermen, just as a little dust which is unable to resist the force of strong winds. Let us learn, therefore, so to speak with the heathens as not to be like a herd of sheep or cattle, but let us be prepared to prove the hope which is in us. And, meanwhile, let us insist on the chief point, which is no small one, and say to them, How was it that the weak circumvented the strong, that twelve men conquered the world, not in the strength of their own weapons, but in their nakedness fighting armed men? For, say, if twelve men, inexperienced in war, breaking in upon a huge array of armed warriors, not only weaponless themselves, but feeble in body, were to suffer nothing at their hands, and were to escape scatheless from a thousand missiles, and, standing in their midst with unprotected bodies, were to put them all to flight, not using weapons, but fighting with their hands, slaying some and taking others into captivity, and not receiving a scratch themselves, nor reached by a thousand blows aimed at them—who would ascribe this to man alone? Yet the victory of the Apostles was far more wonderful than this. For it is much more stupendous that an unlearned man, an untaught man, and a fisherman should circumvent so much cleverness, than that an unarmed man should come scathless out of the fight: that they should be held back neither by their small numbers nor their poverty, nor by dangers, nor by force of habit, nor by the difficulty of the enterprise which they had undertaken, nor by death looking them daily in the face, nor by the multitude of those deceived, nor by the fame of deceivers.

In like manner, then, let us overthrow them, and fight against them, and let us strike them down rather by our life than by arguments. For this is the great strife, and the most unanswerable argument is that of works, since we may philosophise with our tongues in a thousand ways, and yet if we show not forth a better life than theirs, we gain nothing whatever. They do not give heed to our reasonings, but take note of what we do, and they say, 'First yield obedience to your own words, and then advise others. If you speak of the innumerable goods of the next world, and yet seem to be given up to present ones, as if those others did not exist, your deeds are more convincing to me than your words. For when I see you seizing others' property, grieving inordinately over the dead, committing many other sins, how can I believe you when you tell me that there is a resurrection?' Even if they do not put this into words, they think it, and bear it in their minds. And this it is which prevents infidels from becoming Christians. Let us, then, lead them by our life. Many illiterate men have thus struck down the mind of philosophers, by showing them the philosophy of works, sending forth a voice louder than a trumpet through their own manner of life and conduct: this voice is indeed much more powerful than the tongue. Whenever I say that it is not lawful to bear malice to anyone, and then injure a heathen in a thousand ways, how shall I be able to persuade him by my words since I frighten him away by my deeds? Let us, therefore, catch them by our daily life, and build up the Church through these souls, and collect this wealth. Nothing whatsoever is of so much worth as a soul, not even the whole world. If you should give thousands of pounds to the poor, you do nothing in comparison to the one who converts a soul. *He who makes an honourable man out of a worthless one shall be as My mouth,* God says. Compassion for the poor is also a great good, but it is nothing compared to withdrawing a soul from error; the man who does this becomes like Peter and Paul. For we may point out the Gospel which they preached; not that we be imperilled as they were, and have hunger and pestilence and other evils to endure, for this is a time of peace, but so that we may show forth the zeal of a willing spirit. *This* fishing may, indeed, be carried out by those who sit at home. If any man have a friend, or relation, or servant, this let him do and say, and he will become like Peter and Paul. And why do I say Peter and Paul? He will be the mouth of Christ. For *he who makes an honourable man out of a worthless one shall be as My mouth*, He says. If you should not persuade to-day, you will to-morrow, and, even if you never persuade at all, you will have the full reward. And if you cannot persuade all, you can persuade a few out of many, since the Apostles themselves did not convince all the men of their day; but still they conversed with them all, and have the reward for all. For God is wont to bestow His crowns, not according to what is accomplished by good deeds, but according to the intention of those who do them. If you put down only two mites He receives them, and He will do for those who teach what He did for the widow. Therefore, because you are not able to save the world, do not despise the few, nor turn away from small things in your desire for great things. If you cannot give a hundred, look after the ten; and if you cannot give ten, do not despise the five; and if five are beyond you, do not overlook the one; and if you cannot even give the one, do not lose courage, and do not neglect your part.

. . . .

The Victory of Our Faith.

(*Homilies on St. Matthew*, lxxv., vol. ii., p. 376.)

. . . .

We may wonder the more at the power of Christ, and at the courage of the Apostles, because they were announcing the Gospel at the very time when everything Jewish was particularly attacked, and the Jews were proscribed as seditious, and the Roman emperor commanded their total dispersion. And this happened in a state of things which we may describe in this way. There is a great tempest at sea, the whole atmosphere is wrapped in darkness, wreck follows upon wreck, on board all the sailors are in open rebellion, and from below monsters are darting up, and together with the waves are destroying the men; thunderbolts are falling, pirates attacking, and on board all is mutiny. Suppose that in this extremity anyone should order men who were ignorant of nautical matters, nor even knew the sea, to sit at the rudder, to guide the helm, and to fight their way. And then, in the face of an experienced crew equipped with much labour suppose that these men should use a light boat, in the state of tumult which I have described, and overcome and master it. For as Jews they were hated by the Gentile world, and as the enemies of their own laws they were stoned by the Jews; nowhere was there any standing-ground. Thus, on all sides there were precipices, chasms, and rocks; cities, country-places, dwelling-houses, offered them nothing else; one and all opposed them—commander, and magistrate, and the man in private life, all races and all peoples—and there was a disturbance with which men could not reason. For, indeed, the Jewish race was exceedingly hateful to the Roman rulers, inasmuch as it had caused them trouble in a thousand ways, and yet the Gospel tidings were not prejudiced thereby, but the city itself was ravaged and set on fire, and numberless ills fell upon its inhabitants. Nevertheless the Apostles, going forth from that city, bringing in new laws, mastered even the Romans. Oh, what new and wonderful deeds are these! The Romans at that time subdued countless thousands of Jews, and they did *not* circumvent twelve poor unarmed men. What words can adequately express this wonder? For there are two things which teachers should possess—the being worthy of confidence and the love of their disciples; and over and above these, that what they say should be well received, and the time in which they say it free from agitation and fear. But then everything was just the reverse. For neither did they appear to be worthy of confidence, and yet they were to detach those whom men, apparently thus worthy, had deceived. They were not loved, but even hated, and they drew men off from those things which they clung to, from habits of life, and from country, and from laws. Moreover, their injunctions were exceedingly hard, but those from which they took men were most pleasant. Many were the dangers and the deaths to be encountered both by them themselves and by those who listened to them; and with all this, the time itself was a time of great trouble, fruitful in wars, tumults, and agitation, so that if there had been no one of the things which we have enumerated, it alone might have upset everything. We may say, pertinently: *Who shall declare the powers of the Lord? who shall set forth all His praises?* For if the friends of Moses did not listen to him when he spoke with miraculous signs simply because of bricks and clay, who was able to withdraw from an idle life men who day after day are killed and slaughtered, and are suffering intolerable evils? Who was able to make them prefer this insecure life of blood-shedding and death even to the other, the heralds of these tidings being of another race, and on all accounts most hostile? Let a man bring in, not to a race, or city, or people, but into one small household, one who is hated by everybody in it, and let him try hard through that person to withdraw men from those he loves, from father and wife and children, will he not be seen torn to pieces before he opens his mouth? And if he bring to the house contention and strife between husband and wife, will they not take and stone him before he again crosses the threshold? If besides he is contemptible, and yet enjoins disagreeable things, ordering luxurious men to practise an ascetic life; and with all this, if the combat be against men much more numerous and powerful than himself, is it not evident that he is wholly undone? And yet this very thing which it was impossible to do in one household is what Christ has done in the whole world, through precipice and fire, and chasm and rock, with earth and sea fighting against Him, by introducing the healers of the world. And if you wish to learn these things more accurately,—I mean famines, and plagues, and earthquakes, and other visitations,—go over the history of these things as it is contained in Josephus, and you will see it all most clearly. This is why He Himself said: *Be not disturbed, for all things must come about;* and *He who perseveres unto the end shall be saved;* and again, *This Gospel shall be preached throughout the whole world.* For He revives those who are discouraged and drooping for fear at what He has told them, by saying, that whatever happens, the Gospel must be preached in every part of the world, and that then the end will come. Do you see what a state things were in at that time, and how war was everywhere? And this at the outset, when that which is established most especially requires much peace. Now, what was this state? There is no reason why we should not recapitulate the same things. The first war was that of deceivers, for He said: *There shall arise false Christs and false prophets;* the second, that of the Romans: *You are about to hear wars;* the third was that which was to bring in famine; the fourth, that of plagues and earthquakes; the fifth, *They shall give you up to fear;* the sixth, *You shall be hated by all;* the seventh, *They shall traduce and hate each other;* hence clearly civil war; hence false Christs and false brethren; hence *Charity shall grow cold,* which is the cause of all evils without exception. Do you see how war was there in every shape, both novel and marvellous? Still, with all this and much more (for war amongst kindred was added to civil discord), the Gospel tidings took possession of the whole world. *For*, He said, *the Gospel shall be preached in the whole world*.

. . . .

MARRIAGES AS THEY WERE AND AS THEY ARE.

(*Homilies on St. Matthew*, lxxiii., vol. ii., p. 355.)

. . . .

Have you not heard that men and women were assembled together in the upper room, and that that gathering was worthy of heaven? And with reason. The women of those days put in practice a high ascetic life, and men were grave and wise. Listen at least to the seller of purple saying: *If you have judged me to be faithful to the Lord, come unto my house and abide there*. Listen to the women who followed the Apostles about from place to place with the spirit of true men—a Priscilla, and a Persis, and the others—from whom the women of to-day are as far removed as the men are from the men. For then even when going about they gave no scandal, but now, delicately nurtured in their houses, they hardly avoid this suspicion. These scandals arise from people decking themselves out and from luxury. Those women of old made it their business to spread abroad the Gospel tidings: *now* women's anxiety is to have fine figures and comely faces. They care no more for their good name than for their salvation; and as to high and great deeds of goodness, they do not even dream of them. What woman shows eagerness to make her husband better? What man is anxious to bring his wife to amendment? Not one; but the wife's whole anxiety is about jewels and clothes, and the other adornments of the body, and how she may increase her substance; and the husband's is the same, except that he has many more cares, and they are all worldly cares. Who that is about to marry would inquire into the girl's manners and education? No one; but he would be particular enough about money and land, and the accurate estimate of her fortune, as if he were going to buy something, or to carry out some low contract. This is why they speak of marriage as a contract. For I have heard many say, ' Such a man has made a contract with such a girl; that is, he has married'. They trample upon the very gifts of God, and marry and are married, as if they were buyers and sellers. Indeed, deeds require more accuracy than the business of buying and selling. Consider how men married of old, and emulate their example. Now, *how* did they marry? They enquired about the ways and habits of their bride, and about her goodness of heart. Therefore they had no need of contracts, nor of pen-and-ink settlements; the bride's character was everything to them. So I admonish you, too, not to look for money and wealth, but for disposition and goodness. Seek out a virtuous and earnest girl, and she will be of more worth to you than thousands of pounds. If you look for the things of God, the other things will come of themselves; but if you pass over the former and insist on the latter, you will not gain even these. But you will say, 'Such a man became rich through his wife'. Are you not ashamed to bring forward such instances? I have heard many say, 'I would rather be poor a thousand times over than grow wealthy through my wife'. For what is more unacceptable than that wealth? What is more pungent than that abundance? What is more humiliating than to be the man thus noted and pointed at by everyone as the 'man who became rich through his wife'. I would set forth the domestic vexations which would of necessity befal this man from his act, viz., his wife's temper, his state of slavery, their contentions, the scoffs of servants who call him 'a poor beggar, a nobody sprung from nowhere, for what had he to offer? Did not everything belong to the lady?' But these words make no impression on you, for you have not an independent spirit. Since toad-eaters, too, have to hear what is still more outrageous, and do not care, so neither are these men troubled, but they glory in their shamelessness, and when we talk to them about it, one of them answers, 'Let me alone, it is very pleasant; and it can put an end to me for all I care'. Oh! the malice of the devil for making certain sayings commonplaces in life, which are capable of poisoning the whole existence of such men. See, at least, what deadly havoc this one diabolical phrase works; for it says in so many words, 'Have no care for sobriety or for justice: let everything of the kind be thrown aside, and look only for one thing—pleasure'. Even if this pursuit oppress you, choose it; even if all who meet you spit upon you, and throw mud in your eyes, and drive you about like a dog, bear it. What else could swine say if they had a voice? or unclean dogs? Indeed, often *they* would not give voice to those things which the devil has induced men to rave about. Therefore I strongly advise those who know the heartlessness of these words to fly from such proverbial sayings, and to confute them by the contrary ones of Holy Scripture. Which are they? *Go not after thy lusts, and turn away from thy own will.* And, again, concerning the harlot, its words are opposed to that other phrase: *Mind not the deceit of a woman. For the lips of a harlot are like a honey-comb dropping, and her throat is smoother than oil. But her end is bitter as wormwood, and sharp as a two-edged sword.* Let us listen to these, and not to those words. For on the latter base-minded and servile men ground their sophistry; hence, in this, men become unreasoning things, in that they elect to seek pleasure everywhere according to the world's standard, which is despicable even apart from our showing. For after the surfeiting, what is the gain of a sweet taste? Cease, then, from this mirth, and from committing yourselves to hell and the unquenchable fire, and let us look forward as we ought to the things to come, putting off the scales from our eyes, so that we may reach that future life in due time in great piety and contentment, and may gain its good things through the love and kindness of Our Lord Jesus Christ, to Whom be power for ever and ever. Amen.

"USE A LITTLE WINE."

(*Homilies de Statuis*,[1] xxi., *preached at Antioch*, tom. ii., p. 2.)

. . . .

Since, therefore, we melt down the gold of the Apostle's mines, not throwing it into the furnace, but putting it by in the understanding of our soul, not enkindling a flame, but the fire of the Spirit, let us pick up diligently even the tiny shavings. For if the word is brief, its power is great. If the special worth of pearls lies not in their bulk but in their beauty, so is it in the reading of the Divine Scriptures. On the one hand, secular education has a care for much that is trifling, is full of silly talk to its pupils, and sends them away empty-handed, without gain small or great. It is not so with the grace of the Spirit, but just the contrary. By a few words it brings asceticism before all, and often one

---

[1] Translated from Greek Benedictine Edition in folio, tom. ii., p. 2.

word is sufficient for the provision of a whole lifetime.

Since we have this wealth before us, let us rouse ourselves, and receive these words with a pure mind. And I am prepared to show that this word (of St. Paul to St. Timothy) contains a great deal. This advice has seemed to many superfluous and trifling, and they make some such remark as, 'Might not Timothy have known himself how much wine he was to take, without waiting to be told it by his master?' Now, as the master not only gave the order, but enforced it by letter, as on a metal slab, in the epistle which he wrote to him, was he not ashamed to establish a rule for such things in writing to his disciple? Learn, then, that this advice, far from being superfluous, was necessary and most useful. It is not Paul's doing, but the grace of the Spirit. I am speaking not only of its having been said, but also of its having been made emphatic in writing, and published by this same epistle to all future generations. I shall come presently to this proof. Together with the remarks I have noted, some people question another and a not less important point, asking themselves why God allowed a man of so great courage, whose bones and body put forth devils, to fall into this great bodily weakness; for he was not merely ill, he was always and persistently ill with illnesses following close upon each other, so as to leave him no breathing time. How do we know this? From Paul's own words; for he did not say, *because of thy infirmity*, nor thy infirmities alone, but to show that they were constant he said, *thy frequent infirmities*. Let as many as are given up to a long sickness, and are in great distress and weariness, listen to this. Our enquiry does not concern itself only with the fact that, being a holy man, he was sick, or that he was so thus constantly, but that he was entrusted with the concerns of the world. If he had been one of those dwellers on the mountain heights, or bound fast to a tent in the desert, and thus leading a life without business, the question would be less puzzling; but exposed to view as he was, with the cares of churches so great upon him, traversing entire cities and countries, and the whole world itself, with so much readiness, that *he* should have been given up to the powerlessness of illness, this it is which is the most perplexing of all to a man without reflection; for if not for himself, he wanted his health for others. He was an excellent general: he had waged war, he said, not against unbelievers only, but against demons and the devil himself. All his enemies were fiercely assailing him, dispersing his army, and taking it captive. This man could lead thousands to the truth, and he was sick. If no further harm than this had been done to our work by that illness, a man says, that alone was sufficient to make believers grow more careless and negligent. If soldiers see their general confined to bed, they grow careless and less eager for battle; so it was much more natural that the faithful of those days, seeing the master who worked signs so great constantly ill and weak in his body, should suffer, humanly speaking, at the sight. This is not all; but enquiries go on to something else, and ask again why neither he cured himself, nor his master, who saw him thus prostrated, cured him either; whereas they were raising the dead, and casting out demons, and conquering death with authority, they did *not* cure this one sick body; and whilst in life and in death they were showing forth a wonderful power in other bodies, they did not restore *this* ailing stomach. And, what is more, Paul was not ashamed, after wonders so great as he had shown forth, by a mere word writing to Timothy, of advising him to try the remedy of wine-drinking. Not that drinking wine is bad. Far from it. This is what heretics assert; but that he deemed it not beneath him that the cure of one sick member could not be affected without this help. He was so far from being ashamed of this that he made it clear to all succeeding generations. Do you see how deeply we have gone into the matter: how that which appears a small thing gives rise to endless questions? Let us, then, add the explanation, for we *have* gone into it thus deeply in order to rouse your minds and establish them in security.

You must allow me, before coming to the explanation in question, to say something about Timothy's goodness and Paul's care for him. What was kinder than he, who at so great a distance, and in a round of so much business, made the wellbeing of his disciple's stomach his care, and told him clearly what to do for his restoration to health? And what could equal Timothy's virtue? He so looked down on luxury and scorned a rich table as to grow weak from his extreme severity and excessive fasting. Listen to Paul's words plainly showing that he was not this by nature, but that he had lost his strength of stomach through fasting and water drinking; for he did not merely say, *Use a little wine*, but saying in the first place, *Do not still drink water*, he added his counsel about drinking wine. The *still* was a proof that until then he had drunk water, and had so become weak. Who would not be struck with his mortification and severity of life? Timothy was taking heaven itself by storm, and pressing on to the height of virtue, and to this his master bears witness in the words: *I have sent you Timothy, who is my beloved child and faithful in the Lord.* Now, when Paul calls him his child, and his faithful and beloved child, these words sufficiently show all his worth; for the judgments of the saints are not given either out of love or hatred, but are free from all prejudice. If Timothy had been Paul's child according to nature, he would not have been as enviable as he is now renowned, for whereas Timothy was nothing to him according to the flesh, through the attraction of piety he drew him into his sonship, preserving carefully in all things the characteristics of Timothy's asceticism. Just as a calf yoked with a bull, so did Timothy bear the yoke with him all over the world, and made no difference as he grew older, but his ardour induced him to vie with the labours of his master. Paul, again, witnesses to this, saying: *Let no one set him at nought, for he is doing the Lord's work as I am myself.* Do you see how he proclaims Timothy's zeal as equal to his own? And that you may not think that favouring prompted him so to speak, he makes his listeners themselves witnesses of his child's goodness, saying: *You know what his test has been; how he has served with me in the Gospel as a child his father. You have had a proof by this of his virtue and of his tried spirit.* Yet whilst Timothy was rising to these great heights of goodness, he did not presume of himself. On the contrary, he was in wrestling and fear. On this account he was diligent in fasting, and did not act as the majority of men do, who, having given themselves up to fasting, some for ten months only, others for twenty, suddenly break up everything. He did not suffer this, nor did he say anything of this kind within himself: 'Why should I go on fasting? I have got the better of myself: I have conquered my desires, I have mortified my body, I have terrified demons, I have cast out the devil, I have raised the dead, I have cleansed lepers, the opposing powers hold me in fear, what further need have I of fasting and of the weakness which it brings?' He said none of these things, nor were they in his mind; but the greater his abundance of good deeds, the more he feared and trembled, and this asceticism he had learnt from his master; for he who had been rapt into the third heaven and taken into paradise, who had heard ineffable words and had participated in mysteries so high, who had traversed the whole world as if with wings, said, in writing to the Corinthians: *I fear lest, having preached to others, I myself should be cast out.* Now, if Paul, who was able to say, *The world is crucified to me and I to the world*, is in fear after all these his wonderful deeds, how much more should *we* fear, and this should increase in proportion to the number of our good actions. For the devil storms and rages the more when he sees us ordering our lives with care. When he sees much goodness pressed together and an accumulation of merits, then it is that he sets himself to bring about a completer shipwreck. For a poor and abject man, even if he be supplanted and fall, does not so injure the common good. Now, when he who stands, as it were, gloriously on the heights of virtue, seen and known to all, the object of general admiration, falls into temptation, he effects great ruin and havoc, not only because he fell from a high place, but also because he made those who looked up to him more slothful. Just as in the body, when a member withers up, the harm is not great, yet, if the eyes fail or the head is injured, the whole body becomes useless, so is it with the saints and with those who do great things. When these are extinguished, when they admit any stain, they work immense harm to the whole body.

Now, Timothy had all this before him, and he fortified himself on all sides; for he knew that youth is hard to manage: unstable, easily deceived, unsteady, and that it needs a strong bridle; for it is a pyre which embraces all external things and is easily ignited. Therefore, he was careful to put a check upon it on all sides, and he tried in every way to quench this fire, and he drove the horse, which was unruly and refractory, with much spirit, until he had broken him in and made him obedient, and brought a strong hand to bear upon him, so that he listened to reason's word of command: 'Let my body be weak but not my soul,' he said. 'Let the flesh be bridled, and my soul in its course heavenwards not be impeded.' Together with this, what we should especially wonder at in him was, that weakened down as he thus was, and fighting with weakness, he did not neglect God's work, but was more active than those in full and robust health. He was seen with his master, now at Ephesus, now at Corinth, often in Macedonia, in Italy, everywhere by land and by sea, ever taking part in his toils and in his continual dangers, nor did his weakness of body get the better of his asceticism of spirit. This is zeal according to God, which makes high-soaring easy. Thus, they who are in good case and sound in body will gain nothing by it if their soul be cast down, and soft, and slothful; so the weak will not be harmed by their want of health if their soul be strong and alert. Now, this advice and counsel seem to some to warrant unlimited wine-drinking, which is by no means the case. If anyone would weigh the word carefully, he would find it is rather an exhortation to fasting. For consider, this advice of Paul's was given not from the first and at the outset. It was given when he knew that Timothy's whole strength was broken, and even then not unrestrictedly, but with a condition. He did not merely say, *Use wine*, but, *a little wine*, and this not because Timothy required the advice, but because *we* do. Therefore, in writing to him, he limits and restricts wine-drinking, telling him to drink as much as would overcome weakness, and restore health to the body; not what would encourage another complaint. Immoderate wine-drinking breeds complaints no less than excessive water-drinking, or rather much worse ones, both in soul and body. It incites the war of passions, and leads a tempest of foolish fancies into the mind, weakens and enervates strength of body. An abundance of water falling on the earth does not more persistently break up the soil than constant wine-drinking does bodily strength by weakening and wasting it. Let us, therefore, avoid both extremes, and take care of our health, whilst we keep it within due bounds. For wine was given us by God, not that we should be drunk with it, but that we should be temperate, that we should be made glad and not sorry. *Wine rejoices the heart of man*, the Scripture says.

Now, you turn it into a course for despondency. Those who drink too much are sullen, and their reason is overclouded. Used with moderation, it is the best medicine. This will be a useful argument against heretics who attack what God has made. If it had been forbidden, Paul would not have counselled it, nor have said, *Use wine*. And not against heretics only is it good, but against our own simpler brethren, who, when they see certain men degrading themselves by drink, instead of blaming *them*, attack God's gift, saying, *Let there be no wine*. Then we may answer them: 'Let there be no drunkenness'. For wine is God's, whilst drunkenness is the devil's. It is not wine which makes inebriety, but intemperance. Do not slander God's creature, but the madness of your fellow-man. Will you neglect to punish and correct the sinner whilst you despise the Benefactor?

. . . .

Possessing the Land.

(*Homilies on Second Epistle to Corinthians*, ix., vol. iii., p. 110.)

. . . .

Since, then, the things which we see are temporary, but the things which we do not see eternal, let us turn our minds to these. For what excuse should we have for choosing passing things instead of eternal ones? If the present time be indeed pleasant, it does not last, whilst the pain which it produces endures relentlessly.

How will those who have been made worthy of the Spirit be justified, enjoying so great a gift, if they remain crawling upon the earth and clinging to it? For I hear many men making use of foolish speeches, such as: 'Give me to-day and take to-morrow; for, if things are what you pretend hereafter, it is one thing against another; but, supposing there is no hereafter at all, it is two things instead of nothing'. What is more senseless or more idle than such words? We are talking about heaven and the ineffable goods of eternity, and you bring before us the arguments of a racing-course, and are not ashamed to speak words worthy of madmen. Do you not blush so to cleave to present things? Will you not desist from madness and foolishness, and from wasting your youth? That heathens should speak in this way is not astonishing, but what will believing men who so rave have to say for themselves? Would you call in question those immortal hopes or doubt them altogether?

And what is your excuse? 'Who has ever come, you say, 'and told us about the next world?' No man ever did; but God, Who is the most worthy of belief, has revealed these things. 'But we cannot see them.' Neither can you see God; and do you doubt His existence because you cannot see Him? 'I believe in it most thoroughly,' you say. Now, then, if an unbeliever ask you, 'Who has ever come from heaven and told us these things?' what will you answer? How do you know that there is a God? 'From visible things,' you reply; 'from the order which is in the whole creation; from the fact that this is evident to all.' Therefore, apply the same argument to that which concerns judgment. 'How am I to do this?' you ask. I will tell you, and you will say if I am right. Is God just, and does He give to each one according to his works, or, on the contrary, is it His wish that the wicked should do well and feast, and the good be in trouble and want? 'Certainly not,' you say; 'for not even a man would suffer this.' Then where are those who are upright here to enjoy good things? Where are the wicked to suffer, if there is to be no future life and no retribution after this world? Do you see that so far it is one against one, and not two things instead of one? I am showing you that the just will have not one thing rather than another, but two things rather than nothing, and that with sinners and those who feast here just the reverse is the case. For those who feast in this world have not even one thing against another, but those who persevere in virtue have two things instead of nothing. Who will be in refreshment—those who misuse this present life or those who lead an ascetic one? You say the former, but I point out the latter, and call in as witnesses those very people who have enjoyed present things, and they will not be ashamed of what I am going to say. For they have often cursed match-makers and the day on which the marriage-tie was completed, and have envied the unmarried. Many young men, who could easily have married, have desisted for no other reason except its irksomeness. I say this, not in disparagement of marriage—for it is honourable—but against those who misuse it. For if married people have often called their life insupportable, what shall we say of those who have fallen into the abysses of lust, and who have led a life more slavish and miserable than any captivity?—of those who have rotted in luxury, and drawn down a hundred disorders upon their body? 'Still,' you answer, 'it is pleasant to be somebody.' Nothing in the world is bitterer than this servitude. The vain man and he who wishes to please all-comers is more servile than any slave; whereas he who looks down upon vainglory is exalted above all, and troubles himself not with what others say. 'But having money is delightful.' We have often shown you that those are in greater plenty and refreshment who have given up these things and are rather possessors of nothing. 'But drunkenness is pleasant.' Who would say so? Therefore, if poverty is pleasanter than riches, the unmarried rather than the married life, obscurity rather than reputation, fasting than feasting, it follows that those have the most who do not cleave to present things. I mean that the one, although he may be torn with numberless cares, rests on a good hope; whereas the other, even if he enjoy luxury a thousand times over, has fear of the future to spoil and mar his pleasure. And this is indeed not a slight punishment, as it is destructive to feasting and enjoyment. Together with these there is a third sort of punishment. What is this? That earthly feasting is seen to have no real existence, since nature and the action of time disprove it; whereas eternal things not only do exist, but remain unchanged. Do you see that it is not only two things against nothing, but three, five, ten, twenty, or a thousand against nothing. In order to teach you this from an example, take the case of Dives and Lazarus: the one enjoyed the present life and the other eternal life. Now, does it seem to you that you can set the one thing against the other: to be chastised for ever and to suffer hunger for a short time; to be sick in a perishing body, and to be burnt in a fierce fire with an immortal body; to be crowned, and to feed on eternal goods after short suffering, and to be tortured endlessly after a brief enjoyment of temporal things? Who would say so? What would you have me reckon? Quantity, quality, order, God's determination respecting each of us? How long will you speak as an insect might who is always wallowing in the mire?

It does not belong to consistent men to throw away so precious a soul for anything whatsoever, when a little labour is required to conquer heaven. Shall I show you by another example that a formidable tribunal is awaiting us there? Open the door of your conscience and see the judge who is sitting in your mind. If you exercise judgment upon yourself, selfish as you are, and could not bear the judgment not to be just, how much more will God have a care for the righteous, and judge every man impartially rather than allow all things to be carried out for nothing and in vain! Who, indeed, would say this? No man whatsoever, but heathens, barbarians, poets, philosophers, and all the human race will agree with us in these matters, if not in the same way, and will admit that there is some kind of tribunal in hell, because the thing is so clear and evident.

'And why,' you ask, 'does He not chastise in this world?' In order that He may show forth His own long-suffering, and give us an opportunity of salvation by contrition; that He may not use harshness with our race, nor deprive of salvation those who may be saved by a perfect conversion. If He immediately chastised sins and destroyed sinners, how would Paul have been saved or Peter, the chief teachers of the world (οἱ κορυφαῖοι τῆς οἰκουμένης διδάσκαλοι)? How would David have reaped salvation from his repentance? or the Galations? or many others? This is why He does not demand the payment of every penalty here, but some of the whole number, nor all there, but one man pays in this world and another in the next, in order that He may arouse the most insensible through those whom He chastises, and prove the future state through those whom He does not chastise. See you not how many men have received their punishment here—those, for instance, who were buried by the tower, those whose blood Pilate used for the sacrifices, those amongst the Corinthians who died a premature death for partaking unworthily of the mysteries; or again, Pharaoh, or those amongst the Jews who were slaughtered by the Gentiles, or so many others then, and now, and at all times? And, again, many great sinners have departed hence without paying any penalty here, like the rich man in Lazarus' case, and numerous others. This he does, and so leads unbelievers to future things, and makes believers more fervent. *For God is a just, and a strong, and a long-suffering judge, and remembers not His anger day by day.* Yet, if we misuse His long-suffering, a time will come when He will be patient no more, and will instantly apply the penalty. Let us not then encounter chastisement during endless ages for the enjoyment of one moment, which is our present life, but let us labour during this critical moment that we may be crowned for ever. Do you not see that this is how the majority of men act in worldly things? And they choose a short labour in preference to a long rest, even if the issue be unfavourable to them. Here there is equality of labour and gain, or, on the other hand, there is often endless labour and a small harvest, or none at all; whereas in the case of the kingdom the travail is little, and the pleasure great and never-ending. For consider, the husbandman toils all the year round, and towards the end of it he is often defrauded of the fruits of his many labours. Again, the sailor and the soldier are in wars and toils till extreme old age, and it often chances that each dies, the one without his wealth of cargoes, the other losing his life as well as victory on the battlefield. Now, tell me what excuse shall we have if we choose labours in worldly things, that we may rest for a while, or not even that, because hope is uncertain, whereas in spiritual things we do the very contrary, and draw down upon us an unspeakable chastisement for the sake of short ease?

. . . .

THE WORD OF PRAISE.

(*Homilies on Second Epistle to Corinthians*, i., vol. iii., p. 8.)

. . . .

Let us not lose heart in temptation. For no man that feasts, and slumbers, and flags, is united to Christ, nor any of those who lead this soft and dissolute life; but the man in tribulation and temptation, he who walks on the narrow path, is near to Christ. For this was His path, and so He said: *The Son of man hath not whereon to lay His Head.* Therefore do not grieve that you are tried, seeing Whom you are like in this, how you are purified by temptations, and what great things you gain. Nothing is grievous except falling out with God. Short of this neither tribulation, nor snares, nor anything else, has power to afflict the wisely-tempered soul; but just as a small spark falling into a deep abyss goes out at once, so the force of despondency sinking into a good conscience is destroyed and quickly disappears. Thus it was that Paul always rejoiced, since he drew his courage from the things of God, and did not even perceive human evils: he was grieved as a man, but did not fall. Thus, too, that patriarch of old was in gladness whilst suffering many painful things. For consider: he was exiled from his country, he went through long and grievous journeys, and coming to a foreign land, he had not a place for the sole of his foot. After that he was a prey to hunger, and it made him a wanderer, and his hunger was followed by the taking of his wife, by the fear of death, by childlessness, and war, and dangers, and plottings, and at last by the crowning and most bitter grief of all, the slaughtering of his only son, the heir.

Do not think that, because he had so much endurance, he went through these things without suffering. For if he was just a thousand times over, as indeed he was, he was still a man, and he had the feelings of a man. Yet no one of these things overthrew him, but he stood like a valiant combatant with the laurel wreath, acclaimed with applause in each race. Thus, too, blessed Paul, exposed day by day to the snowstorms of temptation, as if feasting in the midst of paradise, rejoiced and exulted. Now, just as a man who is glad with this gladness does not fall a prey to despondency, so one who is not glad in this way is easily overcome by everything, and he suffers as a man would, who having insufficient armour should be wounded by a chance shot. Not so the man who is safely armed from head to foot: he wards off every assailing dart. For, indeed, joy, according to God, is stronger than any armour, and nothing can make such a man downcast or sad, but he bears all things with fortitude. What is more destructive than fire, or more painful than constant tortures? Even if a man lose a hundred possessions and children, and anything else, this is the sharpest suffering: *Skin for skin, and all that a man hath he will give for his life.* Nothing could be harder to bear than pain. Still, that which men deem unbearable becomes tolerable and desirable through the gladness coming from God. If you lead the martyr whilst still alive away from the cross or the cauldron you will find this same joy within his breast, which is not even to be described.

'And why should I suffer,' you ask, 'since this is no age for martyrdom?' What are you saying, 'This is no age for martyrdom'? It has never ceased, but is always before our eyes if we will be on the look-out. It is not only hanging on the wood which makes a martyr, for if this were the case, Job would be deprived of this particular crown. He neither appeared at a judgment-seat, nor heard the voice of a judge, nor saw an executioner, nor raised in the air and disjointed on the cross, were his ribs worn away.

Yet he bore stripes harder than many martyrs did, and the voices of ceaseless messengers urged and tormented him more sharply than any stripes, and those worms devoured his flesh more rapidly than countless executioners. Was he then not fully equal to a martyr? He *was* a thousand times a martyr. He wrestled in every single way, and was crowned; he was tried by money losses, and by children, and bodily sickness, and wife, and friends, and enemies, and servants, for they also insulted him to his face; by hunger, and curses, and pains, and stench. On this account I should say that he would equal not one, or two, or three, but many martyrs. Besides all this, the time added greatly to his crowns: for instance, it was before the law and the dispensation of grace, and he suffered during many months and with intensity, and all his misfortunes were laid upon him at once, although each was in itself overwhelming, and that which seemed the most grievous of all, the loss of his wealth. Many at least have borne stripes but have not borne the loss of property, and have chosen to be scourged for it, and would rather have endured a thousand other evils than any diminution of it, as the loss of money appeared to them the greater stripe. So this constitutes another kind of martyrdom for the man who bears its loss with endurance. And how shall we be sure of the endurance, you ask? By understanding that you gain more than you have lost by a single word, that of thanksgiving. If, when we hear of our loss, we are not agitated, but say, 'Praised be God,' we have found something of much greater worth. Indeed, you could not gain rewards so high by distributing your riches to the poor, nor by going about to seek out the needy, and by lavishing your good things upon them, as you gain by this one word. Hence, I admire Job not so much when he opens his house to the poor, as I proclaim and wonder at him for bearing the loss of his wealth with thanksgiving. The same is evident in the case of his children's death. You will receive a reward not less than his was who led out his son to sacrifice him, if seeing *yours* dead, you give thanks to the God of mercy. How is such a man less than Abraham? He did not see *his* son lying dead, but only expected it; so that if he carries off the palm for his readiness to sacrifice, and for putting out his hand to seize the knife, he is surpassed by the fact of *your* son being actually a corpse before your eyes. And, besides, the inward consciousness of his good deed bore him up with consolation, that heroic action being produced by his own fortitude, and the listening to the voice from above increased his readiness; in this case there is nothing of this kind. Thus it requires a most steadfast soul in the man who looks upon his only son, brought up in wealth and giving much promise, lying stretched across the threshold, in order to bear it meekly. He who can do this has overcome the tempest of natural emotion, and is able to speak tearlessly those words of Job: *The Lord has given, the Lord has taken away;* he will take his place even with Abraham, and be proclaimed with Job for this one word alone. And if you put a stop to the wailing of women and break up the bands of weepers, and lead them to the voice of praise, numberless rewards will follow both from above and below; men will be in admiration, angels will applaud, God will be your crown.

. . . .

———

Sufferings of the Just.

(*Homilies de Statuis*, xxi., *preached at Antioch*, t. ii., p. 13, *Benedictine Edition*.)

. . . .

Blessed are ye when men reproach you, and pursue you, and say every evil thing against you, lying. Rejoice and be glad, because your reward is very great in heaven; for this is what their fathers did to the prophets. And again, Paul, wishing to encourage the Macedonians, said: *You, brethren, are become the imitators of the churches of God in Judea, because you have suffered from your own countrymen the same things as they suffered from the Jews.* And again, exhorting the Hebrews in the same way, he enumerates all the just; those who were in furnaces, in water, in deserts, in mountains, in caves, in hunger, those living in anguish; as a community of suffering is in itself some consolation to its victims. And listen again to Paul urging the same thing when speaking of the resurrection: *If as a man I fought with the wild beasts at Ephesus, what do I gain by it if the dead are not to rise again?* And again: If we hope in Christ in this life only, we are more miserable than all men. We suffer a thousand evils according to this world, he says; if then we may hope for no other life, what can be more wretched than we? Whence it is clear that our lives do not end here, and this is evident from temptations, for God would never allow those who have suffered so much and so greatly, and have passed their whole lives in temptations and numberless dangers, not to be rewarded with gifts much greater. And if this be the case, it is evident that He has prepared another life which is happier and more glorious, in which He means to crown and to proclaim the champions of piety in the face of the whole world. Therefore, when you see a just man spending this present life in great trouble, when you see him ill-treated, in sickness, poverty, and enduring all sorts of misfortunes, say to yourself, that if there were no resurrection and no judgment, God would not allow him to leave this world after suffering so many evils and enjoying no good. Hence it is evident that He holds in reserve for them another life far pleasanter and higher than this. If this were not the case He would not allow so many sinners to feast in this life, nor so many just to be in a sea of troubles. But since there *is* another life, in which He designs to give to every man according to his deserts, whether they be those of wickedness or those of goodness, He suffers the one to be persecuted and the other to enjoy himself. I will endeavour to prove another reason (why suffering is tolerated) from the Scriptures. And what is it? That we who are called to the same virtue may not say that *they* had a different nature to ours and were not men. So in speaking of the great Elias it is said that Elias was a man of like feelings to ourselves. Do you see that he is shown to be a man like to us from similarity of feelings? And again: *For I am a man of like nature to yourselves.* This is a pledge of similarity. Clearly He is teaching you here the lesson that He makes us happy in the right way. When you hear Paul saying, *Up to the present time we are in hunger, and thirst, and nakedness, and we are chastised, and homeless, and weary;* and again: *that the Lord chastises the one He loves, and scourges every son He receives,* it is evident that we should exalt not those who are enjoying rest, but those who are tried and afflicted for God, and that we should emulate those who live holily, and care for piety. So spoke the prophet: *Their right hand is the right hand of iniquity. Their daughters decked out, adorned round about after the similitude of a temple. Their store-houses full, flowing out of this into that. Their sheep fruitful in young, abounding in their goings forth; their oxen fat. There is no breach of wall, nor passage, nor crying out in their streets. They have called the people happy that hath these things.* What do you say, O prophet? *Happy,* he says, *is that people whose God is the Lord.* I call blessed, not the man who abounds in money, but him who lives for piety, even if he suffer a thousand evils. And if we ought to speak of another[1] reason, I should say that tribulation increases the worth of the tried. *Tribulation worketh patience, and patience probation, probation hope, and hope is not shamed:* see you how the probation produced by tribulation makes us hopeful concerning the future, and how remaining in temptations puts us in good hope of what is to come? Therefore, I said, not unadvisedly, that tribulations themselves strengthen the resurrection in our hearts, and make those who are tried better. For as, he says, gold is tried in the fire, so is an acceptable man in the fire of humiliation. There is yet another[2] reason. What is this? One which I have often spoken of already: that, if we have any stains, we may put them off in this world. The Patriarch clearly said to the rich man that Lazarus had received his bad things, and was therefore consoled. And, added to this, we may find another reason. What is it? The strengthening of our crowns and rewards, for the more searching the tribulation, the greater will be the rewards, or, rather, they will far surpass the comparison. *The sufferings of this time are not worthy to be compared to the glory to come, which shall be revealed in us.* Having, then, all these reasons to give for the affliction of the saints, let us not be cast down in temptations, nor distressed, nor

---

[1] I have ventured to change ἐννάτην into *another*. It is part of a long argument.

[2] δεκάτην αἰτίαν.

harassed, but let us instruct our own souls, and teach these things to others. Even if you see a man leading a good life, practising asceticism, pleasing God, and he be suffering a thousand evils, be not scandalised, O beloved. Again, if you see some one overthrown who is engaged in spiritual works and about to complete something useful, be not troubled. For I have often heard many men remark upon it in this way: 'So and so,' they say, 'went to a shrine, taking all his money to the poor, and he was shipwrecked, and lost everything; another, again, did the same and fell among thieves, and barely escaping with his life, he got away in nakedness'. What should we say? That none of these things need trouble us. For if he *did* perish by shipwreck, the fruit of justice is perfect above: he had done his part, he had put together his possessions, given them up, and taking them, had set out. He had begun his journey, but the shipwreck was not of his own making. Why, then, did God allow it? That it might prove him. Still the poor were deprived of their money, you say: you do not care for the poor as God their maker does. If they were indeed deprived of this money, He is able to offer them an opportunity of a much greater treasure.

Therefore, do not let us call Him to account for what has happened, but glorify Him in all things. For not by chance, or in vain, does He allow such things often to come about, nor does He despise those who are to enjoy solace from money, but instead of this He puts another means of support in their way, and, besides the trial, gives the shipwrecked man a greater reward. Indeed, giving thanks to God in trials of this kind is much higher than alms, for we do not give by alms alone, but if we bear bravely the losses inflicted by others, we shall gain immense fruit from it. In order to prove this to you I will make it clear to you from what happened to Job that patience is better than alms-giving. When Job was rich, he opened his house to the poor and gave away all that he possessed, but he was not so magnificent at the time he was opening his house to the needy, as when he heard unmoved that it had fallen to the ground: he was not so renowned when he covered the naked with the fleece of his sheep as when, hearing that fire had broken out and consumed all his cattle, he gave thanks. *Then* he was kind, now he became mortified: *then* he had compassion on the poor, now he gave thanks to his Lord. Nor did he say to himself: 'What is the meaning of this? The sheep, from which thousands of poor were fed, are destroyed: for if *I* was unworthy to enjoy this abundance, I should have been spared, at least, for the sake of those who shared it.' He neither said nor thought anything of the sort, but he knew that God was ordering it all for the best. And to show you that he beat the devil more effectually by giving thanks when despoiled than by showing mercy when rich, consider that, at the time of his wealth, the devil had some reason, even if falsely, for saying,

Does Job worship Thee for nothing? Now when God took away everything, and stripped him completely, and Job kept his good-will towards God, then was that shameless mouth stopped, and he had nothing more to say: that just man was more glorious than before. To bear with fortitude and thanksgiving the being despoiled is a much greater thing than for a rich man to give alms, as has been shown in the case of this just man. Then his kindness to his fellow-man was overflowing, now he proved his exceeding love for God. I insist on this, not without reason, but because many men by frequent alms have supported widows, and then been deprived of their substance. Others have lost everything through a fire breaking out; others have encountered shipwreck; others through slanderings and abuse have, after generous alms-giving, fallen into the extreme of poverty, and into weakness and disease, and have been helped by no one in any way. In order, therefore, that we should not say, as many often do, 'No man knows anything,' what I have said will suffice to put an end to this difficulty. 'So and so, who gave so much in alms,' you say, 'lost everything.' And what if he did? For, if he give thanks for this great loss of his, he will propitiate God's good-will the more, and reap not double riches, as Job did, but the hundred-fold in eternal life. If he *does* suffer here, the very fact of his bearing it all bravely will increase his reward. God, in calling him to greater trials and struggles, allowed him to fall from abundance into poverty. Has fire perchance often broken out in your house and destroyed your substance? Remember what happened to Job, give thanks to the Lord, Who was able to stop it and did not stop it, and you will receive a reward as great as if you had poured forth all those things into the hands of the poor. Or, are you living in poverty and hunger, and a thousand dangers? Call to mind Lazarus, who was hard pressed by sickness, and poverty, and solitude, and numberless things of the kind, and all this after so much goodness; call to mind the Apostles, who passed their lives in hunger and thirst and nakedness; and the prophets, and patriarchs, and just, and you will find them one and all, not amongst the rich, not amongst those who feast, but amongst those suffering hunger and affliction and anguish.

Pondering on these things, give thanks to God for the share He has allotted to you, not in hatred, but in tender love, since He would not have allowed those men to suffer evils so great, if He had not loved them dearly, because He made them more illustrious through these evils. No good is so great as thanksgiving, as nothing is worse than blasphemy. Let us not be astonished that, when we are paying much attention to spiritual things, we suffer a great deal. It is as with thieves, who do not break into places where mud and chaff and reeds are, but where gold and silver are, and are ever on the watch. Thus the devil gives his special attention to those who are taken up with spiritual things. Snares are numerous where goodness exists, and envy is to be found where there is alms-giving. But we have one great weapon by which we may resist all these machinations, the giving thanks to God in all things. Tell me, did not Abel, who reserved the first-fruits for God, fall by his brother's hand? Yet God allowed it, not hating the man who had honoured him, but loving him much, and adding to the crown of Abel's beautiful sacrifice the further crown of martyrdom. Moses wished to succour some one who had been wronged, and he confronted the greatest dangers on this account, and fled from his country, and God allowed it, to teach you what the patience of the saints is. If, knowing beforehand that we should suffer no evil, we were thus to give ourselves up to spiritual things, we should not appear to be doing a great thing, possessing this pledge of security. Now, it so happens that those who do this are chiefly admirable because, foreseeing dangers, and penalties, and deaths, and a thousand evils, they have still neither desisted from their good deeds nor grown faint-hearted through fear of the terrors to come. As the three children said, *There is a God in heaven Who can deliver us, and even if He do not, know, O king, that we do not worship thy gods, and do not adore the golden statue which thou hast set up*, so when you are about to do something for God, expect many dangers, many penalties, many deaths, and wonder not nor fear at them. *Son*, he says, *when thou comest to serve*

God, prepare thy soul for temptation. For no one who has chosen a hand-to-hand fight may expect to bear off the crown without wounds. And you who are to wrestle with the devil in every possible way, live not a life of ease and luxury. Your rewards and promises are not here, but God promises you all glory in the world to come. When, therefore, either you yourself do a good action and reap contrary effects, or you see another enduring them, rejoice and be glad, for the deed becomes a source of greater reward to you; only be not cast down, do not lose your fervour, grow not faint-hearted, but rather go on your way with greater readiness. Since the Apostles, also, were scourged and stoned and perpetually in prison for what they preached, not only after their liberation from dangers, but in the very midst of them, they announced the tidings with all the more willingness. We may see Paul catechising and instructing even in prison, even in his chains, and again before the tribunal, and in the shipwreck, and the storm, and in a thousand dangers. Do you also emulate these saints, and, as long as you can, hold to good works. Even if you see the devil assailing you on a thousand sides, never turn away. In distributing your money, you may perhaps have suffered shipwreck, yet Paul, who was more precious than any money, in preaching the word, went to Rome, suffered shipwreck, and endured numberless evils. And this he clearly says in the words: *We have often wished to come to you, but Satan has prevented us.* And

God allowed it by an abundant manifestation of His power, showing that, in spite of the devil's making and unmaking in a thousand ways, the Gospel was by no means lessened or impeded thereby. So Paul gave thanks to God in everything, knowing that God was proving him by these things; and he showed his burning zeal everywhere by allowing no obstacle to stand in his way. Now, the more we meet with failure, the greater will be our hold of spiritual works; and do not let us say, 'Why did God allow there to be impediments?' He allowed them that He may prove your zeal the more to the multitude, and your true love. For lovers are remarkable for never departing from the good pleasure of the beloved one. He who is remiss and luxurious is prostrated by the first touch of tribulation; but the fervent and watchful man, even if he be impeded in a thousand ways, sets himself the more to work at God's business, doing his part perfectly, and giving thanks in every thing. This let us also do. Thanksgiving is an immense treasure, great riches, an inexhaustible good, a strong weapon. Blasphemy has a present penalty, and causes our destruction over and above what we have suffered. Have you lost money? If you have given thanks, you have gained your soul and won greater riches for yourself, and propitiated God the more; but, if you have blasphemed, you have destroyed your own salvation without gaining any of those things, and have slain your own soul.

. . . .

The Folly of the Cross.

(*Homilies on First Epistle to Corinthians*, xiv., vol. ii., p. 36.)

. . . .

Showing the power of the Cross, St. Paul says: *The Jews too ask for signs, and the Greeks seek after wisdom: but we preach Christ crucified, a scandal to the Jews, a folly to the Gentiles, but to those who are called, both Jews and Gentiles, Christ the power of God and the wisdom of God.* There is a deep meaning in these words. For he wishes to say how God conquered by contraries, and that the promulgation of the Gospel does not come from man. What he says amounts to this. When we say to the Jews, 'Believe,' they reply, 'Raise up the dead, cure those who are possessed, show us signs'. How do we answer these things? By saying, that He Whom we preach was crucified and died. This was sufficient not only not to move those who did not wish to be moved, but also to repulse those who had the will; yet still He is not repulsed, but draws men after Him, and conquers and gets the better of them. Again, the Gentiles demand of us eloquent discourses and elaborate reasonings, and we reply to them also by preaching the Cross, and that which seems to be weakness to the Jews, the Gentiles consider folly. Now, when we not only do not offer them what they ask for, but the very contrary, for the Cross not only does not seem to be a sign tested, according to human reason, but the destruction of signs: not only not a manifestation of power, but a proof of weakness: not only not an embodiment of wisdom, but a personification of folly; when, then, those who look for signs and wisdom not only do not receive what they seek, but listen to things which are the exact contrary of their desires, and, furthermore, are persuaded by them, is not the power of Him Who is preached beyond words? It is as if some one were to show those who are tossed on the waves and longing for harbour, not the land, but a more angry sea, would he induce them to follow him? Or if a physician were to tell a man broken by pain and desiring remedies that he will restore health, not by medicine but by again using the knife, would his patient yield himself to his guidance? This implies very great power. So the Apostles made their way not only by signs, but by a line of action seemingly in opposition with signs, as Christ had done in the case of the blind man. For wishing to cure him, He used a course which increased the affliction, as He put clay upon his eyes. Just, then, as He cured the blind man by putting clay upon him, so he drew the world to Himself through the Cross, which indeed was an increase, not a removal of scandal. So He acted in the Creation, preparing contraries by contraries. He built up with sand the limits of the sea, curbing the strong with the weak; He placed the earth upon the water, causing that which was hard and firm to be upborne by flowing and liquid matter. Again, through the prophets He made iron float with a little wood. Thus He drew the world after Himself through His Cross. For as water supports the earth, so the Cross supports the world. Therefore it is a great proof of power and wisdom to persuade by contraries. And if the Cross seems to be a subject of scandal, still not only it does *not* scandalise, but it draws to itself. St. Paul had all these things in his mind and was struck with astonishment when he said that *the folly of God is wiser than man, and the weakness of God is stronger than man,* applying this folly and this weakness to the Cross, not that it was really foolish and weak but that it seemed so: for he answers them according to *their* estimate. That, in fact, which philosophers had been unable to do by their reasonings was effected by this apparent folly. Now who was the wiser? He Who persuaded many, or he who persuaded a few—or rather no one? He Who convinced man of the greatest things, or he who used his powers of persuasion about things which do not exist at all? How Plato and his school laboured about the line, the angle, and the point, and about even numbers and odd numbers, and about their being equal and unequal, discoursing to us about such like cobwebs, for such things are less profitable to our life than even cobwebs, and so helping us neither much nor little, he came to the end of his life.

How he wearied himself to show that the spirit is immortal, and did he not die without making any clear statement or convincing a single man amongst his disciples? But it was through unlearned men that the Cross brought conviction, and drew the world to itself. It spoke to men, not of chance things, but of God, and of piety in the truth, of the Gospel polity, of future judgment, and it made uncouth men and unlearned men philosophers.

This is how the folly of God is wiser than man, and His weakness stronger. How is it stronger? It is stronger in that it spread over the whole earth and seized all men by force, and whereas thousands and thousands did their utmost to stamp out the name of the Crucified One, just the contrary came to pass. For this name took root and was propagated all the more, whereas *they* were destroyed and consumed, and living men fighting a dead One, gained not a stroke. Consequently when a heathen tells me that I am a fool, he proves that he himself is doubly one; inasmuch as considered by him to be a fool, I appear wiser than the wise; and when he calls me weak, he shows himself to be weaker. For publicans and fishermen set up those very things by the goodness of God which philosophers, and orators, and despots, and the whole world vainly striving with all its might could not even devise.

What, indeed, has the Cross not introduced? The belief concerning the immortality of the soul, and the resurrection of the body, the despising of present things, the desire of eternal. And it made angels out of men, who practise everywhere the philosophy of all endurance. But amongst heathens, too, you say, 'There have been many who have despised death'. Tell me who they are. Do you allude perchance to the drinker of hemlock? But, if you like, I will show you thousands of such men in the Church. For if, when a persecution came, all men could get off by taking hemlock, they would all have been more illustrious than he was. Besides, he drained the cup, not being free to drink or not to drink: willing or unwilling, he had to suffer, which was not courage, but necessity. Thieves and murderers under sentence of their judges have suffered harder things. It is just the very contrary amongst us; for the martyrs endured, not in spite of themselves, but willingly, and having it in their power not to suffer, showed forth a fortitude beyond all proof. Therefore it is not surprising if Socrates drank hemlock, both because he could not do otherwise, and because he had reached extreme old age, for he said that he was seventy years old when he despised life, if this be indeed despising it; *I* should not say so, nor would anyone else. But show me a man rejoicing in torments for his belief, as I can show *you* thousands all over the world. Who bore bravely the tearing out of his nails, the racking of his joints, the hacking asunder of his members, one after the other, the stretching upon a gridiron, or plunging into a caldron? Show me this. For death by hemlock is equivalent to slumbering quietly away, as it is said to be an end which is sweeter than sleep. And if certain men have even endured torments, they have forfeited the praise due to them by dying for criminal causes: some for betraying secret things, others for aiming at domination, others for being taken in the most shameful deeds; others, again, either vainly or foolishly, without any cause, have destroyed themselves. But it is not so with us. And this is why their deeds have been hushed in silence, whilst ours are flowering and increasing day by day. This was in Paul's mind when he said: 'The weakness of God is stronger than all men put together'. For the divinity that was in the tidings is clear from this. How, indeed, was it that twelve unlettered men attempted things of this importance, twelve men, whose life was spent on seas and rivers and in deserts, who scarcely entered city or market-place? How did they manage to set themselves in battle array over the whole world? The recorder of their deeds shows them to have been faint-hearted and unmanly, and himself to have no desire to conceal their shortcomings, which were themselves the greatest proof of the truth. Now, what does he say about them? That when Christ was taken, after seeing Him work countless wonders, some fled, and the one who remained, the chief of all, denied Him. How was it, then, that those who, whilst Christ lived, could not endure Jewish anger, should have been able to range themselves against the whole earth after He was dead and buried, if, as heathens say, He did not rise from the dead, nor have any communication with them, nor infuse courage into them? Would they not have said to themselves, 'How is this? He was not powerful enough to save Himself, and will He help us? He did not help Himself whilst alive, and will He, now that He is dead, put out His hand to us? In life He did not gain over even one people, and shall we persuade the whole world by speaking His name?' And, indeed, how would it be reasonable not only to do these things, but even to conceive the doing? Whence it is evident that if they had not seen His resurrection, and had not witnessed a very great proof of His power, they would not have made such a venture. For if they had, indeed, numberless friends, would they not have made enemies of them all by disturbing ancient customs and removing ancestral landmarks? Now, they had all for enemies both at home and abroad. But if they had been in universal veneration on account of outward gifts, would not all men have detested them for introducing a new manner of life? Seeing, however, that they were without all these things, this in itself would have been enough to make them hated and despised by all.

. . . .

The Abode of the Humble.

(*Homilies on St. Matthew*, lxxii., vol. ii., p. 344.)

. . . .

He who humbleth himself shall be exalted. Where shall we find this humility? Would you like to go once more to the abode of goodness, to the tents of the blessed, I mean, to the mountains and forests? For it is there that we shall see this perfection of humility. They are men, some famous for outward position, some for wealth, who humble themselves in every particular, in their food, in their dwelling, in their servants, and so in all their life they are writing the word *humility* as if with pen and ink. Just as smart dressing and a fine house and a large establishment are incentives to vainglory, which thrust men into it, often in spite of themselves, all these things are cut off in the desert. Those men light their own fire, hew their wood, do their own cooking, and themselves wait upon guests. Insult is neither given nor taken, no man is ruled, no man rules, but all are ministering. Each man washes the stranger's feet, and there is much contention as to who shall do it. This he does, not seeking to find out who the stranger is, whether a slave or a free man; in each case he carries out this service. No man is either great or small. Is there confusion then? God forbid, it is rather the perfection of harmony. If, indeed, a man there be of small account, he who is great does not regard it, but deems himself inferior, and so becomes greater.

Both servers and served eat at one and the same table, have the same food, the same clothes, the same lodging, the same rule of life. He is great there who is eager over a lowly task. Mine and thine do not exist, and the thing itself, the cause of endless strife, has been banished. And why do you wonder that there is one rule, one table, and one dress for all, where there is one spirit in all, not according to the body only (for this is the case with all men), but according to charity? For how could charity ever be set against itself? Neither poverty nor riches are to be found there, neither fame nor disgrace. How, then, could folly or vainglory creep in? Some are great, some are little amongst the number according to a moral reckoning, but as I was saying, no one takes note of it. The weak man does not grieve as being despised, for there is no one to despise him. Even should anyone insult another, this is their principal training, bearing contempt and contumely and shabby treatment both in word and act; they live with the lowly and the maimed, for these are the guests of their repasts, and thus they are worthy of heaven. One dresses sores, another leads the blind, another supports the lame. There are neither flatterers nor parasites, or rather they do not even apprehend what flattery is. How, then, could they ever be puffed up? For a great equality reigns among them, consequently the contentedness produced by goodness. In this way the most wretched are better taught than by being obliged to give them the first places. Just as a meek man schools an impetuous man to lowliness, so does a man who makes no account of reputation, but despises it, teach the ambitious. This they do lavishly, for, in proportion as we fight over the first places, do they wrestle not to have them, but to be hindered; and their burning zeal is, not who shall be honoured, but who shall not be honoured. Moreover, their very works incline them to moderation, and do not tolerate vanity. For, tell me, how can a man who is tilling and watering and planting the earth, or plaiting baskets, or weaving a sack, or doing any other manual labour, ever think great things of himself? Who, that is living in poverty, and struggling with hunger, will be sick with this complaint? No man. Therefore their lowliness is well contented. And just as moderation is difficult here, through the crowd of flatterers and admirers, so is it perfectly easy *there*. They have only the desert before them: they see birds flying, and the breeze through the trees, and the soft wind blowing, and streams flowing through ravines. How, then, could a man living in so great a solitude be puffed up? Neither can *we* find any excuse, that, being in the thick of the fight, we think great things of ourselves. For Abraham, when in company of the Chananæns, said, *I am dust and ashes*, and David, in the din of arms, *I am a worm and no man*, and the Apostle in the midst of the world, *I am not worthy to be called an apostle.* Therefore, what shall we have to say for ourselves, if, even with these great examples before us, we are not sober? As *they* are worthy of a thousand crowns for being the first to walk upon the path of goodness, so do we deserve as many chastisements for not arriving at a like zeal, neither for the example of those who have departed hence and lie in their sepulchres, nor for the living who are wonderful through their deeds. What could you allege for not being converted? Are you unlettered, and have you not read the epitaphs so as to know the goodness of those men of old? This is indeed the chief point of accusation, the church being ever open, not to go in and partake of those pure waters. Besides, if you did not know the dead through their epitaphs, you should have had these living men before your eyes. 'But if there was no one to point them out to us?' Come with me and I will show you the dwelling-places of these holy ones: come and learn a useful lesson from them. They are shining lights throughout the world, they surround cities like strong walls. They have taken possession of deserts in order to teach you to look down upon worldly agitations. They, then, in this strength of theirs, are able to enjoy peace in the midst of the tempest: you, who are tossed about on all sides, should be at rest, and have a short breathing time from the ever rolling waves.

. . . .

The Prisoner of Jesus Christ.

(Homilies on Epistle to the Ephesians, viii., vol iv., 175.)

It is the virtue of teachers to seek not honour nor glory from their disciples, but their salvation, and to do all things unto that end; for he who seeks the former would be a tyrant, not a teacher. It was not for your greater personal glorification that God set you over them, but that your business should be forgotten whilst theirs is strengthened. This is a teacher's part; this was what blessed Paul did, who was removed from vanity and considered himself as one of the multitude, or rather as the least of all. Thus he calls himself their slave, and generally speaks in the attitude of a suppliant. Look at him, at least in this instance, writing nothing imperiously, nothing authoritatively, but mild, conciliating words. *I, a prisoner in the Lord, beseech you that you walk worthy of the vocation in which you are called*, he says. Tell me, what do you beseech, O Paul? That you may get something for yourself? 'Certainly not,' he answers, 'but that I may save others.' Yet they who beseech do it for what concerns themselves. 'And this *does* concern me,' he says, 'as I have written distinctly in another place: *Now we live, if you stand in the Lord.*' He was always most eager for the salvation of his disciples. *I, the prisoner in the Lord.* Great and wonderful dignity, surpassing consulships, and kingdoms, and all things else. This he wrote also to Philemon, saying: *As Paul, an old man, and now a prisoner also of Jesus Christ*. Nothing is so glorious as a chain for Christ's sake, as the fetters which hang round those hallowed hands. Better than being an apostle, or a teacher, or an evangelist, is it to be a prisoner for Christ's sake. If there be a lover of Christ, he will know what I say;[1] if any man be foolish and on fire for his Lord, he understands the power of chains, he would choose to be a prisoner for Christ rather than to dwell in paradise. Paul has shown us those hands of his more glittering than gold or than any royal crown. A band of precious stones does not ennoble a head as iron chains for Christ's sake. *His* prison was more glorious than kingly palaces, or than heaven itself. Why do I say 'than palaces'? That place contained Christ's prisoner. A lover of Christ knows what this privilege is, he is acquainted with this virtue, he knows what a gain the being in chains for His sake has been to the human race. More glorious far than sitting on His right hand, more solemn than sitting on one of the twelve thrones, is the being imprisoned for His sake. And why do I speak of human things? I shame to put riches and golden ornament in comparison with those chains, but with regard to those great ones, if their deed had no reward, this alone is a great reward and a powerful antidote, the suffering these evils on account of the Beloved. Lovers, I say not of God but of man, know the proverb which speaks of those who take pleasure rather

---

[1] Compare with St. Augustine, *Da amantem et sentit quod dico.*

in suffering evils from the loved ones than in being honoured by them. This is seen only in the case of the holy band: I mean the Apostles. Listen to what blessed Luke says: *They went from the council rejoicing that they were accounted worthy to suffer reproach for His Name.* Now to others it seems ridiculous that dishonour should be accounted honour and a joy, but to those who follow Christ this desire is held to be most blessed of all. If anyone would give me all heaven or those chains, I would choose the chains. If anyone were to place me with the angels above or with Paul in chains, I would choose his prison. If anyone were to make me one of those heavenly Powers or Thrones, or a prisoner as Paul was, I would choose to be a prisoner. Nothing is more blessed than those chains. Would that I could now be in those regions; for it is said that the chains are preserved, as well they may be, and I am in admiration of those men full of desire for Christ; would that I could see those chains, which devils have feared and trembled at, which angels reverence. Nothing is better than suffering some adversity for the sake of Christ. I deem Paul blessed not so much because he was ravished into paradise as for being thrown into prison. I call him blessed not so much because he heard ineffable words as for enduring chains. I hold him blessed not so much for being carried into the third heaven as for his chains. That these were greater than those things, understand what he himself thought of them. He did not say, 'I, who have heard mysterious words, beseech you,' but what? *I, the prisoner in the Lord, beseech you.* And if he did not use the expression in all his epistles, it is not astonishing, for he was not always in chains, only at certain times. I would choose rather to suffer adversity for Christ than to be honoured by Christ. This is true honour and glory, higher than any other. If he became a servant for my sake and divested Himself of His praise, nor deemed that He was glorified except in being crucified for me, what ought I not to suffer? Listen to Him as He says, *Glorify Me, O Father.* What sayest Thou, Lord? Thou art led to the cross between thieves and malefactors, to suffer the most shameful death; Thou art to be spit upon and struck, and this Thou callest glory? 'Yea,' He answers, 'I suffer these things for those whom I love, and account them a glory indeed.' If He Who loves the wretched and miserable calls this glory, if He finds His glory, not in being on His Father's throne, nor in honour, but in being dishonoured, and prefers it, how much more am *I* bound to hold these things a glory! O happy chains, O blessed hands which those chains adorned! Those hands of Paul's which raised up the lame man in Lystra and made him walk were less honourable than when covered with chains. If I had been living in those days, it is then that I would have embraced them and placed them on my eyes; I would not have ceased caressing the hands which had been found worthy to wear chains for my Lord's sake. Do you wonder at Paul because the serpent fastened upon his hand and did no harm? Wonder not: the serpent reverenced the chains, and so did the ocean, for then he was in fetters. If anyone were to give me now the power of raising the dead I would not have it, but I would have those chains. If I were free from the cares of the Church, and were sound in body, I would go that long journey only to look at those chains, to see the prison in which he was bound. Although amongst his wonderful deeds there are many signs everywhere, they are not so enviable as the marks of Christ. And in the Scripture he does not encourage me so much by wonder-working as he does when he is suffering persecution, being scourged, and dragged away. *So that*, he says, *they brought handkerchiefs and aprons from his body to the sick*. These were truly wonders, but not so great as those others: *They scourged him and laid many stripes upon him, they cast them into prison;* and again: *They gave praise to God in their chains;* and again: *They stoned him and drew him out of the city, thinking him to be dead*. Would you know what a privilege it is for the body of a servant to wear an iron chain for Christ's sake? Then listen to Christ's words: *Blessed are ye*. Why blessed, O Lord? When you raise the dead? No, not for this. When you cure the blind? Not at all. Then why? *When they shall reproach you, and pursue you, and say every evil against you, lying, for My sake*. And if evil report makes men so blessed, what will suffering evil not do for them? Listen to that holy one who says this in another place: *For the rest a crown of justice awaits me.* Yet the chains are brighter than this crown; they will make me worthy of it, he says, and I value nothing so much. Suffering for Christ's sake is a perpetual remedy to me. May it be given to me to utter those words, *I make up in my flesh what is wanting to the sufferings of Christ:* and I shall want nothing more.

. . . .

The Seed not vivified unless it dies.

(*Homilies on First Epistle to Corinthians*, xli., vol. ii., p. 517.)

. . . .

But some one asks, how are the dead to be raised to life? With what sort of body will they come? Senseless man, that which thou sowest is not quickened, except it die first. Whereas the Apostle is everywhere so gentle and humble, he makes use of stronger language in this place on account of the adversaries' unreasonableness. Nor is this enough but he adds arguments and examples, and in this way gets the better even of the most contentious. He had already said: *Whereas by man came death, by man came also the resurrection from the dead;* and now he dissipates an opinion prevalent amongst heathens. And consider again how he cuts away that which is most plausible about it. He did not say, '*you* ask,' but made the adversary indefinite, that, using strong language with effect, he might not unduly crush his hearers. He stated two difficulties: the manner of the resurrection and the quality of bodies. And indeed they were in doubt concerning both points by their words: 'How can that which is dissolved rise again?' and, 'With what sort of body will they come?' How, *with what sort of body?* Will it be like this corruptible mortal body, or like some other? Then, to show that they are not seeking to clear up doubtful points but to dispute what is indisputable, he uses still stronger language, saying, *Foolish man, that which thou sowest is not vicified unless it dieth.*

This is also our way of answering those who call in question what is indisputable. Why, for instance, does he not at once take refuge in the power of God? Because he is talking to unbelievers. Whenever he has to deal with believers he is in no great need of arguments. For instance, saying in another place that *He shall transform the body of your humility into becoming conformed to the body of His glory*, and showing forth something further than the resurrection, he made use of no examples, but, instead of any proof, brought forward the power of God, adding, *according to the efficacy of His power and to bring all things into subjection to Him*. Here, however, he sets arguments in motion. For since he provided this one from Scripture, he used the same with authority against those who did not believe in the Scriptures, and said: *Foolish man, that which thou sowest;* that is, you see from what you yourself do day after day the proof of these things, and do you still doubt? This is why I call you foolish, that you ignore what happens every day to yourself, and that whereas *you* can work a resurrection, you doubt concerning God; therefore he said most emphatically: *That which thou sowest;* you, that is, who are a mortal and corruptible man.

And see how the words he uses bring home the point in question. *It is not vivified*, he says, *unless it dieth*. Passing over the terms which are proper to seeds, such as the sprouting and growth and rotting and withering, he takes those points which correspond to our flesh, the 'vivifying' and 'death,' which belong properly not to seeds but to bodies. And he does not say that it is vivified after dying, but what is more, that it is quickened *because* it has died. You see how, as I am always saying, he brings his argument as a proof against itself. That which they made out as conclusive against the resurrection *he* makes an earnest of it, for they said, 'He will not rise because he is dead'. Now, how can you meet this? If, indeed, he had not died, neither would he rise again, and *because* he has died, therefore he rises again. In the same way Christ points this out still more clearly, saying: *If the grain of wheat, falling into the earth, doth not die, it remaineth alone, but if it dieth, it beareth much fruit;* so here, in illustrating this example, Paul does not say that it does not live, but that it is not 'quickened,' making again the power of God his theme, and showing that it is He Who does all, not the properties of the soil. And why did he not at once speak of something more personal—I mean of human seed? For our coming into the world also begins in corruption just as that of the corn does. It was because it was still stronger in our case than in the latter. What he wants is something quite perishable: the corn was partially so, and that is why he introduced it. Besides, the human seed proceeds from a living person, and falls into a living womb, but here the seed is cast into the earth, not into a living body, and becomes dissolved in it, just as in the case of the mortal body. Thus the example was the more pertinent.

And the sower does not sow the body which shall be. That which has been said so far is to answer the objection, 'How shall they rise again?' this is directed to the question, 'What sort of body will they have?' Now what is, *Thou sowest not the body which shall be?*—not a full ear of corn, nor new grain. For here they were not disputing the resurrection, but the manner of the resurrection, what sort of body the risen one should be, whether like our present one, or more perfect and splendid, and he embraces both points in the same example, and shows that it *is* a much more perfect one. But heretics, admitting none of these things, retort by saying that it is one body which is sown and another which is risen. How, then, could it be a resurrection since a resurrection refers to something sown? What is there wonderful or awful about the victory over death, if one thing is sown and another thing rises again? Death would not seem to be giving back the trophy which he took. How would the illustration be carried out in what they say? Not one substance is sown and another raised up, but the same substance in an improved condition. Supposing that Christ did not resume the same body when He became the first fruits of the risen; but according to you He cast off His former body although it was without sin, and took another. Whence, then, did this other come from? The first was from the Virgin. Whence the second? Do you see what an unnatural argument it is? Why did He show the marks of the nails? Was it not because He wished to prove that the same body which was crucified had also risen again? How does the sign of Jonas affect him? I presume that it was not one Jonas who was swallowed up, and another who was washed to land again? And what were His words? *Destroy this temple, and in three days I will raise it up again.* It is plain that He *did* raise up this temple when destroyed. Therefore, the Evangelist went on to say that *He was speaking of the temple of His body.* Now, what does St. Paul say? *Thou sowest not the body which shall be;* that is, not the ear of corn, which is the same and not the same: the same as being the same substance, and not the same inasmuch as it is perfected, and whereas the same substance remains, it rises in renewed vigour. If this were not the case,

He would not have required a resurrection at all, unless He had meant to raise up something better. Why, indeed, should He dissolve the house if He did not intend to make it a more striking dwelling-place? This, therefore, St. Paul said in answer to those who look upon it as corruptible. Moreover, lest any man should imagine that he means another body, he softens the difficulty, and himself interprets it so that his hearer should not in any way bring the wisdom of the world to bear upon the point. What need is there, then, of our arguments? Listen to his interpretation of the words, *Thou sowest not the body which shall be,* to which he added pertinently, *but bare grain, as of wheat, or of some of the rest.* That is to say, *thou sowest not the body which shall be:* the corn, for instance, as we look upon it, with stalk and ear, *but bare grain, as of wheat, or of some of the rest. And God giveth it a body as He wills.* 'Granted,' you say, 'but in that case the work of nature comes in.' Tell me, what sort of nature? Here it is God Who works everything, not nature, nor soil, nor rain. Hence He makes this clear, and leaving earth, rain, air, sun, and the labour of the agriculturist out of the question, adds: *God giveth it a body as He willeth.* Seek not, therefore, to understand or to scrutinise the why and the how, when you hear that God's power and good pleasure come into play. *And to each of the seeds its own body.* Why then another? He gives each his own. So that when St. Paul says, *Thou sowest not the body which shall be,* he does not mean that He raises up something else of a different substance, but something better and more splendid: *To each one of the seeds its own substance.*

. . . .

THE RESURRECTION IN CREATION.

(*Homilies on First Epistle to Corinthians*, xvii., vol. ii., p. 199.)

. . . .

Let no man disbelieve in the Resurrection, but if any man be in doubt, let him consider what great and wondrous things God made out of nothing, and receive *them* as a pledge of *it*. That, indeed, which has already taken place is much more marvellous and awe-inspiring. For, consider, He took the earth and moulded it, and made man and earth which was not before. How, then, did earth become man? How did the earth come out of nothing? How all those things proceeding from the earth, the endless families of unreasoning animals, of seeds and plants, which came forth without travail, without rains falling upon them, with no apparent cultivation, neither oxen nor plough nor anything else contributing towards their production. On this account He brought forth in the beginning, from that which was without life and without substance, such great things, both of the physical and animal creation, in order that He might teach you from the first the doctrine of the Resurrection. For this is far more difficult than the Resurrection. It is not indeed an equivalent proof of power to rekindle a smouldering flame and to light a fire by invisible means; it is not the same thing to restore a dilapidated house and to build one from the foundations. In the one case, if there was nothing else, there was material to work from; but in the other not even that. Consequently, He began by the more difficult thing, in order that you might receive that which was easier. I say *more difficult*, not that it was so to God, but according to our manner of reasoning. For nothing is hard to God; and just as the sculptor who makes one statue can as easily produce a thousand, so it is as easy to God to create a thousand endless worlds, or, rather, as easy as it is to you to *think* of a city or countless worlds, and indeed much more so. *You* spend a little time upon the thought, but it is not so with God. In the same proportion as stones are heavier than the swiftest birds, or rather than this mind of ours, so much is our mind removed from God's swiftness of action. Have you wondered at His power with regard to the earth? Consider again how the heavens were made from nothing, the countless stars, the sun and moon: none of these things were previously in being. Again, tell me how, after they were made, they remained in place, and on what they rested? What was their basis, and what is the earth's basis? And what comes after the earth? What is that something? Do you see to what a giddy height the light of your reason leads you if you do not hold eagerly to the faith and to the inscrutable power of the Creator? If you will make a guess from human things, you will shortly be able to give wings to your reason. 'What human things?' you ask. See you not what potters do? How they remould a broken and shapeless thing into a vessel; how melters make gold and iron and brass out of earth? Again, how others who manipulate glass transform sand into one compact and transparent body? Let me mention dyers of leather, who dress garments: they produce one piece after the other, which they have received, with the dye. Again, as to our own generation: is not the seed, formless and shapeless at first, implanted in the mother's womb? Whence, then, comes so wonderful a formation of the living man? And what about wheat? Is not a mere seed put into the ground? And does it not rot after it has been put there? Whence come the ear of corn and the stalk and all the rest? Does not a small grain of fig, which is often scattered into the earth, take root and put forth branches and fruit? You receive each one of these things, and do not trouble yourself about them, but would subject God alone, Who disposes of our bodies, to scrutiny! What can justify such a demand?

These and such like things are what we say to heathens, for I need no argument with those who are convinced of the Scriptures. For if you were able to understand all that He does, how would God be more than a man? Indeed there are many men whom we fail to understand. But if this happens to us in the case of men, and we do not grasp them, how much more are we to abstain from scrutinising the wisdom of God and from fathoming His reasons —the former, because He Who acts is worthy of confidence; the latter, because the acts themselves are above reasonings. God is not so abject as to do only those things which *you*, in the weakness of your reasonings, are able to encompass. For, if you cannot grasp a mechanic's work, how much less that of God the Sovereign Architect! Therefore, do not disbelieve the Resurrection, for you will be so much the further away from the future hope. But what clever thing do opponents say, or rather what exceedingly foolish thing? 'How,' they ask, 'when the body has been mixed with earth, and become earth, and it again has been changed into something else, can it rise again?' This seems to *you* to be impracticable, but not so to the Eye which never sleeps, for to It all things are laid bare. In that corruption *you* see no distinction, but He knows everything; you, again, are ignorant concerning your neighbour's heart: He is familiar with all. Since, then, you do not know how God raises from the dead, you doubt that He *does* raise, and will doubt that He knows what is in the human mind; for neither are these things apparent to our bodily eyes. If, indeed, in the case of the body, matter is visible even if it be dissolved— but those conceptions are invisible—therefore, shall

He Who is perfectly cognisant of invisible things not see the visible ones and not easily raise up the body? No one will say so! Do not disbelieve in the Resurrection, for this disbelief is in truth a diabolical temptation, and the devil urges it, not only that the Resurrection may be doubted, but also that he may dissolve and destroy virtuous actions. For if a man imagines that he is not to rise again, and not to give an account of his works, he will not easily be righteous, and not being righteous, he will thoroughly mistrust the Resurrection. Each paves the way for the other: wickedness comes from want of faith, and want of faith from wickedness. For when a conscience has burdened itself with much wickedness, and since it is not willing to provide itself with consolation by change to a better course, in fear and anguish at the future punishment, it seeks to ease itself in unbelief. If you say there is neither Resurrection nor Judgment, another man's comment is: 'Then I shall give no account of my actions'. But what are Christ's words? *You err, not knowing the Scriptures nor the power of God.* In truth, God would not have worked things so great if He had intended not to raise us up again, but to dissolve and annihilate us: He would not have stretched the heavens above our heads, nor the earth under our feet, nor have made all other things for this brief period of life only. But if He has done this for the life which now is, what will He not do for the life to come? If there is to be no future life, then are we far less considered, according to our present condition, than those things which were called into existence for our sakes. For heavens, and earth, and ocean, and rivers are more abiding than we, as also some unreasoning animals: the crow, the elephant, and many others are much longer lived than we. *Our life is short and full of labour*: it is not so with them, but they have a long life free from despondency and care. Tell me, how is this?—has He made the servants happier than their masters? I repeat it, do not reason in this way, nor humble your intellect, nor disregard the riches of God, having so great a Master. It was God's design from the beginning to make you immortal, but you were not willing. The being with God, the living a life without suffering, or grief, or care, or labour, or any other anxiety,—all this pointed to immortality. Adam had no need of clothes, nor of shelter, nor of any other protection, but he was more like an angel, and he had a fore-knowledge of many things to come, and was endued with much wisdom. He knew what God had done in secret, as to the creation of woman, and so he said, *This is bone of my bone, and flesh of my flesh*. Afterwards came labour, and sweat, and shame, and cowardice, and bondage: *then* there was neither grief nor pain, nor effort. But he did not remain in this high state.

. . . .

Resurrection confirmed by Signs which followed.

(Homilies on the New Testament,[1] viii., t. iii., p. 89.)

. . . .

The reason, beloved brethren, why we read immediately after the Crucifixion and the Resurrection of the wonders worked by the Apostles is that we may have a clear and unambiguous proof of the Resurrection. You did not look upon Him rising from the dead with your bodily eyes, but you see Him rising with the eyes of faith. You did not look upon Him rising with this physical eyesight of yours, but you will see Him rising through those signs. For their manifestation will lead you to faith's contemplation. Hence the working of signs in His name was a much greater and stronger testimony than seeing Him as He rose from the dead. Would you know how this establishes the Resurrection more firmly than if it had been seen by all men with their bodily eyes? Listen with attention, for many men make this objection and say, 'Why, when rising from the dead, did He not show Himself immediately to the Jews?' But this argument is trifling and vain. If He had meant to enforce faith upon them, He would not have omitted to appear to all men after the Resurrection. Now He showed that He did *not* mean to put force upon them by appearing after the Resurrection: in the case of

[1] Translated from the Greek Benedictine Edition in folio.

Lazarus, He raised up this man, who had been four days dead, and was corrupt and stinking, and He made him, who was bound, come forth before all; and not only He did not induce them to believe, but He provoked them to anger. When they came they wished to put Him to death on this account. Now, if they were faithless when He raised up another, would they not also have been mad with Him if He had shown them Himself risen from the dead? If they had not been able to accomplish anything, they would still have been guilty of impiety. Thus, wishing to save them from a useless madness, He concealed Himself. For He would have made them deserving of chastisement if He had appeared to them after the Cross. Consequently, to spare them, He hid Himself from their eyes, but manifested Himself through signs. Hearing Peter say, *In the Name of Jesus Christ arise and walk*, was not a less thing than seeing Him rise again. And that this *was* a great proof of the Resurrection, and more conducive to faith than the first, that seeing signs taking place in His Name was better able to persuade the minds of men than the sight of Him risen is evident from what I am going to say. Christ rose and showed Himself to the disciples. Yet one of their number, Thomas, who was called Didymus, was unbelieving, and he demanded to put his hands into the marks of the nails. Now, if that disciple, who had spent three years with Him, who had partaken of his Lord's table, witnessed great signs and wonders, and heard his Lord's words, did not at first believe when he even beheld Him risen, until he felt the marks of the nails and of the wounds, tell me how would the whole world have believed it if it had seen Him risen? Who would say as much? But I will give you further proof than this that signs were more persuasive than the physical sight of the risen Lord. The crowd hearing Peter's words to the lame man, *In the Name of Jesus Christ arise and walk*, three thousand, and five thousand believed in Christ; on the other hand, the single disciple seeing Christ risen was unbelieving. Do you see that the signs much more furthered faith in the Resurrection? In presence of the one His own disciple doubted, whereas in contemplating the signs even enemies were persuaded. Hence they were more powerful and clearer; they attracted men and won them over to the Resurrection. And why do I speak of Thomas? For understand fully that neither were the other disciples persuaded by their first sight of Jesus risen; but condemn them not, dear brethren. If Christ did not reproach them, neither should you, for the disciples saw a strange and wonderful thing; they saw Him rising the First-Born from the dead. Signs so great as this are wont at first to stupify, until in process of time they take root in the souls of the faithful. Now, this is what happened to the disciples. Whilst Christ risen from the dead spoke to them the words, *Peace be to you*, the Evangelist says they were troubled and frightened, imagining they saw a spirit, and Jesus said to them, *Why are ye fearful?* And after that He showed them His Hands and Feet, and He said to them, whom joy and wonder made unbelieving, *Have you anything to eat?* wishing to convince them through these material things of the Resurrection. 'Do neither My Side nor My Wounds persuade you, then let even food persuade you.' That you may clearly understand that He said, *Have you anything to eat here?* in order to show them they beheld not a vision, nor a spirit, nor a phantom, but a true and substantial resurrection, consider how Peter is convinced of it in this very way. For in saying that *God had raised Him from the dead and had given Him to appear in a glorious form to us His preordained witnesses,* he added, as a proof of the Resurrection: *we who ate and drank with Him.* This was why whenever Christ raised anyone from the dead, in order to prove the Resurrection, He said: *Give him to eat.* When, therefore, you hear that He offered Himself to them in the body during forty days, appearing to them and living with them, understand His reason for eating with them. It was not that He required food, but He wished to strengthen the weakness of the disciples; whence it is plain that the signs and wonders of the Apostles were the greatest proof of the Resurrection. Therefore, His own words were: *Amen, Amen, I say to you, he who believeth in Me shall do the works which I do, and greater works than I do.* For since the Cross coming between had scandalised many, He required even greater signs after it. If, indeed, Christ in ending His life had remained in death and the tomb, and had not risen, as the Jews pretend, nor ascended into heaven, not only were greater signs not required to come after the cross, but even the former ones should have been blotted out. Follow my argument attentively, as what I have said is an irrefutable proof of the Resurrection, and therefore I repeat it. First, Christ did wonders, He raised the dead and cleansed lepers, and cast out devils: after this He was crucified, and, as the lawless Jews assert, He did not rise from the dead. Now, how are we to answer them? That if He did *not* rise, how after this did greater signs take place in His Name? No living man at his death ever worked greater wonders after it, but in this case they *were* greater after it, both in manner and in matter. They were greater in matter, for never had the shadow of Christ raised from the dead, yet the shadows of the Apostles did many things of this kind. And they were greater in manner when at His command signs took place; but after the crucifixion His servants, using His awful and all-holy Name, did greater and more wonderful things, so that their power shone forth more conspicuously than His. For it was much more striking that another should do these things by invoking His Name than that He should command them to be done. See you, dear brethren, how the signs of the Apostles after Christ's Resurrection were greater both in manner and in matter? Therefore, the proof of the Resurrection is irrefutable. As I was saying, and now repeat, if Christ had died and not risen again, wonders also should have ceased and been extinguished: now, not only were they not quenched, but they became more evident and more glorious after these things. And if Christ had not risen, others would not have worked signs so great in His Name. One and the same power did wonders both before and after the Cross, first through Himself and afterwards through His disciples; but the greater and more wonderful signs took place after the Cross in order that the proof of the Resurrection might be the clearer and more renowned. 'And how,' the unbeliever asks, 'is it certain that signs *did* take place?' 'How is it certain that Christ was crucified?' 'From Holy Scripture,' you answer. And it is also evident from Holy Scripture both that signs took place then and that Christ was crucified, for they say one and the other. And if the adversary assert that the Apostles did no signs, he shows their power and divine grace to have been the greater, inasmuch as without wonders they were able to win such a world to the service of God.[1] For this is the greatest sign and the crowning wonder of all, that the lowly, and poor, and despised, and ignorant, and unlearned, and needy, twelve men in number,

---

[1] Compare with St. Augustine: Unde temporibus eruditis, et omne quod fieri non potest respuentibus, sine ullis miraculis nimium mirabiliter incredibilia credidit mundus?--*De Civitate Dei*, l. xxii., c. viii.

seem without signs to drag in their train cities so great, and races and peoples, kings, tyrants, philosophers, and orators, and, so to speak, the whole world. Would you like to see signs taking place now? Then I will show you signs more striking than the former ones—not one dead man raised to life, not one blind man restored to sight, but the whole world freed from the darkness of error; not one leper cleansed, but entire nations washed from the leprosy of sin and purified through baptism to regeneration. What greater signs than these would you have, O man, contemplating so radical a change over the face of the earth?

Would you know how Christ restored sight to the world? Men began by looking at wood and stone, not as wood and stone, but were so blinded as to invoke material things as gods: now, however, that they have seen what wood is and what stone is, they believe what God is, for that high and blessed nature is contemplated by faith alone. Would you have another sign of the Resurrection? You will find it in the knowledge of the disciples, which was increased after the Resurrection. For it is admitted by all that one who is well-disposed towards a living man thinks no more of him when he is dead, but if he dislikes the living man, and if he deserts him whilst present, much more will he forget him when dead. Hence, no one who neglected a friend and counsellor when living will make much of him when dead, especially when he finds a thousand dangers threatening himself if he should be so minded. Yet, what took place in the case of no other man *did* take place with Christ and His Apostles and those who had denied and forsaken Him during His life, who had left Him when apprehended, and turned their backs upon Him after numberless reproaches, made so much of the Cross, as to give up their own lives for their testimony and for their faith in Him. If Christ did not die and did not rise again, what reason was there that those who had fled from Him when living, on account of impending danger, should have encountered a thousand dangers for Him when dead? Now they all fled from Him, and Peter, besides, denied Him thrice with an oath, and he who denied Him thrice with an oath, and was frightened at a poor maid-servant, after His death, wishing to persuade us through their acts that he had seen Him risen, became so thoroughly changed that he defied all the people, and went out into the midst of the Jews and proclaimed that He Who was crucified and buried had risen from the dead on the third day, and had ascended into heaven, and that he himself feared no evil. Whence came this courage of his? Whence, if not from his conviction of the Resurrection? For since he had seen Christ, and spoken with Him, and had heard future things foretold, risking the rest of his life as if for a living man, he so confronted all adverse things that he took fresh strength and courage, so as to die for Him, and to be crucified with his head downwards.

Therefore when you see greater signs taking place, and the disciples showing more feeling for Him Whom they at first deserted, and a bolder fearlessness, and the change in morals becoming everywhere more marked, and bringing everything into a secure and happy state, learn through practical experience that the personal history of Christ did not stop at the death of Christ, but a Resurrection received Him, and He lives and remains immutably the crucified God for ever. If He had not risen and were not living, the disciples would not have worked greater wonders than had taken place before the Cross. *Then* the disciples even had left Him: *now* the whole world seeks Him out, and not Peter alone, but thousands of others; and after Peter many more, who never saw Him, have given up their lives for Him. They have lost their heads and suffered numberless evils in order to maintain a pure and entire belief in Him until their death. How then could a dead man lying in his tomb, as you say, O Jew, have shown forth so great a strength and power even in those coming after Him, persuading them to adore Him alone, and to be willing to endure and suffer anything rather than to give up their faith in Him? Do you not see this clear proof of the Resurrection in every particular? Through the signs then and now, through the affection of the disciples then and now, through the perils in which believers passed their lives? Would you see His enemies too fearing His strength and His power, and in much greater straits after His crucifixion? Give your minds, then, to this also. The Jews seeing the courage of Peter and John, the Scripture says, and considering that they were ignorant and untaught men, wondered and were dismayed, not that they were illiterate, but that, being illiterate, they got the better of all the wise, and seeing the man who had been healed standing with them, they could say nothing against it, although before this they *had* had something to say against it when they saw signs taking place. Now, why had they nothing to say then? The invisible power of the Crucified had sealed their tongues. He it was Who had silenced their mouths and put down their boldness, so that they stood there, and could not gainsay them. And when they *did* speak, see how they admit their own cowardice. *Would you draw down upon us the blood of this man?* For if He be a mere man, why fear His blood? How many prophets have you removed, O Jew, how many just have you slain, and have you feared the blood of any one of them? Why, then, did you fear in this case? The Crucified awed their conscience; and not being able to conceal their struggle, they reveal their own weakness towards their enemies in spite of themselves. And when they crucified Him, they cried out, saying, *His blood be upon us and upon our children.* Thus did they despise His blood. But after the Cross, seeing His power shine forth, they are afraid and distressed, and say, *Would you draw down the blood of this man upon us?* If indeed he was a deceiver, and impious, as you false Jews say, why did you fear His blood? If He were this you should have prided yourselves on putting Him to death but because He was not this, therefore, are you in fear.

Do you see how everywhere His enemies are distressed and afraid? Do you see their anguish? Learn, too, the kindness of the Crucified. They said, *His blood be upon us and upon our children.* Not so Christ, but, supplicating the Father, He said, *Father, forgive them, for they know not what they do.* For, if His blood had indeed fallen upon them and upon their children, the Apostles would not have been made out of their children; neither three thousand nor five thousand would have believed on the spot. See you how barbarous and cruel as they were towards their descendants, they ignored even nature itself, whilst God was more loving than all fathers put together and tenderer than any mother? Still His blood *was* upon them and upon their children, though not upon all their children, but on those alone who emulated the impiety and unrighteousness of their fathers. Those alone were liable to the evils who were sons, not according to nature, but through their own foolish choice. Look with me at another side of the goodness and lovingness of God. He did not at once let the chastisement and penalty fall upon them, but He allowed forty years and more to pass after the Cross. Our Lord

Himself was crucified under Tiberius, and their city was destroyed under Vespasian and Titus. Now, why did He allow so long a time to elapse after these things? Because He wished to give them time for repentance, so that they might put off their iniquities and be quit of their crimes. As, having a respite for conversion, they remained in their impenitence, He at last inflicted punishment upon them, and, destroying their city, sent them out wanderers over the face of the earth. And this He did through love. He dispersed them that they might everywhere see that Christ Whom they had crucified adored, and that, seeing Him adored by all, they might learn His power and acknowledge their own exceeding wickedness, and in acknowledging it might come to the truth. And indeed their humiliation became a teaching to them and their chastisement a remedy, for, if they had remained in the country of the Jews, they would not have recognised the truth of the prophets. What had the prophets said? *Ask of me and I will give you the gentiles for your inheritance and the ends of the earth as your possession.* Thus it behoved them to go out to the ends of the earth that they might see with their own eyes that Christ reigns even there. Again, another prophet says, *Each one shall adore Him from his own place.* Therefore it was necessary that they should be dispersed into every corner of the earth, that with their very eyes they might see every man adoring Him from his own place. Again, another says, *The earth shall be filled with the knowledge of the Lord as the waters cover the sea.* Therefore, it was fitting that they should go forth unto all the earth, that they might see it all filled with the knowledge of God, and *seas*, that is, these spiritual churches, with His fear. On this account God dispersed them throughout the earth. If they had established themselves in Judæa, they would not have known these things. He wishes too that they should experience with their eyes both the truth of the prophets and His own power, so that, if they be right-minded, they may be thus led to the truth, whilst, if they follow impiety, they may have no excuse in the terrible day of judgment. Therefore, God dispersed them over the earth that we too may draw profit hence, that, seeing the prophecies concerning their dispersion and the destruction of Jerusalem, which Daniel, in recalling the abomination of desolation, and Malachias, in saying, *The gates shall be shut in you*, and David and Isaias and many other prophets have foretold, and how those are chastised who did not receive their Lord, cut off from their national liberty, from all their domestic ties and hereditary customs, may understand the power which accomplishes and works these things, and that enemies may see His strength through our gain. May we indeed learn through their chastisement His infinite kindness and power, and may we be constant in giving Him praise, so that we may arrive at eternal and unspeakable goods by the grace and goodness of Our Lord Jesus Christ, to Whom, with the Father and the Son, be honour and power, now and for ever. Amen.

PART II.

THE KING'S HOUSE.

"Thou art Peter."

(*Homilies on St. Matthew*, liv., vol. ii., p. 108.)

. . . *Thou art Simon the son of Jona: thou shalt be called Cephas.* Since thou hast proclaimed *My* Father, He says, so will I name *thy* father to thee: which was almost saying, 'As thou art the son of Jona, so am I the Son of My Father'. For it was superfluous to say, 'Thou art the son of Jona'; but as He had spoken of the Son of God, in order to show that as Peter is the son of Jona so He is the Son of God, of the same substance as the Begetter, He added further: *And I say to thee thou art Peter, and upon this rock I will build My Church*—that is, on the faith of this confession. Then He shows him many men who are ready to believe, and He strengthens Peter's will and makes him pastor. *And the gates of hell shall not prevail against it.* 'If they shall not prevail against *it*, how much less against Me. So be not troubled, for thou art soon to hear that I am to be betrayed and crucified.' He goes on to speak of another honour: *And I will give thee the keys of the kingdom of heaven.* What does *And I will give thee* signify? As the Father gave thee to know Me, so do *I* also give it to thee. He did not say: 'I will invoke the Father,' although the power shown forth was so great and the gift was so unutterably magnificent, but *I will give thee.* Tell me what hast Thou given? The keys of the kingdom of heaven, that whatsoever thou dost bind on earth shall be bound in heaven, and whatsoever thou dost loose on earth shall be loosed in heaven. How, then, was it not His to give to sit on His right and on His left Who said, *I will give?* Do you see how He leads Peter up to the most ineffable knowledge, how He reveals Himself, and shows Himself to be the Son of God, through that double promise? For that which belongs only to God, namely, the remission of sins, the setting up of an immutable Church in the midst of waves, and making a fisherman more enduring than the hardest rock, with the whole world against him, these are the things which He promises to give, as the Father said to Jeremias: *I have made thee a pillar of iron and a wall of brass;* but Jeremias was commissioned for one people, whilst Peter is charged with the whole universe. I would ask those who wish to depreciate the dignity of the Son, which were the greater gifts to Peter, those of the Father or those of the Son? The

Father vouchsafed to Peter the manifestation of the Son, but the Son's gift it was to make known that manifestation of the Father and of Himself throughout all the world, and He entrusted to a mortal man authority over the whole kingdom of heaven, giving those keys to him who propagated the Church in all parts of the earth and showed it forth more powerful than heaven. *For heaven and earth shall pass away, but My words shall not pass away.* How, then, was the Giver of such gifts, the Worker of such triumphs, in any way less than the Father? I speak of them, not separating the works of the Father from the Son, *for all things were made through Him, and without Him nothing was made,* but in order to silence the shameless tongue of those who would so venture. Consider the authority which He manifests here throughout all He says. *I say to thee, thou art Peter: I will build My Church: I will give thee the keys of the kingdom of heaven.* And at the time when He said these things, He charged them to tell no man that He was the Christ. Why did He thus charge them? That when those who took scandal were removed, the work of the Cross over, and all His other sufferings completed, when there was no man left to disturb or trouble the faith of the multitude in Him, His worship, undefiled and immutable, might be grafted on the minds of those who listened. For it was clear that His power had not yet shone forth. On this account He willed to be preached by them at a time when the unerring truth of deeds and the strength of things accomplished should support the testimony of the Apostles. For there was a difference between seeing Him, now working wonders in Palestine, now despised, now driven about (more especially at the time when the Cross was about to follow the wonders accomplished), and seeing Him adored and trusted by the whole world, His former suffering no more. This is why He enjoined them to tell no man. For that which has once been rooted and is then torn up, would with difficulty, if planted again, be received by the many, but that which has once been secured, and which remains immutable, and is not threatened from any quarter, is in easy progress and gives good promise of growth. If, indeed, those who enjoyed many signs, and who took part in these ineffable mysteries, were scandalised by merely being told of the Cross, and not those only, but Peter too, the head of all,[1] consider what the multitude were likely to suffer when they learnt that He was the Son of God, and saw Him spit upon and crucified, and yet did not know the sacred nature of these high mysteries, and had not received the Holy Ghost. If He said even to the disciples, *I have many things to say to you, but you cannot bear them now*, how much more would the rest of the people have fallen if He had revealed to them the secret of these hidden things before the due time. On this account, then, He orders them to be silent. And that you may see how much there

---

[1] Μᾶλλον δὲ οὐκ αὐτοὶ μόνοι, ἀλλὰ καὶ ὁ πάντων κορυφαῖος Πέτρος.

was to be learnt after these things to complete the teaching, when those who offered scandal were removed, consider the behaviour of Peter, the chief of all. For this very Peter, after wonders so great, showed himself weak enough to deny Our Lord and to fear a poor maid-servant. Then, when the crucifixion was accomplished, and he had received clear proof of the resurrection, and there remained nothing to scandalise or terrify him, he embraced the unspeakable teaching of the Spirit in order to leap with greater eagerness than a lion upon the Jewish people, although he was threatened by a thousand dangers and deaths. It was reasonable, therefore, that He bade them not to tell the multitude before the Cross, since He did not venture to impart everything before the Cross even to those who were to teach. *I have many things to say, but you cannot bear them now.* And they were ignorant concerning many things spoken by Him which He did not clearly explain before the Cross. But when He rose from the dead, then they came to a knowledge of some of the things which He had said.

. . . .

"Peter Rose Up."

(Homilies on Acts of Apostles, Benedictine Edition, iii., tom. ix., p. 23.)

* * *

And in those days Peter rose up in the midst of the disciples and said. As one eager and as entrusted by Christ with the flock, and as the first of the choir, he ever first begins to speak. *And the number of names together was,* he says, *about a hundred and twenty. Men and brethren, this Scripture must needs have been fulfilled, which the Holy Ghost spake before.* Why then did he not singly ask of Christ to give him some one in the place of Judas? And why do they not make the election of themselves? Peter had now become better than his old self. This is what we may say on the subject. We will give two reasons why their asking for one to fill up their band was no chance but a matter of revelation: the first, that they were engaged about other things; the second, that this was the greatest proof of Christ's presence with them. For being absent He made the election as He would have done if present. And this was no small matter of consolation. But observe Peter doing this with common consent; nothing authoritatively, nothing arbitrarily. And he did not say simply thus: 'Instead of Judas we elect this man,' but consoling them about what had passed, see how he manages his discourse. For what had happened had caused no small distress.

And do not wonder at this. For if many at present twist about this fact, what may we expect that they said? *Men and brethren*, he says: if the Lord called them brethren, how much more he? . . . This is why he began by saying, *Men and brethren, we must choose one of us.* He commits the judgment to the multitude, both to invest with respect those who were chosen, and to escape himself odium from the rest. . . . What, then, might not Peter himself have elected? Certainly. But he does not do so, that he might not seem partial. Moreover, he had not as yet received the Spirit. *And they appointed two, Joseph that is called Barsabas and Matthias.* He did not appoint them, but all. He introduced the matter, showing that it was not even his own, but from above, according to prophecy. So that he was an interpreter, not a master.

. . . .

Built upon the Rock.

(*Homily before he went into exile*,[1] tom. iii., p. 415.)

Numerous are the waves, and great the tossing of the sea, but we have no fear of going down, for we stand upon the rock. Let the ocean rage as it will, it is powerless to break the rock. Let the

---

[1] Ὁμιλία προ τῆς ἐξορίας. Benedictine Edition. There is a doubt about the authenticity of the latter part of this Homily, which has not been translated.

waves roll, they cannot sink the bark of Jesus. Tell me, what should we fear? Death? *To me to live is Christ and to die gain.* Is it exile perchance? *The earth is the Lord's, and the fulness of it.* Is it confiscation of property? We brought nothing with us into the world, and it is clear that we can take nothing away with us. I despise what the world fears, and hold its good things in derision. I do not fear poverty, nor do I desire riches. I am not afraid of death; I do not pray to live, if it be not for your good. This is why I speak of what is now taking place, and exhort your charity to be of good cheer. For no man shall be able to separate us. No man can part that which God has joined together. If, speaking of man and wife, He says: *On this account a man shall leave his father and his mother and shall cleave to his wife, and the two shall be one flesh; for that which God has joined together man shall not separate;* if you cannot dissolve marriage, how much less shall you be able to break up the Church of God. You may fight her, you will not be able to harm the object of your attack. 'But whilst you make me more illustrious, you are undermining your own strength by fighting against me.' It is hard for you to kick against a sharp goad. You do not take the edge off it, but you make your own feet bloody; and the waves do not break through the rock, but are dissolved in foam. There is nothing more powerful than the Church, O man; give up fighting her, lest she overpower your strength. Wage not war against heaven. If you fight a man, you conquer or are conquered. But if you fight the Church, you cannot conquer. For God is stronger than all. *Do we provoke the Lord to jealousy?* Are we stronger than He? Who will venture to subvert the order which God has established? You know not His power. He looks down upon the earth and causes it to tremble. He commands, and that which was shaken becomes firm. If He can establish in peace a city torn by factions, how much more is He able to establish the Church! The Church is stronger than heaven. *Heaven and earth shall pass away, but My words shall not pass away.* What words? *Thou art Peter, and upon this rock I will build My Church, and the gates of hell shall not prevail against it.*

If you distrust words, believe in facts. How many tyrants have wished to get the better of the Church! How many frying-pans, and furnaces, and fangs of wild animals, and sharp swords have there not been! Yet they have not succeeded. Where are the oppressors? Silence and oblivion have passed over them. But where is the Church? It is more dazzling than the sun. *Their* deeds are no more, hers are immortal. Now, if being few they were not conquered, how will you get the better of them, now that the world is filled with the service of God? *Heaven and earth shall pass away, but My word shall not pass;* and with good reason. The Church is more pleasing to God than heaven; He did not take a body from heaven, but He *did* take flesh of the Church.[1] Heaven is made for the Church, not the Church for heaven. Be not disturbed by anything which has taken place. Gain me the grace of an immutable faith. See you not Peter walking upon the waters, beginning to doubt and being on the point of drowning, not through the surging waves, but through the weakness of his faith? Did we come here by vote of man? Did a man bring us in, that a man might displace us? I say this, not out of pride, nor to boast—God forbid!—but wishing to give courage to what is faint in you. Since the city has become quiet, the devil aimed at disturbing the Church. Wretched and most wicked demon, you could not master walls, and do you think to shake the Church? Is the Church made up of walls? The Church is in the multitude of the faithful. What an array of immutable pillars, not clasped by iron, but bound by faith! I say not that so vast a multitude is more ardent than fire, but if it consisted of one, you would not overcome that one. You know what wounds the martyrs inflicted on you. Many a time a tender maiden has been brought into court; she was softer than wax, and she became harder than a rock. You tore her sides, yet you took not her faith. The flesh languished whilst the strength of faith was not weakened: the body was being spent, the spirit was renewed: the physical frame was perishing, yet piety endured. You have not conquered a single woman, and do you

---

[1] Ἐκκλησίας δὲ σάρκα ἀνέλαβε.

hope to conquer so numerous a people? Do you not hear the Lord saying, *Wherever two or three are gathered together in My name, there I am in the midst of them.* Where is *not* this people whom charity binds? I have a proof of it. Am I in good heart by my own strength? I hold His written word. This is my staff, this is my courage, this is to me a calm harbour. Even if the world be troubled, I hold that written word; I look up to those words, they are a wall of strength to me. What are they? *I am with you always until the consummation of the world.* Christ is with me, what shall I fear? If waves are raging against me, and the fountains of the deep and the passions of princes, all these things are more insignificant than a cobweb. And if it were not for your charity, I would not refuse to depart to-morrow, for I always say, 'Lord, may Thy will be done'; not what this man or that man wishes, but as Thou wilt. This is my tower of defence, this is my immutable rock, this is my sure staff. If this be God's will, so be it. If He wish me to remain here, I am grateful to Him. Wherever it may be, I give Him thanks.

. . . .

The Priest a Man, not an Angel.

(*Homily on Peter and Elias, Benedictine Edition*, tom. ii., p. 730.)

Why is it that so few are here to day? We commemorate the martyrs, and no one comes; the distance has made man soft, or rather not the distance, but their softness has been the impediment. Just as nothing can hinder readiness and alertness of will, so everything serves as a hindrance to an irresolute and desponding man. The martyrs shed their blood for the truth: can *you* not make light even of a long way? They laid down their head for Christ: will *you* not even come out of the city for your Lord? He died for you, and are you lukewarm in His service? You are commemorating the martyrs, and are you discouraged and remiss? You should come and see the devil humbled, and the martyr triumphing, God glorified, and the Church crowned. What is your excuse? 'I am a sinner and I cannot come.' That is the very reason why you should come so that you may not be quite lost. Tell me what man is without sin? This is why there is a sacrifice, and a Church, and prayer, and fasting. Because the soul has many wounds, therefore remedies have been devised for them, and for every single wound of the soul a corresponding medicine has been prepared. You have the Church offering sacrifices, the prayers of the fathers, the administration of the Holy Spirit, the memory of the martyrs, the assembly of the faithful, and many things of the kind which have power to recall you from iniquity unto justice. If you do not come to invoke the martyrs, what excuse have you got? . . . You say, 'I am a sinner and cannot come'. *Because* you are a sinner, come. Or do you not know that those very men who stand before the altar have contracted sins? They are clothed in flesh and blood, yet we do not refuse to teach when we cast our eyes on the ocean of God's goodness. If you enter in, you have not this against you, for you are subject to teaching. As for us, the higher our dignity, the greater is our guilt. It is one thing for the man, who is subject to teaching, to sin, and another for the teacher. Nevertheless, we do not refuse to impart discipline, or fall into negligence under pretext of humility. It was a divine ordering that priests themselves should fall into sin. Now listen to what I mean. If the teachers themselves, if priests had not sinned and been subjected to the ordinary passions of life, they would have become inhuman and relentless towards others. Therefore, He designed that priests, too, and rulers should be under the dominion of their feelings, so that from what they themselves experience they should extend pardon to others. God has always pursued this course, not only now but of old: He allowed those to whom He was going to entrust His Church and His people to fall into sin, so that on account of their own shortcomings they might become merciful to others. If they had *not* sinned, they would not have made a single excuse for sinners, but, wholly merciless, would have excluded all from the Church. Let me show you by an example that it *is* so, and that I do not speak from conjecture. Peter was to be entrusted with the keys of heaven and with the multitude of the people. For what were the Lord's words to him? *Whatsoever thou shalt bind on earth shall* be bound in heaven, and whatsoever thou shalt loose on earth shall be loosed in heaven. For Peter was somewhat severe, and if he had been faultless how would he have excused his disciples? This was why the Divine Goodness brought about a certain fall on his part, that from what he himself experienced, he might become kind to others. And consider the man who is allowed to fall into sin,—Peter, the chief of the Apostles, the irremovable foundation, the immutable rock, the leader of the Church, the sure harbour, the invincible pillar. Peter it was who had said to Christ, *Even if I should die with Thee I will not desert Thee;* Peter who had confessed the truth by divine revelation: *Thou art Christ the Son of the living God:* this Peter going in on the night of Christ's betrayal and standing by the fire to warm himself, a certain maid-servant went up to him and said, *Yesterday thou wert with this man,* and Peter answered, *I know not the man.* Just before he had said, *Even if I should die with Thee;* now he denies Him and says, *I know not the man.* O Peter! is this thy promise? Thou hast not endured torments nor stripes, but at a single word from a maid-servant—thou hast denied. Wilt thou deny, Peter? As yet there are neither torments, nor stripes, nor blows, nor angry passions, nor princes, nor outstretched swords, neither edicts, nor threatening emperors, nor sentence to death, neither prisons, nor precipices, nor seas. There are none of these things, yet thou hast already denied Him: *I know not the man.* Again the maid said to him,

Yesterday thou wert with this man. And he answered her: *I know not the man.* Who is making thee deny? No one in authority, but a woman, and she a poor doorkeeper, a captive unworthy of an answer: at *her* word thou deniest! This is wonderful indeed! A maid-servant, a harlot going up to Peter disturbed his faith. Peter, the pillar, suffered no temptation: she only opened her mouth and that pillar was shaken, that bulwark was moved. What seest thou before thee, Peter, whilst thou deniest? A miserable maid-servant, a wretched doorkeeper. This is what thou seest, and dost thou deny? Now for the third time she says: *Yesterday thou too wert with this man*, and he denied for the third time. And Jesus looking at him, recalled his own words to his mind, and he began to weep tears of contrition for his sin. Still Jesus pardoned him, knowing that as a man he had had a human weakness. But as I have said, on this account He was about to entrust him with a whole people, so that, not being hard or without sin, he might not be without mercy for his own brethren. He fell into sin, that, considering his own fault and his Lord's pardon, he also might extend a merciful forgiveness to others, which, according to divine dispensation should reconcile them to God. He who was to be entrusted with the Church was allowed to sin; the pillar of the churches, the harbour of faith, Peter the teacher of the world, was allowed to sin in order that his forgiveness might become the basis of mercy for others. Why do I say these things? Because we priests who sit upon a throne and teach are fettered by sins. This is why neither angel nor archangel has been entrusted with the priesthood, for *they* are without sin, in order that they should not through severity at once strike down sinners amongst the people. A man born of man was entrusted with this throne, a man held subject himself to pleasure and to sin, so that in receiving a sinner, mindful of his own failings, he might be gentler to that sinner. For if the priest were an angel and were to receive a dissolute man, he would kill him on the spot, not being acquainted with this passion. On this account if an angel had the sacerdotal authority, he would not teach, but he would kill the man in anger through his not being an angel: for this reason it was a man with the knowledge and experience of his own faults, that he might pardon sinners, and not be moved by anger, that the Church might not be vacant through the Synagogue.

. . . .

The Authority of the Priest.

(*On the Priesthood*,[1] b. iii., c. iv., p. 24.)

The priesthood performs its functions on earth but ranks with heavenly things. And indeed most rightly, for neither man, nor angel, nor archangel, nor any other created power has ordained this series

---

[1] Translated from the Greek German Edition, Περὶ Ἱερωσύνης. Leipzig, 1872.

of actions, but the Paraclete Himself, and He it is Who has inspired those still in the flesh to represent visibly the ministry of angels. Therefore, since the priest stands in the very heavens in the midst of those powers, he should be as pure as they. The ordinances before the law of grace, such as bells and fringes, and precious stones on the breast, those on the shoulders, the mitre, the girdle, the long garment, the gold plate, the holy of holies, the intense quiet of the holy place, were awful and sacred, but if any-one would examine those of the law of grace, he would find the former terrible ordinances were as nothing, and that what was then said concerning the law was in this also true, that *even that which was glorious in this part was not glorified by reason of the glory that excelleth.* For when you see the Lord sacrificed and lying before you, and the priest standing over the sacrifice making supplication, and all present dyed in the precious Blood, do you feel as if you were still amongst men and on earth, and not rather transported straight into heaven? Casting aside from your mind every carnal thought, do you not consider the things of heaven with a naked soul and a pure heart? Oh, what a wonder this is! What man-loving kindness of God! He Who is sitting with the Father above is received in that hour into the hands of all men. And He gives Himself to those who wish to hold Him to their hearts in close embrace, and all do this through their eyes. Now would these things appear to you worthy of contempt, as if a man could possibly feel anger against them? Would you like to realise the surpassing sacredness of this holy place through another wonder? Picture Elias to yourselves, an immense crowd surrounding him, the sacrifice lying upon stones, all men holding their breath, and the prophet alone in prayer, then fire coming swiftly from heaven upon the offering. This is a marvel which is most awe-inspiring. Pass on from this to the rites which are now being carried out, and you will see not marvels alone but things beyond awe itself. For the priest is standing there, not bringing down fire but the Holy Spirit: and he makes a long prayer of supplication, not that fire from above may consume the offering, but in order that grace, coming down upon the sacrifice, may through it enkindle all souls, and make them purer than silver purified in the fire. Now, such being this most tremendous rite, who that is not utterly mad and out of his mind will be able to show contempt for it? Do you not know that never could soul of man have borne that fire of the sacrifice, but all would have been consumed if it had not been for an abundant assistance of God's grace? If, indeed, anyone would consider what a great thing it is for a man still clothed in flesh and blood to be able to approach nearer to that high and perfect nature, he would then clearly see what honour the grace of the Spirit has vouchsafed to confer upon the priest. For through his ministry both these things are accomplished and other things which, in regard to our dignity and salvation, are in no way inferior. Dwellers on the earth, sojourners here, are entrusted with the things of heaven, and have received an authority which God has given neither to angels nor to archangels. Not to them are those words said: *Whatsoever you shall bind on earth shall be bound in heaven, and whatsoever you shall loose shall be loosed.* It is true that those in power on earth have authority to bind, but in the case of bodies only: now *that* chain affects the soul, and penetrates into heaven, so that whatsoever the priest does here below, God ratifies it above; the Lord of all sanctions the action of His servants. What indeed did He give to them if not all authority in heaven? *Whose sins*, He says, *you shall forgive they are forgiven, and whose sins you shall retain they are retained.* What could be greater than this authority? The Father has given all judgment to the Son: now I see them set over all judgment by the Son as if they were already in heaven, and had passed beyond nature, and had thrown off our passions also, to so great an authority have they been raised. Thus, if a king entrusts to one of his subjects power to throw into prison those whom he chooses, and to release them, that man will be an object of singular distinction to all. He who receives from God an authority greater in proportion as heaven surpasses earth and souls bodies, has seemed to some to be favoured with an honour so small as to make it credible that some one might look down upon the gift of men so trusted. God forbid such unreason, for it *is* a consummate unreason to despise so exalted an authority, without which we can arrive neither at salvation nor at the promised goods. If a man cannot enter into the kingdom of heaven unless he be born again of water and the Spirit, and if he who does not eat the Flesh of Christ and does not drink His Blood shall have no part in eternal life, and all these things are brought about by no one else, but only by those sacred hands, those of the priest, I mean, how without them will it be possible for a man either to escape hell-fire or to reach the crowns which are laid up for us? For priests are those who have been trusted with throes of the Spirit, and they generate through baptism: through them we put on Christ and unite ourselves to the Son of God, and become members of that august Head. Hence they might justly be held by us in greater veneration than not rulers and kings only, but than our own fathers. These have generated us by ties of the flesh and of inclination: priests are the authors of our birth from God, of that blessed regeneration of our true liberty, and of our adoption according to grace. Priests amongst the Jews had power to cleanse the leprosy of the body, or rather not at all to cleanse it, but only to proclaim who *were* cleansed, and you know how sought after the priestly office then was. Now these have received power with regard to, not the leprosy of the body, but impurity of the soul, not to examine it when cleansed but to entirely effect the cleansing. Hence, those who hold them in contempt would be under a worse curse and would deserve a greater chastisement than Dathan and his companions. The latter, indeed, even if they claimed an authority which did not belong to them, were still impressed with its being something extraordinary, and showed this by desiring it with great warmth; but the former, since a better order has been brought about and divine worship has received so wonderful an increase, have ventured on a deed the opposite to that of the others, of much greater audacity. To desire undue honour and to disregard it are not forms of showing contempt; but the one is as far removed from the other as is the measure of contempt from admiration. What soul so unhappy as to disregard goods so great? I cannot say, unless anyone should be goaded on to it by a demon. Now I will go back to my starting-point. God has given greater power to priests than to parents, according to nature, not only for chastising but also for conferring benefits, and there is as great a difference between the two as between this present life and the life to come. Earthly parents generate for this present life, priests for the life to come: the former are unable to preserve their children from death even of the body or to ward off illness from them; but the latter have often saved a soul which was sick and about to be lost, procuring for some a milder chastisement, and keeping others out of trouble from the first, not only by teaching and advising, but also by helping them with prayer. Not only do they generate us anew, but after this they have authority to remit sins. *Is any man sick among you*, the Apostle says, *let him call in the elders of the Church, and let them pray over him, anointing him with oil in the Name of the Lord: and the prayer of faith shall save the sick man, and the Lord shall raise him up, and whatever sins he may have committed shall be forgiven him.* So parents in the order of nature can do nothing to help their children if these should chance to offend people in high places; but priests have reconciled them not to rulers or kings only, but to God Himself, Who was angered against them. After this will anyone venture to accuse us of folly? For my part I conceive that what has been said will inspire the souls of hearers with such respect that they will no longer charge with folly and audacity those who shrink from acquiring this honour for themselves, but those who seek and pursue it.

. . . .

The Priest a Shepherd of Souls.

(*On the Priesthood*, b. vi., c. i.)

You have heard what is to be expected here on earth, but how shall we bear what is to come hereafter, when we shall be compelled to answer for everyone who has been entrusted to us? The punishment there does not stop with shame, but is a chastisement which never ends. If I began by quoting the words, *Render obedience and submission to those who are over you, and who are responsible for your souls, as giving an account for them*, I will not now withhold them. Fear of this judgment keeps me in a state of perpetual trembling. If, indeed, for scandalising one, and that one the least of all, it is better for a man to have a millstone about his neck and to be cast into the sea; and if all who inflict a blow upon the conscience of their brethren sin against Christ Himself, what will be the suffering on their account of those who destroy not one, or two, or three, but so great a multitude? It will not do to throw the blame on want of practice or to take refuge in ignorance, or to allege necessity or main force: it would be easier for a subject, if he required it, to make use of this excuse for his own sins than for rulers in those of others. What is meant by this? That he whose part it is to correct the ignorance of others, and to guard against the devil's coming attack, may not allege his own ignorance, or say, 'I did not hear the trumpet,' or 'I did not foresee war'. As Ezechiel said, this is the very reason why he is seated in his place, that he may sound the trumpet to others and warn them of coming troubles. On this account the chastisement is inexorable, even if only one be lost. For if, when the sword is brandished, the watchman does not sound the trumpet to the people, nor signal to them (he says), and the sword appearing destroys a life, that life has been lost through the man's own lawlessness, but I will require his blood at the watchman's hand.[1] Cease, then, to push us into that inevitable judgment. We have to do, not with armies and kingdoms, but with an action which requires angelical goodness. The soul of a priest should be purer than the very rays of the sun, so that the Holy Spirit may never leave him to himself, that he may be able to say : *I live, not I, but Christ liveth in me.* If dwellers in the desert, who are removed from the cares of city, market-place, and all that these entail, and are ever in rest and peace, are unwilling to presume of their security in such a life, but add numberless cautions, fortifying themselves on all sides, ardent to do and to speak with much care, so that they may approach God as fearlessly and purely as it lies in human capacity to do, what think you the power and strength of the priest should be, to enable him to put off all defilement from his soul and to preserve spiritual beauty undamaged? For he ought to be much purer than they, and the more so as he incurs greater necessities than they, which may sully his purity, unless by constant watchfulness and strenuous effort he makes his soul inaccessible to their influence. Thus, there are fair faces, and luxurious movements, and a studied walk, and a mincing tone of voice, and painted eyes, and rouged cheeks, beautiful plaits, dyed hair, rich clothes, variegated golden ornaments, fine precious stones, the perfume of scents,

[1] See Ezekiel, c. xxxiii., v. 6.

and all other things of the kind, dear to the female sex, which are calculated to upset a soul that is not armed in the austerity of wisdom. It is no wonder if a man be troubled by *these* things; but that the devil should be able by the contrary things to wage war against the souls of men and to wound them,—*this* is most surprising and embarrassing. Already some who have escaped the former snares have allowed themselves to be taken by that which was so different. For an unstudied address, neglected hair, a dirty garment, a disordered appearance, a careless demeanour, a natural manner, frank language, an unartificial gait, an artless voice, a life of poverty, the being despised, and unprotected, and in solitude, have inspired a man at first with pity, and from that have led him to utter destruction. And many who have escaped the former snares, the snares of gold, and perfume, and clothes, and the rest which go with them, as I said, have fallen into these so far removed from those, and have been lost. Now, when the battle strikes on the spectator's soul, and weapons of war surround him on all sides, whether by poverty or by riches, by adornment or by simplicity, by a studied manner or by unaffectedness, or in any other of the ways which I have enumerated, whence is refreshment to come to him who is thus hemmed in? How are we to meet the case, not of being taken by force, for this is not so very difficult, but of keeping our mind in tranquillity from impure thoughts? I pass over honours, which are the causes of a thousand evils. Those which come from women lower the tone of the tempered mind, and often work ruin whenever a man is not wholly on his guard against such plottings. And as to honours coming from men; if they be not received with much high-mindedness, they involve a man in two opposite sufferings—the slavishness of flattery and the foolishness of boasting. On the one hand, he is forced to stoop to those who serve him; on the other, he is puffed up against his inferiors through these honours of theirs, and thrust into an abyss of folly. We say this, but the harm of it can only be properly ascertained by experience. And, necessarily, things much worse and more dangerous than these would happen to those who are in the midst of the fight. The lover of the desert is exempted from all this, for if a foolish thought *did* suggest something of the kind to him, this imagination is weak and easily overcome, because the flame of the eyes is not fed by outward things. Now the monk fears for himself alone: even if he were obliged to think of others, these would be very few. Or if they were many, they would be fewer than those in churches, and give their superior little anxiety, not through their small numbers alone, but because they are removed from worldly business, and have neither children, nor wife, nor anything else of the kind to trouble about. It is this and the common life which have made them disposed to obey their rulers. Thus they are able to see and to correct their faults, for the constant watchfulness of the teacher is no slight thing towards increase of virtue. Now, the majority of men under the priest's charge are taken up with worldly cares, and this makes them slack in the fulfilment of their spiritual duties. Hence the teacher should scatter the seed, so to speak, day by day, in order that the teaching by constantly falling should take root in the listener's mind. For superfluous wealth, and great power, and the softness arising from luxury, and many other things joined to these, suffocate the seeds, and often the density of thorns does not allow the seed to shoot forth so as to be seen. Moreover, excessive tribulation, the necessities of poverty, constant reproaches, and everything else of the kind which is opposed to the former things, lead a man away from a holy zeal. Not even the smallest part of sins incurred can become manifest to them. How should it not be so when they know not the greater number even by sight? Thus onerous are a priest's duties towards the people. But if anyone would consider duties towards God, he will find the others nothing at all, so much more careful and diligent a zeal do these require. For what sort of man should he be who rules an entire city—and why do I say a city?—the whole world rather—and has to propitiate God for the sins of all—not the sins of the living only, but those of the dead also. I hold that the courage of Moses and Elias is all insufficient for this ministry. Entrusted as if with the world itself, and the father of all, the priest thus approaches God in order to extinguish wars in every place and to appease strife, to bring about peace and plenty, and to ask both privately and publicly a speedy deliverance from the evils which are pressing upon every man. He himself ought to be as much above what he asks for as the ruler should be in everything above the ruled. Now, what place are we to asign to him when he calls down the Holy Spirit, and offers up the most tremendous Sacrifice, and continually holds in his grasp the common Lord of all? What purity shall we not expect him to have, what piety? Think what the hands should be which thus minister! What the tongue which utters those words! What should be purer or holier than the soul which receives so great a Spirit? Then angels surround the priest, and the sanctuary and all the place about the Sacrifice are filled with heavenly powers in honour of Him Who is lying there. And this can be sufficiently believed from the rites. But I once heard some one say that an old man, who was held in veneration and accustomed to revelations, told him he himself had been made worthy of this vision. At the time of the sacrifice he had suddenly seen a multitude of angels, as many as his eye could grasp, in shining garments surrounding the altar, bending low, as a man might see soldiers in the presence of the king, and this I believe. And another man told me, not what he had learnt from a third person, but what he himself had been allowed to see and to hear. This was it. When the departing, who have chanced to partake of the mysteries with a pure conscience, draw their last breath, angels, serving them as a body-guard for the sake of what they have received, lead them out of this world. Do you not tremble to come with this soul to this holy sacrifice, and to be at these solemn rites the man in soiled garments whom Christ cast out from the rest of the guests? The soul of the priest should be a light of justice to the world, but ours is so surrounded with the darkness of an evil conscience as to be always overclouded and unable to look fearlessly at its Lord. Priests are the salt of the earth; who could bear easily with our folly and our ignorance in everything if you were not accustomed to give us an exaggerated love? And it is not enough that he who has been entrusted with so wonderful a ministry should be pure; he should also be wise and experienced in many things; he should know worldly business not less than those engaged in the midst of it, and still be further removed from all things than monks in their desert. As he must come into contact with men who are married and have children to bring up, and keep servants and have much wealth, who are engaged in public business, who are in power, he should be many-sided. I say many-sided, not a schemer, neither a flatterer nor a hypocrite, but made up of much liberality and fortitude, knowing how to lend a useful hand whenever circumstances demand it, at once kind and austere. All subjects are not to be used in the same way, since the children of physicians deem it not good to apply one treatment to all the sick, nor has the pilot only one course at his command against the wind. Storms are ever hanging over *this* bark, and these storms assail not only from without, but arise also within, and we need to have much condescension and much care. All these things which are different in themselves have one end in view—the glory of God and the strengthening of the Church.

. . . .

One Sacrifice.

(*Homilies on Epistle to the Hebrews,*[1] xvii.)

. .   .   .

Tell me what need was there of having many sacrifices when one is sufficient? That there being many which were constantly offered might show their inefficacy for purification. Just as a powerful remedy, which is productive of health and able to remove all the malady, does everything by one application, and when this one application does everything, it shows its strength in not being applied again; and this is also its work, for if it be always used it is a sign that it has no efficacy. The merit of a remedy consists in being applied once and not often. And so it is here. Why, then, are they

[1] Benedictine Edition, t. xii., p. 167.

always cured by the same sacrifices? If they had been free from all sin, sacrifices would not have been offered up every day. Therefore, they were fixed things, so as to be invariably offered up for all the people both in the evening and in the morning. Thus, it was a confession of sins, not a remission of sins; a confession of weakness, not a manifestation of strength. Since the first sacrifice availed nothing the second was offered up, and that also proving ineffectual another followed, so that it was an acknowledgment of guilt. On the one hand, the act of offering was a confession of sin, and the ever-recurring offering was a confession of weakness. Now, with Christ it was the contrary. He was once offered up, and His one oblation sufficed for all time. He expressed it well by calling them images, for they present the figure only and not the strength of the reality. Just as an image represents the likeness of a man but not his power, so the truth and the figure have something in common with each other. The likeness is the same but not the living power. So it was in the matter of heaven and the tabernacle. The figure was equal, for it was holy; but the power and the other qualities were not the same. What is the meaning of *He hath appeared for the putting away of sin by the sacrifice of Himself?* What is the *putting away?* Contempt; for sin has no longer any assurance. It has been put away. How? Whereas it should have paid a penalty it did not, that is, force was put upon it; for just when it was likely to destroy all men it was itself taken away. *He hath been made manifest*, he says, *by the sacrifice of Himself;* that is, He was manifested to God and went to God. Now, because the priest did this many times in the year, do not think that this has taken place by chance and not through weakness. If not through weakness, why then did it take place? If there are no wounds, then neither are remedies necessary. Therefore, He enjoined that the sacrifice should be always offered up on account of weakness, and that it should take place as a commemoration of sins. What then? Do we not offer up sacrifice day by day? We do indeed, but we commemorate His death. This sacrifice is one, not many. How one and not many? Because it was once offered up, just as that one sacrifice in the holy of holies. This is a type of that, and that of the other. We are ever offering up the same Person. Not one sheep to-day and another to-morrow, but ever the same sheep, so that the sacrifice is one. Now, in virtue of this argument, since the sacrifice is offered up in many places, are there many Christs? By no means, but there is everywhere one Christ, as perfect in one place as in another, one body. Therefore, as He Who is offered up in many places is one Body and not many bodies, so is it one Sacrifice. He is our High Priest Who offered up the sacrifice which purifies us. This is that which now also we offer up; the One then offered up, the Inconsumable. This is done in commemoration of what was then done, for He says, *This do in commemoration of Me.* We are ever offering not another sacrifice, as the high priest then did, but always the same; or rather we make a commemoration of a sacrifice. And since I have spoken of this sacrifice, I would say a few things to you who are initiated, a few things in volume though possessing great power and help. What we speak is not ours but the Divine Spirit's. What, then, is it? Many partake of this sacrifice once in the whole year, some twice, some often. Now, we speak to all, not only to those who are here, but to those who dwell in the desert. For they receive once a year, often, indeed, once in two years. Well, then, whom shall we prefer? Those who receive once, or those who receive twice, or those who receive often? Neither those who receive once, nor those who receive often, nor those who receive seldom, but those who receive with a pure conscience, and an undefiled heart, and an irreproachable life. Let such as these ever approach, and those who are not so not even once. Why? Because they take judgment to themselves, and condemnation, and chastisement, and penalty. Wonder not at this. For just as food, which by its nature is nourishing, if taken by a diseased stomach, destroys and withers up everything and prepares disease, so is it with this case of the tremendous mysteries. You are partaking of a spiritual table, of a royal table, and do you again fill your mouth with mud? You use perfumes, and do you again fill yourself with ill odours? Tell me, I beseech you, if you receive communion once a year, will forty days suffice you for the atonement of your sins during all that time? Again, at the end of a week perhaps, you return to your former ways. Now, tell me, if you were to enjoy good health for forty days after a long illness, and then were to go back to unwholesome food productive of disease, would you not waste your trouble? Evidently you would. If physical things are so changed, how much more those which belong to the will. Thus for instance, we see by nature, and we have naturally a healthy sight. But often our eyes fail from disease. If, therefore, natural things are so mutable, how much more that which is a matter of free-will! You give up forty days to the care of your soul's health, often not even that, and you think to have appeased God? You are trifling, man! I say this, not forbidding you the one communion in the year, but wishing rather that you should always approach the holy things. So it is that the deacon raises his voice to call the holy, and, in doing this, scrutinises all, so that no one should approach unprepared. As with a flock of sheep, where many of them are sound and many are diseased, these latter have to be separated from the sound ones, so is it in the Church. Since here, too, some sheep are sound and some diseased, through this cry which is everywhere heard, this most awful voice, the priest separates the one from the other, invites and urges the holy to approach. As, however, man cannot know his fellow-man—for *what man has known that which is in man, if not the spirit of man that is in him?*—this cry he raises after the sacrifice is completed, so that no one should approach the spiritual fountain negligently or as if by chance. In the case of the flock—for there is no reason why we should not again make use of the same illustration—we shut up the sick ones within the fold, and keep them in a dark place, and give them different food. We allow them neither fresh air, nor pure grass, nor water in the open. Hence that voice is instead of a chain. You will not be able to say, 'I was in ignorance of any danger following upon this act'. We have, too, the special witness of Paul in the matter. But you say, perhaps, 'I have not read about it'. This is an accusation rather than an excuse. You are coming into the church every day and still do not know these things.

. . . . .

The new Pasch.

(31*st Homily on St. Matthew*, lxxxi., vol. ii., p. 459.)

. .

And whilst they were at supper, Jesus took bread, and blessed, and broke, and gave to His disciples, and said: Take ye and eat: this is My Body. And taking the chalice, He gave thanks, and gave to them, saying: Drink ye all of this; for this is my Blood of the new testament, which shall be shed for many unto remission of sins. Consider what great hardness of heart the traitor showed. Partaking of the mysteries, he remained the same, and enjoying that most tremendous Banquet, he was not converted. This Luke plainly intimates when he says that after these things the devil entered into him, not despising the Lord's Body, but scorning the traitor's shamelessness. For his sin was the greater for two reasons: that he approached the mysteries with such a mind, and that, approaching them, he grew no better. Neither fear, nor gratitude, nor the honour received, had any influence over him. And although Christ knew all things, He did not forbid his approach in order to show you that He leaves no means of conversion untried. Therefore, both before this and after this, He continued to exhort and to check Judas both by actions and words, by fear and by kindness, by threat and by benefit. But nothing availed against that grievous sickness of his. Hence, leaving Judas to himself, He again reminds the disciples through the mysteries of His death as victim, and during the progress of the table discourses about the Cross, seeking, by His insistence in foretelling His passion, to find an entrance for it in their minds. If, with all that was done and foretold, they were troubled, what would they have suffered if they had heard none of these things? *Whilst they were eating, He took bread and broke it.* Why did he carry out this mystery at the time of the Pasch? In order to teach you everywhere that He is Himself the Lawgiver of the old dispensation, also, and that its ordinances were made to foreshadow these things. On this account He adds the reality to the type. The evening signified the fulness of time, and the end itself to which things were coming. He gives thanks, teaching us how we are to carry out this mystery, and showing us that He goes not unwillingly to the Cross. And He instructs us that, whatever we may suffer, we should bear it with thanksgiving, and opens out from this good hopes for us. For if the type released men from so grievous a slavery, how much more will the reality set the world free, and be bestowed for the blessing of our nature. For this reason He did not institute this mystery until the enactments of the Law were to cease, and He brings to a conclusion the chief of their feasts by translating them to another and a most awful Table, and says: *Take and eat, this is My Body which is broken for many.* How should they not have feared when they heard this? He had spoken to them often and much before on the same subject. Therefore, He no longer prepares them for it, for they had heard of it sufficiently; but He tells them the reason why He suffers—the remission of sins. He calls His Blood the Blood of the new Testament, that is, of the promise, of the gospel, and of the new law. For this both had been promised of old, and is the bond of the new Covenant. And as the old Covenant had sheep and heifers, so the new Covenant had the Lord's Blood. Then He goes on to show them that He is about to die, and therefore He commemorates the Covenant, and recalls the old Covenant to their minds, for that too was consecrated through blood! And again He tells them why He is to die, *which is shed for many unto the remission of sins*, and He says: *Do this for a commemoration of Me*. Do you see how He leads them away and withdraws them from Jewish customs. 'As you did that,' He says, ' for a commemoration of the wonders in Egypt, so do this for a commemoration of Me.' That blood was shed to save the first-born sons: *this* Blood for the remission of the sins of the whole world. *This is My Blood*, He says, *which is shed for the remission of sins*. He said this to show by this also that His sufferings and His cross are a mystery, and again, to comfort His disciples through it. And as Moses had said: *Let this be to you a perpetual memorial*, so *He* said, *For a commemoration of Me*, until I come. And again, *With desire I have desired to eat this Pasch*, that is, ' to give you the new gifts, that Pasch by which I intend to make you spiritual '. And He Himself drank of it. In order that men, hearing this, might not say: 'How is this? Are we drinking blood and eating flesh?' and then be troubled (for words of His on this subject had already disturbed them, and many had been scandalised by them); to remove, I say, their trouble, then also He did it first Himself, and led them gently to a participation of the mysteries. Therefore,

He drank His own Blood. 'How is this?' you ask. 'Did men of old do it?' Certainly not. Therefore, He says: *Do this*, that He may draw them away from the other. For if this work the remission of sins, as indeed it does, the other is superfluous for the future. Now, as in the case of the Jews, so was it here. He bound up the commemoration of the benefit with the mystery, thereby stopping the mouths of heretics. For when they say, 'How do we know that Christ suffered?' amongst other arguments, we silence them also with the mysteries. If, indeed, Jesus did not die, what do the things involved in the rites symbolise?

. . . .

The 'Eyes of Rome'.

(*Homilies on Epistle to the Romans*,[1] xxxiii., vol. i., p. 489.)

. . . .

A good teacher makes it his special duty to help those he is teaching, not by word only, but by prayer also. Hence Paul's words: *Let us give ourselves continually to prayer and to the ministry of the word.* Who will pray for us now that Paul has departed? Those who emulate Paul: let us only show ourselves worthy of so great an advocacy, that we may not alone hear Paul's voice in this world, but when we depart hence may deserve to look upon that soldier of Christ. Or rather, if we listen to him here

[1] Greek Oxford Edition.

we are sure to see him there, and if we are not near to him we shall undoubtedly see him resplendent in glory close to the King's throne, where the cherubim give praise, where the seraphim unfold their wings. There with Peter we shall see Paul, the head and leader of the choir of the saints, and we shall be in possession of true charity. For if in this world he so loved men as when he might have been dissolved and with Christ he chose to be here, how much more potently will he show forth the love-charm in that place. This is why I cherish Rome, although I have other grounds for my admiration in its size, and age, and beauty, and population, and power, and wealth, and its successes in wars; apart from all these things, I hold it blessed because Paul wrote to the Romans in his lifetime and loved them so much, because he spoke to them in person, and there finished his life. This is why that city is famous rather than for all other reasons put together: it is like a strong and beautiful human body with two shining eyes, which are the bodies of these two saints. The heavens are not so splendid when the sun is sending forth its rays as the city of Rome transmitting these two lights of hers to the whole world. Rome will yield up Paul; Rome will yield up Peter. Consider in awe what a sight Rome will witness when Paul rises in a moment from that tomb, together with Peter, and is borne away to meet Christ. Think what roses Rome presents to Christ, what a double crown surrounds the city, how it is girt with golden chains, and what the fountains of its being are. This is why I am in admiration at that city, not for its abundance of gold, not for its columns, nor for any other beauty it has, but for these pillars of the Church.

Who could now give me to embrace Paul's body, to be nailed to his tomb, and to see the dust of him who completed what was wanting to the sufferings of Christ, who bore His marks, and sowed the earth with the Gospel? Who could give me to see the dust of that body in which he went over the world, through which Christ spoke, through which a light shone forth brighter than any lightning, and a voice arose more terrible to the devils than loudest thunder, through which he gave utterance to those blessed words: *Would that I could be anathema for my brethren*, which he used before kings and was not ashamed, through which we have known Paul and Paul's Lord? We do not dread the thunderbolt as devils dread that voice. For if they trembled at his garments, how much more at his voice. This voice led them in chains, purified the world, cured diseases, put forth evil, set up truth, had the indwelling Christ, and with Him made itself everywhere heard. That voice of Paul's was like the cherubim. As God took up His seat on those powers, so did He on the tongue of Paul. It became worthy to receive Christ, speaking those things which were dear to Christ, and soaring to an unspeakable height like the seraphim. For what is beyond those words of his: *I am sure that neither angels, nor principalities, nor powers, nor present, nor future, nor height, nor depth, nor any other creature shall be able to separate us from the love of God in Christ Jesus?* How many wings does that voice seem to you to have? How many eyes? Therefore he said: *We are not ignorant of his devices;* and so the devils fled, not merely when they heard his voice, but when they saw his cloak from a distance. Would that I could see the dust of this mouth in which Christ did great and unspeakable things, and even greater things than by Himself—for that He *did* work greater things by His disciples was what He said—through which the Spirit gave those wonderful oracles to the world. For what good thing did that mouth not accomplish? It put forth demons, remitted sins, curbed tyrants, silenced the tongues of philosophers, led the world to God, induced barbarians to be ascetic, and changed all things on earth; nay, in heaven too he did his will, binding and loosing those whom he chose to bind and to loose there, according to the power which was given to him. Would that I could look upon not only the dust of his mouth, but of that heart, which we might not wrongly call the heart of the world, the source of endless good, the beginning, fountain-head of our own life. From thence the spirit of life was poured out upon all, and was diffused amongst the members of Christ. It was sent forth, not through arteries, but through the free choice of good.

That heart was so broad that it could embrace whole cities, and peoples, and nations. *My heart is enlarged*, he says. Yet, large as it was, his all-embracing love often urged and troubled it. *For out of much affliction and anguish of heart I wrote to you*, he says. This heart, even dissolved in dust, is what I long to see—the heart which was consumed for each individual sinner, suffering afresh the agony of child-birth over every abortive child, the heart which sees God: *For the clean of heart shall see God:* the heart which has become a sacrifice: *An afflicted spirit is a sacrifice to God:* that heart higher than the firmament, wider than the universe, brighter than sunshine, hotter than fire, stronger than adamant, giving forth fruitful streams: *For*, he says, *out of his belly shall flow rivers of living water:* hence arose the fresh spring which watered not the face of the earth, but the souls of men; hence sprung forth not rivers alone, but fountains of tears by day and by night: that heart which lived a new life, not this physical life of ours: *I live*, he says, *not I, but Christ liveth in me.* So that Paul's heart was His heart—a tablet of the Holy Spirit, a book of charity, a heart in anguish over the sins of men: *I am afraid of you*, he says, *lest perhaps I have laboured in vain among you, and as the serpent seduced Eve, lest coming I should not find you as I wish:* a heart fearful about itself whilst full of courage: *I am afraid*, he says, *that after preaching to others I myself shall be cast out;* and, again: *I am sure that neither angels nor archangels shall be able to separate us:* the heart which was made worthy to love Christ as no one else has loved Him, despising death and hell, and torn by the tears of his brethren. *What are you doing,* he says, *weeping and filling my heart with anguish?*—that strongest of hearts, which could not endure for a moment to be away from the Thessalonians. Would that I could see the dust of those fettered hands through which the imposition of the Spirit was given and the divine words were written: *See what a letter I have written to you with my own hand;* and, again: *A greeting from the hand of Paul,* of those hands at sight of which the viper fell into the fire. Would that I could look upon the dust of those gloriously-blinded eyes which saw the light again for the world's salvation and were made worthy in the body to behold Christ, and saw earthly things without seeing them, those eyes which looked upon unseen things, which knew not sleep, which were watching in the midst of night, and which did not suffer what other eyes suffer. Would that I could see the dust of those feet which toiled over the world and wearied not, which were chained to a pillory when he was imprisoned, of those feet which traversed known and unknown regions and were often on the way. And why should I speak of each member separately? Would that I could see that tomb in which the armour of justice is stored up, the armour of light, those members which are now in life, which were dead whilst living, in all of which Christ lived, which were crucified to the world, those members of Christ which had put on Christ, the temple of the Spirit, the dwelling-place of holiness, which were chained to the Spirit and nailed to the fear of God, bearing the marks of Christ. This is the body which protects that city and is stronger than any tower of defence or any number of fortifications, and with it is that of Peter, whom he honoured in life, *for he went up to consult Peter.* In death, therefore, charity made him worthy to be Peter's companion. Would that I could see this lion according to the Spirit. For like a lion breathing fire on troops of foxes so did he spring upon the tribe of devils and philosophers and fall like a heavy thunderbolt upon the devil's ranks. Nor did the devil stand against Paul in battle, but so great was his fear and trembling that he retreated from his shadow or his voice. So it was that, being far off, Paul gave the fornicator up to him and again snatched him from his hands, and so he did others too, that they might be taught not to blaspheme. Consider how he ranges against the foe those who are under his own command, rousing and spurring them on. Thus, when he said to the Ephesians, *Our warfare is not against flesh and blood, but against principalities and powers*, he added the reward also, by the words *in heavenly things. For*, he said, *our warfare is not for earthly things, but for heaven and heavenly things.* And to others his words were: *Know you not that we shall judge angels, how much more things of this world?* Taking all this to heart, let us stand bravely.

For Paul was also a man and of the same nature as we are, having everything else in common with us; but because he showed a great love for Christ he scaled the heavens and found his place with the angels. If, then, we wish to rouse ourselves a little and to kindle that fire within us, we should emulate that holy one. He tells us himself that this is not impossible: *Be imitators of me as I am of Christ.* Therefore let us not only admire him and wonder at him, let us also imitate him, that at our departure hence we may be made worthy to see him and to share that unspeakable glory. May this be granted to all of us through the grace and love of Our Lord Jesus Christ, to Whom, with the Father and the Holy Ghost, be praise for ever and ever. Amen.

. . . .

'THIS IS MY BODY.'

(*1st Homily on the Betrayal of Judas, Benedictine Edition,* t. ii., p. 381.)

Then the disciples came to Him. *Then.* When? When these things were taking place, and the betrayal was effected, and Judas destroyed himself, the disciples came to Him, saying, *Where wilt Thou that we prepare to eat the Pasch?* Mark you the difference between disciple and disciples? The one betrays his Lord, the others busy themselves with preparing the Pasch; the one makes a bargain, the others minister for His table: both the one and the others had enjoyed the same miracles, the same teaching, the same authority. Now, how do they differ? In the will: this is everywhere the cause, both of all good and all evil. *Where wilt Thou that we prepare to eat the Pasch? Then* was that same evening. As Our Lord had no house of His own, they said to Him, *Where wilt Thou that we prepare to eat the Pasch?* We have no settled dwelling-place, neither tent nor house. Let those who dwell in splendid houses, and spacious courts, and large precincts be taught that Christ had not where to lay His head. Therefore they asked, *Where wilt Thou that we prepare to eat the Pasch?* What Pasch? This was not our Pasch, but still the Jews' Pasch; it was this Jewish Pasch which *they* prepared; Our Lord Himself prepared ours. Not only did He prepare it Himself, but He became our Pasch. *Where wilt Thou that we prepare for Thee to eat the Pasch?* This was the Jewish Pasch which had begun in Egypt. Now, why did Christ partake of it? Because He accomplished all the observances of the law. At His baptism He said: *Thus it becomes us to fulfil all justice.* I came to redeem man from the malediction of the law. For God sent His own Son, made of woman, made under the law, that He might redeem those who were bound by it, and might put an end to the law. Now, to prevent anyone from saying that He abolished the law because He was unable to fulfil it, as being burdensome, and hard, and oppressive, having first Himself carried it out, He then dissolved it. On this account He held the Pasch also, for the Pasch was an ordinance of the law. And why did the law order the eating of the Pasch? The Jews were ungrateful towards their benefactor, and so immediately after the benefits they forgot God's precepts. When they came out of Egypt, and saw the waters parted, and again closed, and a thousand other wonders, they said, *Let us make to ourselves gods who may go before us.* What say you? You still touch the wonders with your hands, and have you forgotten the benefactor? Since, therefore, they were thus without feeling or understanding, God kept alive the memory of His gifts by the ordinance of feasts, and He commanded the Pasch to be sacrificed, so that if your son ask you, ' What is this Pasch?' you may answer, ' Our forefathers in Egypt sprinkled their doors with the blood of the lamb, lest the angel of destruction, when he came, should enter in and smite with the plague'. Thus the feast was a perpetual memorial of salvation. Moreover, not only did these feasts benefit them by keeping fresh the memory of graces in the past, but something much more, for they foreshadowed what was to come. That lamb, indeed, was the figure of another Lamb, a spiritual Lamb, and that sheep of another Sheep. The one was a shadow, the other the reality. When the Sun of Justice appeared, the shadow forthwith ceased, for at sunrise the shadows depart. Consequently, at that table itself, each Pasch takes place—

the Pasch of the figure and the Pasch of the reality. Just as painters use one and the same canvas for outlining their subject and depicting shadow, and then add colouring to make it life-like, so did Christ act. At one and the same table He showed forth the typical Pasch, and set up the true Pasch. *Where wilt Thou that we prepare for Thee to eat the Pasch?* It was then the Jewish Pasch, but when the sun appears let the lamp be extinguished; with the advent of truth let the shadow languish.

I say these things to the Jews since they seem to celebrate a Pasch, since the uncircumcised in heart put forward their unleavened bread with a gross mind. Tell me, O Jew, how do you sacrifice the Pasch? The temple is destroyed, the altar has been taken away, the holy of holies has been trampled under foot, all show of sacrifice has ceased. Wherefore, then, do you venture to carry out practices so illegal? You went out once into Babylon, and there those who had taken you captive said, *Sing us a song of Sion*, and you would not. And David spoke with the same intent: *We sat beside the waters of Babylon and wept; we hung up our organs on the willows in the midst of it*, that is, our instruments, harps, lyres, and the rest. Men of old used these things, and thus sung hymns, and when they went into captivity took them so as to have a reminder of their life in their own country, not to use them. *For there*, he says, *they who held us captive asked us for words of songs, and we said, How shall we sing the song of the Lord in a strange land?*

What! you will not sing the song of the Lord in a strange land, and yet will you celebrate the Pasch of the Lord in a strange land! What ingratitude and iniquity! Because those who constrained them were enemies, they dared not even sing a psalm in a strange land. And now of themselves, whereas no man puts force upon them, they wage war against God. Do you see how their unleavened bread is unclean and their feast illegal? Now there is no Jewish Pasch. There was one then, but it is dissolved now, and the spiritual Pasch came, which was given then by Christ. For as they were eating and drinking, the Evangelist says, taking bread, He broke and said: *This is My body, which is broken for you unto the remission of sins.* The initiated understand these words. Then, taking the chalice, He said: *This is My Blood, which is shed for many unto the remission of sins.* And Judas was present as Christ spoke thus. This is the very Body which you have sold for thirty pieces of silver, O Judas; this is the very Blood which you have just shamefully bartered to the unfeeling Pharisees. O loving kindness of Christ! O foolish madness of Judas! On the one hand Judas sold Him for thirty pieces of silver, whilst Christ even after this did not refuse to give that Blood, which had been betrayed, to the traitor for the remission of his sins, if he had so willed. And Judas was there, and he partook of the sacred table. For, as Our Lord had washed his feet, together with the other disciples', so did he eat with them of the sacred table, in order that he might have no excuse for remaining obdurate. Our Lord did everything in His power, yet Judas persisted in his wickedness.

But it is now time for us to approach that tremendous table. Let us, therefore, all go to it with becoming sobriety and watchfulness. Let there be no Judas here, no guilty man, no one infected with poison, no man with one thing in his mouth and another in his mind. The same Christ is now here Who prepared that table. And He it is Who is now preparing it. For it is not a man who makes the offerings become the Body and Blood of Christ, but the very Christ for us crucified.[1] Fulfilling what he represents, the priest stands there, speaking those words; the power and grace of them are God's. *This is My Body*, he says, and this word transforms what lies before him;[2] and just as the words, *Increase and multiply and fill the earth*, were once spoken and endue our nature through all time with fruitfulness, so those other words once spoken from that time till to-day and until His coming, make the sacrifice over each table in the churches complete. Therefore, let no hypocrite approach, no one filled with sin, no one with poison in his mind, that he may not receive judgment to himself, for then, too, Judas had partaken of the oblation when the devil leapt into him; not that the devil despised the Lord's Body, but Judas for his shameful conduct.

[1] Ἀλλ' αὐτὸς ὁ σταυρωθεὶς ὑπὲρ ἡμῶν Χριστός.
[2] ... μεταρρυθμίζει τὰ προκείμενα.

This was to teach you that the devil continually attacks and assails those who unworthily partake of the divine mysteries, as he did Judas. For honourable things profit the good, but inflict a greater punishment on those who abuse the use of them. I say this not to terrify but to fortify you. Let there be no Judas, then; let no one enter in poisoned with evil. For the sacrifice is spiritual food; and just as bodily food, when received by a stomach which has bad humours, strengthens disease, not from its own nature but because of that stomach's weakness, so does it usually happen with the spiritual mysteries. They, too, when received by a soul full of wickedness, wither it up and corrupt it the more, not by their own nature, but through the weakness of the participating soul. Let no one, therefore, indulge in bad thoughts; let us rather cleanse our mind, for we are approaching an immaculate sacrifice; let us make our souls holy. This may be done even in one day. How? If you have anything against an enemy cast out your anger, cure your wound, give up your enmity, in order that you may receive a healing from that table, for you are approaching a tremendous and all-holy sacrifice. Reverence the reason which prompts this offering. Christ lies slain before you. Why was He slain, and on what account? That He might bring about peace between the things of heaven and the things of earth; that He might make you the friend of angels, and reconcile you to the God of all; and that, whereas you were a foe and an enemy, He might transform you into His friend. *He* gave up His own life for those who hated Him. *You* continue in enmity with your fellow-servant, and how will you be able to approach the table of peace? He did not refuse even to die for you. Will you not put away for your own sake your anger against your fellow-servant? What excuse has this conduct? 'He has treated me badly,' you say, 'and has been most grasping.' What is this? It was a sheer money loss, but he was far from wounding you as Judas did Our Lord. Yet *He* gave that very blood which poured from Him for the salvation of those who shed it. What have you to put against this? If you do not forgive your enemy you have wounded not him but yourself. You have often done him some harm in this life, but you have prepared for yourself a relentless sentence in the enduring day of eternity. For nothing is so hateful to God as a revengeful man, an unforgiving heart, and an angered mind. Listen to what He says: *When thou offerest thy gift at the altar, and as thou standest there, rememberest that thy brother hath anything against thee, take thy gift from the altar, and going away, be reconciled to thy brother, and then offer thy gift.* What? Do you tell me that I must forgive? 'I do, indeed,' He says; 'this sacrifice was instituted in order that you and your brother should be at peace.' If, therefore, it was instituted that you might be at peace with your brother, and you do not enjoy peace, it is idle for you to take part in the sacrifice, and it has been instituted in vain as far as you are concerned. Do, then, in the first place, that for which the sacrifice is offered, and then you will enjoy its full benefit. The Son of God came down from heaven that He might reconcile our nature to its Lord, and on this account not only did He come, but wished also to make us who should do the same things participators of His Name. *Blessed are the peacemakers*, He says, *for they shall be called the sons of God*. That which the only begotten Son of God did, do you also according to your human power, by becoming a bond of peace to yourself and to others. This is why He calls you who are a peacemaker a son of God; this is why, in the time of sacrifice, He is mindful of no other commandment than that of reconciliation with a brother, showing that it is the greatest of all. Would that I could go on with the argument, but what I have said is sufficient for those who are here present, if they will lay it to heart. Let us always be mindful of these words, beloved brethren, and of the holy kiss of peace, and of the most sacred embrace which we give to each other. For this it is which holds our minds together, and makes us all one body, since we all partake of one Body. Let us then blend ourselves into one body, not mixing our bodies, but uniting our souls in the bond of charity; thus we shall be able to enjoy the table set before us with confidence. For even if we should be righteous a thousand times over, and yet have revengeful spirits, all is vanity and deception, and we shall be powerless to gain fruits of salvation here. Recognising this, let us put off all anger, and, purifying our conscience, let us with all meekness and humility approach the table of Christ, to Whom, with the Father and the Holy Ghost, be all glory, honour, and power, now and for ever! Amen.

THE UNION OF THE HOLY EUCHARIST.

(*Homilies on St. Matthew*, lxxxii., vol. ii., p. 468.)

. . . . .

Let us then trust in God under all circumstances, and never gainsay Him, even when what He says seems contrary to our reasonings and to our sight; but let His word be more powerful than our reasoning and our sight. So let us act in regard to the mysteries, not seeing only that which is before us, but also embracing His words. *His* word is not to be set aside, whereas our senses are easily deceived. *It* has never failed, but our senses have erred over and over again. Since, then, the word is, *This is My Body*, let us trust and believe in it, and gaze at it with our mind's eyes. For Christ delivered to us nothing that is the object of sense, but objects all of the mind, yet dealing with sensible things. Thus, too, in baptism, the gift is made through an object of sense—the water, and that which is accomplished, is an object of mind, viz., birth and renewal. For, if you were bodiless, He would have given you bodiless gifts in their nakedness; but, since the soul is encompassed by the body, He gives you objects of mind, under the appearance of sensible things. How many men say, 'I should like to see His form and features, His garments and His shoes? Well, you see Him, and touch Him, and eat Him. You desire to see what He wore, and He gives you Himself, not to see only, but to touch, and to eat, and to receive within you. Therefore, let no man approach with disgust or carelessness, but all with fire, and zeal, and watchfulness. For, if the Jews ate their Pasch in haste, standing, and holding their sandals and staffs in their hands, how much more should you be wary. *They* were about to go out to Palestine, and so they had the outward signs of travellers, and *you* are going forth to heaven. Hence we must be ever on the watch, for not a small punishment is reserved to those who eat unworthily. Think what your anger is against the traitor, and those who crucified Him, and see if you are not yourself guilty of the Body and Blood of Christ. They slaughtered the all-holy Body, and you receive it with a foul soul after so many loving benefits. He deemed it not sufficient to become man, to be scourged, and put to death, He also blends Himself with us, not by faith only, but in very deed makes us His Body. What, then, should be the purity of him who partakes of this sacrifice? How spotlessly white should not the hand be which divides this Flesh, or the mouth which is filled with spiritual fire, or the tongue which is purpled with that tremendous Blood? Consider what honour has been shown to you, and what that feast is which you enjoy. The angels gaze and tremble, and dare not look back again, because of the lightning which flashes from it; and this is what we feed upon, this is blended with us, and we ourselves become one body and one flesh with Christ. *Who shall declare the powers of the Lord? Who shall set forth all His praises?* Where is the shepherd who feeds his sheep with his own members? And why do I talk of a shepherd? There are many mothers who, after the pains of childbirth, give up their children to be nursed by others. This He would not suffer, but He Himself feeds us with His own Blood, and in everything unites us to Himself. For consider: He was born of our substance. 'Not for all men,' you say. Yes, for all. For, if He came to our nature, it is evident that He came to all, and if He came to all, then He came to each one of us. And why is it, you ask, that all men have not profited by this gift? This was not the fault of Him Who took that nature for all, but of those who had not the will. He unites Himself to each one of the faithful, through the mysteries, and those whom He brought forth He rears through Himself, and gives Himself to no other, persuading you again thereby that it was that very flesh of yours which He took. Therefore, let us not grow negligent who have been made worthy of so great charity and honour. Do you not see how eagerly babies grasp their mother's breast, and how they press their lips upon it. Just so let *us* approach this table and the breast of spiritual drink; or rather, with much more impatience, let us draw near to the kindness of the Spirit, as children to their mother's breast, and let us know one only pain, that of not participating in this food. That which lies before us is no work of human power. He Who did these things at that supper is He Who is now doing them. Our part is to furnish the ranks of servers. He Who sanctifies and prepares these gifts is Himself. Therefore let there be no Judas, no money-lover. If a man be not a disciple, let him withdraw : this table is not prepared for such as he. *I will eat the Pasch,* He says, *with My disciples.* This is that same table, and it offers no less. It was not that Christ instituted the one and a man the other, but He instituted both one and the other. This is that upper chamber in which they were assembled ; thence they went forth into the Garden of Olives. Let us also go forth to minister to the poor, for this is our mountain of olives. The multitude of the poor, who are planted in God's house, are olives, dropping upon us the oil that is to be useful to us, which the five virgins had, and the five who did not take it perished for want of it. Possessing it, let us go in, that we may all meet the Bridegroom, with bright lamps : with it; let us go forth from this world.

. . . .

Bone of our Bone, Flesh of our Flesh.

(*Homilies on First Epistle to Corinthians*, xxiv., vol. ii., pp. 287, 295.)

. . . .

The chalice of benediction which we bless, is it not the communion of the Blood of Christ? What do you say, blessed Paul? Wishing to engage your hearers' attention and commemorating the tremendous mysteries, do you call that awful and most tremendous chalice a chalice of benediction? 'Yes,' he says, 'since what I have said is no slight thing. For when I speak of benediction I speak of the Eucharist, and when I speak of the Eucharist I unfold all the treasure of God's munificence and commemorate His greatest gifts.' And we, recounting over the chalice the unspeakable benefits of God and what mercies we have enjoyed, thus worship Him and hold communion with Him, giving thanks that He has freed the human race from error, that whereas we were far off from Him He drew us near, that when we were without hope and without God in the world He made us His brethren and co-heirs. Thus, in thanking Him for these and all His gifts, we approach Him. How, then, O Corinthians, are you not doing the opposite to this when praising God for turning you away from idols you hasten back to their tables? *Is not the chalice of benediction which we bless the communion of the Blood of Christ?* He spoke these words with an awful assurance. For this is what he says: that which is in the chalice is what flowed from His side, and of that we partake. But He called it a chalice of thanksgiving, since we, holding it in our hands, thus praise Him, wondering and being overwhelmed with this ineffable gift, magnifiying Him for pouring out this very Blood of His that we might not remain in error, and not only that He poured it out, but that He has given to each one of us to partake of it. So, He says, if you desire blood, do not dye the altar of idols with the slaughter of unreasoning animals, but dye My altar with *My Blood*.[1] Tell me what is more tremendous, what is tenderer than this? For this is what lovers do: when they see the loved ones longing for what others have and despising what they themselves have, they give their own gifts, and so induce the beloved to turn away from the things of others. But lovers show this affection of theirs by money, and clothes, and chattels, no one of them ever by his blood; yet Christ gave us even this proof of His solicitude and His burning love for us. Thus, in the old Law, as men were in an imperfect state and offered blood to idols, it remained for Him to receive this (the chalice of the Pasch) that He might turn them away from idols, which, again, was an ineffable tenderness. But here He led them up to a far more awful and magnificent worship of God, and changed the

---

[1] The single word *altar* has to stand for the Greek βωμός and θυσιαστήριον, the former meaning the altar on which a bloody offering is made, the latter the altar on which the sacrifice after the order of Melchisedec is offered.

sacrifice itself, and instead of the slaughtering of unreasoning animals, He commanded them to offer up Himself. *Is not the bread which we break the communion of the Body of Christ?* Why did he not say a participation? Because he wished to set forth something more and to show the closeness of that union. For we communicate not only by receiving and participating, but by being made one with Him. For just as that body is united to Christ, so are we made one with Him through this bread. Why did he add, *which we break?* This is seen to take place in the case of the Eucharist, though not at the Cross, but the contrary. *Not a bone of Him shall be broken*, the Scripture says. That which He did not suffer on the cross He suffers in the Eucharist for your sake, and He endures being broken that He may fill all.

Then after saying *the communion of the body*—for that which communicates is something distinct from the thing communicated—he removed even this seemingly slight difference. For in the words *communion of the body* he sought to say something closer, and therefore added, *That we, being many, are one bread and one body.* 'Why do I speak of communion?' he says; 'we are that very Body itself. For what is the bread? The Body of Christ. What do partakers of it become? The Body of Christ: not many bodies, but one body.' Just as bread is composed of many grains of wheat which are nowhere apparent in it, but still there, presenting no difference by reason of the kneading, so are we joined together with each other and with Christ. You are not nourished by one body and another man by another, but all by the same; therefore he added, 'We are all participators of the same bread'. But if we *are* of the same, and become the same, why do we not all show forth the same charity and become one in this respect also? For this was so formerly in our progenitors. *There was one heart and one mind in the gathering of the faithful.* This is not the case now, but very much the reverse. Dissensions are many and various and well-nigh everywhere, and we show ourselves fiercer than wild beasts towards our members. Christ united you to Himself when you were so distant, and you will not deign to be united with your brother as you ought to be, but thrust yourself away from him, whilst enjoying so great a love and life from your Master. It was not for no purpose that He gave His Body, but as the first human nature, which was made from the earth, became by sin subject to death and to be deprived of life, He introduced, as we might say, another bread and leaven — His own Flesh — in nature, indeed the same, but free from sin and full of life; and He gave to all men to eat of it, that, nourished by it and putting off the old dead nature, we may at this table be blended with the living and immortal nature.

. . . .

This Body He gave to us to take and eat, which

was an act of exceeding love.[1] For it often happens that we bite those whom we love. Thus, when Job pointed out the affection of his household for himself, he quoted those who loved him specially as often saying, *Who will give us to be filled with his flesh?* So it is that Christ has given us to be filled with His Flesh, drawing us to greater love. Let us, therefore, approach Him with fervour and burning love, that we may not encounter the harder chastisement. For the more we are benefitted, the greater will be our punishment whenever we show ourselves unworthy of His generosity. This Body, even lying in the manger, the Magi reverenced: untutored and uncivilised men, leaving their country and their home, undertook a long journey, they came and adored, full of awe and fear. Let us, citizens of heaven, emulate even uncivilised men, if necessary. *They*, seeing Him in a manger, and in a hut, and not seeing Him as you see Him, approached Him with deep reverence: you see Him not in the crib, but on the altar: you see Him not held by a woman, but the priest standing there, and the Spirit hovering with abundant blessings over what is lying there. Nor do you merely see this Body as they did: *you* know His power and all the economy of His providence, nor are you ignorant of anything accomplished through Him, initiated as you are into all His mysteries. Let us therefore rouse ourselves, and tremble, and show forth so much the greater rever-

---

[1] P. 295 of the same Homily.

ence than those men from afar, in order that we may not approach Him heedlessly or casually, and so heap coals of fire upon our heads. This I say, not that we may not approach Him, but that we may not approach Him carelessly. For just as going to Him in a chance way is a danger, so the non-participation in that mystical Banquet is hunger and death. This Feast is the sinew of our soul, the bond of intellect, the basis of fortitude; it is hope, salvation, light, life. With this sacrifice, at our departure from this world to the next, we shall pass through those sacred portals in great fearlessness, as if encompassed with an armour of gold. And why do I speak of the future? Even here this mystery makes the earth a heaven for you. At least unfold the gates of heaven and look through them, or rather not only the gates of heaven, but of the heaven of heavens, and then you will see what I say. For that which is the most precious of all things there, is what I will show you lying on earth. Just as in royal palaces it is not the walls which strike men with the most awe, nor the golden ceilings, but the person of the king sitting on his throne, so in heaven is it the King's Body. Yet this is what you may now see on earth. I am showing you not angels, nor archangels, nor the heavens, nor the heaven of heavens, but the Lord of all these Himself. Do you understand how it is that you see the most precious thing of all upon earth? And not only do you see it, but you also touch it? And not only touch it, but you eat it, and, receiving it, you take it away with you? Cleanse, therefore, your soul; prepare your mind for the reception of these mysteries. If, now, you were judged worthy to carry a royal child in state, with his kingly robes and his diadem, you would give up everything on earth for it. And, here, receiving not a royal child of man, but the very only begotten Son of God, tell me, do you not tremble, and renounce the love of all earthly things, and adorn yourself only for that world to come, or have you still your eyes fixed on the earth, do you still love money, and anxiously crave for gold? What pardon could you look for, or what excuse would you have? Know you not how Our Lord turns His back upon all worldly luxury? Was not this His reason for being born and laid in a manger, and for choosing a mother who was poor? Was it not for this that He said to the man who looked to worldly traffic: *The Son of man has not whereon to lay His head?* And what of His disciples? Did not they carry out the same law, lodging at the houses of the poor, one going to a tanner's, another to a tent-maker's, another to the woman selling purple? They did not seek for illustrious houses, but for upright minds. Let us then emulate their example; looking beyond the beauty of pillars and marbles, seeking only for the mansions above, let us trample under foot all vanities here below, together with the lust for money, and take up a lofty mind. For if we be sober and watchful, the world itself will not be worthy of us, much less the Stoic portico or the Peripatetic walk. Therefore, I repeat, let us adorn our souls, let us prepare this dwelling-place, which we shall take with us when we depart, so that we may possess the eternal tents through the grace and love of Our Lord Jesus Christ, to Whom be glory for ever and ever. Amen.

REMEMBRANCE OF THE DEAD.
(*Homilies on Epistle to the Philippians*, iv., vol. v., p. 36.)

. . . .

Let us, then, not simply grieve for the dead, nor simply rejoice in the living. Then what shall we do? Let us grieve for sinners not when dead alone, but when living also; and let us be glad over the just not in their lifetime only, but when they have departed hence. Sinners even living are dead, whilst the just, who are dead, live: sinners are an object of pity to all men even here because they have quarrelled with God, so are the just blessed in that place, since they have gone to Christ. Sinners, wherever they are, are far from the King, and therefore deserve tears, but the just, whether here or there, are with the King; *there* they are more with Him and nearer to Him, not by their going in, nor by faith, but face to face. Let us, then, not weep simply for the dead but for those in sin: these call for tears, for lamentation and weeping. For, tell me, what hope is there of those who depart in sins to that place where sins are not put off? As long as they were here, the probability was great that they might be converted and become better. But if they go to the other world, there is nothing to be gained from contrition. *In hell*, he says, *who shall give praise to Thee?* Let us weep for those who thus depart. I do not forbid it, only not in an unseemly fashion, not plucking out our hair, nor baring our arms, nor tearing our face, nor wearing black, but only in shedding a bitter tear according to the spirit in secret. Without these accompaniments we may weep bitterly, and not be contented with a show, for what some people have done differs in nothing from a show. For instance, those who beat themselves at the market-place do it not from sympathy, but for display and for self-seeking and vainglory, and many women so treat themselves as a business speculation. Weep bitterly, groan at home when no one is looking: this is sympathy, and this will be helpful to you also. For, in grieving for another, you will be all the more zealous never to fall in the same way, and you will tremble at sin ever afterwards. Weep for unbelievers, for those who are not different from unbelievers, who depart hence without baptism, without being signed with the seal: these should have tears and wailings, they are outside the royal palace with those awaiting judgment and with the condemned. *Amen, I say to you, unless a man be born of water and the Spirit, he shall not enter into the kingdom of heaven.* Weep for those who have died in riches, and have devised no comfort for their own souls out of their wealth, who have received power to wash away their sins, and have not willed to do it. Weep all of you for these both in secret and in public, but with decorum and reverence, not making a show of yourselves. Let us shed tears over these not for one day, nor two, but during our whole life. This is no foolish weeping, but the weeping of affection; the other is senseless, and therefore it soon spends itself. Grief which is born of the fear of God endures for ever. Let us weep for these and help them as much as we can. Let us devise some succour for them; it may be a slight thing, but let us somehow do it. How and in what manner? By praying and inviting others to pray for them, by constantly giving alms to the poor for them. This deed has its consolation. Listen to God's words: *I will protect this city for Myself and for David, My servant.* If the mere remembrance of a just man could do so much, what will works done for him not be able to accomplish? Not in vain was it ordained by the Apostles that the dead should be commemorated at the tremendous mysteries: they knew what a great gain and benefit it would be to the dead. For when a whole people stands with uplifted hands in full and sacred assembly, and the awful sacrifice is lying before us, how shall we not reach God in our prayer for them? But this applies to those who have died in the faith. With regard to catechumens they are not deemed worthy of this consolation; they lack all such succour, save in one particular. What is this? We may give alms for them to the poor, and the action brings them a certain refreshment, because God wills us to be of use to each other. For why did He command us to pray for the peace and well-being of the world, or, again, for all men? Although there are thieves, and tomb-despoilers, and plunderers, and men full of every sort of evil amongst the whole number, yet we still pray for them all. Perhaps there may be a conversion of some. Now, as we pray for the living who do not differ from the dead, so we may pray for the departed. Job offered sacrifices for his children, and freed them from their sins. *Lest perhaps*, he said, *they have sinned in their hearts.* Thus is a man provident for his children. He did not say, as the multitude of men *do* say, 'I will leave them possessions,' nor a fine name, nor, 'I will buy an office,' nor fields, but what, *Lest perhaps they have sinned in their hearts.* For what is the profit of those things? None, of things that remain here below. *I will make*, he says, *the King of all propitious to them: and then nothing is wanting to them. The Lord is my Shepherd, and I shall lack for nothing.* Here are great riches, here are treasures. If we have the fear of God we want nothing, but without it, even if we have a kingdom, we are the poorest of men. A God-fearing man has no equal. The fear of the Lord exceeds all things. This let us possess, and let us do all things unto this end: even if we have to give up our life, or our body to be cut in pieces, let us not fear: let us do all our actions in order to gain this fear. Thus shall we become richer than all, and arrive at the goods to come in Christ Jesus Our Lord, to Whom, with the Father and the Holy Spirit, be honour, power, and glory, now and for ever. Amen.

THE DEPARTED AT THE SACRED MYSTERIES.

(*Homilies on First Epistle to Corinthians*, xli., vol. ii., p. 524.)

. . . .

Since, then, we are to enjoy goods so great, let us join ourselves to that company which is as bright as the sun, and let us not weep for those who depart hence, but for those who make a bad end. For, as the husbandman does not grieve over his seed dissolved, but is in fear and anxiety as long as it remains solid, so he rejoices when he sees that it *is* dissolved. For dissolution is the beginning of the future generating. So let us also rejoice when the corruptible habitation perishes, and man is generated. And wonder not if Paul called the burying a generating, for this is the better generating of the two. Death, labours, dangers, cares, succeed the one; whilst for the other, if we have lived righteously, we receive crowns and rewards: corruption and death succeed the one; incorruption, immortality, and a thousand goods succeed the other. In the one generating there is embracing, pleasure, sleep; in the other there is only the voice coming down from heaven, and all things accomplished in the twinkling of an eye. And he who rises is no more driven to a laborious life, but he will be where pain and sorrow and lamentation have fled away. If, however, you are seeking for a protector, and weep over the man on this account, fly for refuge to God, the common Protector, and Saviour, and Benefactor of all: to the almighty Friend, to the never-failing Succour, to the lasting Shelter, Who is everywhere and always holding us up. 'But,' you say, 'the intercourse was pleasant and fascinating.' I know it was. Still, if you meet your suffering with your reason, and consider in yourself who it is that has taken him, and that if you bear it bravely, you offer up your wish as a sacrifice to God, you will be borne aloft even over this wave, and Christian principle will effect what the action of time does; but if you are pusillanimous, time will weaken your passion without bringing you a reward. Together with these recollections, ponder on the examples offered both in this present life and in Holy Scripture. Consider how Abraham slaughtered his own son, neither shedding tears nor uttering a bitter word. 'But *he* was Abraham,' you say. Yet you are called to greater conflicts. Job, indeed, showed sorrow as a loving father would who mourns over those departing from him. Now *we* show the grief of foes and enemies. For if a man were summoned to a palace and crowned, and you were to beat your breast and be in sorrow at it, I should say you were not a friend to the man crowned, but a determined adversary and hater. 'I am not weeping for him,' you say, 'but for myself.' Neither is this the part of a lover—the wishing him to be still in conflict on your account, to be left in uncertainty as to the future, instead of being crowned, or to be tossing on the sea when he might be resting in harbour. 'But,' you say, 'I know not where he has gone.' How is it that you do not know? This will be evident from the fact of his having lived righteously or the reverse. 'And as he departed in sin, this is the very reason why I am tormented.' What you say is a mere pretext. If this is why you mourn over a dead man, you should have taken pains with the living one and set him right. You are throughout thinking of your own interests, not of his. If, indeed, he departed hence in sin, you should rejoice that his sins were stopped and that he did not continue in evil, and you should help him by those means which are in your power: not by tears, but by prayers, and supplications, and alms-giving, and offerings. It is not by chance that these things have been ordered, nor is it due to haphazard that we commemorate the dead at the sacred mysteries, and that we succour them by supplication to the Lamb, Who is lying there, Who takes away the sins of the world, but that they may derive hence some consolation. Nor is it without reason that he who is standing by the altar, as the sacred mysteries are performed, utters this cry: for all those who have fallen asleep in Christ, and for those who make commemoration in their behalf. For if commemoration were not made for them, this would not be said.

Our mysteries are no theatrical display. God forbid! These things take place by the disposition of the Spirit. Therefore, let us help them, and make commemoration in their behalf. For if Job's sacrifice purified his children, why do you doubt that the departed receive comfort when we too offer sacrifice for them? God is wont to give graces to some on behalf of others. And this Paul also showed, saying *that for this gift obtained for us, by the means of many persons, thanks may be given by many in our behalf.* Let us not weary of helping the departed, both by offering sacrifice and claiming intercession for them. For the sacrifice which saves the whole world is before us. Therefore we pray confidently at it for what concerns the world, and we name them with martyrs, and confessors, and pontiffs. For we are all one body, even if certain members be more resplendent than others; and everywhere we may be gaining forgiveness for them, by prayers, by offerings made for them, by those who are named with them. Why, then, do you grieve and weep, when you are able to apply so great a forgiveness to him who has departed? Is it because you have become lonely, and have lost your protector? But you ought never to say this, because you have not lost God. As long as you possess Him, He will be more to you than any man, be he father, child, or near relation; for even when these were living, it was He in reality Who did everything.

THE TOMBS OF THE MARTYRS.

(Homily on the Martyrs, Benedictine Edition, t. ii., p. 667.)

The feasts of the martyrs are not according to the course of days only, but they are reckoned also by the disposition of those who celebrate them. For instance, have you imitated a martyr, have you emulated his goodness, have you pressed on in the footsteps of his ascetic life? Then, though it is not a martyr's day, you have celebrated a martyr's feast. For to honour a martyr is to imitate him. Just as evil-doers are feastless in the midst of feasts, so the righteous, even if there be no solemnity, have carried out one. The feast is characterised by purity of conscience. This Paul expressed clearly: *Therefore, let us keep the feast not in the old leaven of evil and wickedness, but in the unleavened bread of purity and truth.* There is, then, unleavened bread amongst the Jews, and so there is amongst us; but with them it consists of wheaten flour, with us in a pure life and in remaining spotless. Thus, he who wards off every stain keeps a feast every day, is ever celebrating a solemnity not only on the feast of the martyr or at his shrine, but also sitting at home. Every man can keep the martyr's feast by himself. In saying this I do not mean that we should *not* go to the tombs of the martyrs. I mean that, being there, we should frequent these places with befitting devotion, not only on their days, but that we should show the same piety out of their days. Who would not revere this gathering of ours to-day, this splendid sight, the fervent charity and glowing spirit, the boundless love, which are here manifested? Nearly all the city has been eager to come; fear of his master has not withheld the servant; no straits of poverty, no feebleness of age, have kept the poor or the old away; no tenderness of sex in women, no extreme of luxury has hindered the rich, no folly of power the ruler. But a longing for the martyrs vanquishing all such disparity, both the weakness of nature and the stress of poverty hold together by one bond the vast multitude gathered here, who are moved by the wings of this desire to live the life of the heavenly citizens. For, treading under foot all allurements to excess and wickedness, you are consumed with longing for the martyrs. As with the dawn of day wild animals flee away and take shelter in their own holes, so when the light of the martyrs bursts upon our minds all diseases are put to flight and the bright flame of mortification is enkindled. And let us keep this fire alive not now only, but always, when this spiritual spectacle has been broken up; let us retire to our own homes with the same fervour, not giving ourselves up to taverns, or dissoluteness, or drunkenness, or feastings. You have made night into day through these sacred vigils: do not again make day into night through inebriation, and gluttony, and meretricious songs. You have honoured the martyrs by your presence, your attention, and your fervour: honour them by going modestly home, lest anyone seeing you taking your ease in a low place should say that you came not on account of the martyrs, but to increase your passion and to incite your bad desires. This I say, prohibiting not feasting but sin, prohibiting not wine but drunkenness. It is not the wine which is evil, it is intemperance. Wine is the gift of God, intemperance is the devil's invention. . . . Intemperance is ever an evil, beloved brethren, and most of all on the feast day of the martyrs. Together with the sin, it is a most open contempt and folly and putting aside of the divine words; hence the chastisement would be double. If, therefore, you have come to the martyrs and mean afterwards to drink, you had better remain at home and not shame nor insult the martyrs' feast, nor scandalise your neighbour, nor distort your understanding, nor add to your sins. You came to look upon men who were racked with torments, covered with blood, and adorned with wounds, who gave up this present life and took their flight to the life above. Show yourself worthy of those wrestlers. *They* despised life, do *you* despise luxury; they renounced their life in this world, do you renounce the craving for drink. Do you wish for feasting? Remain by the martyr's tomb, weep there a fountain of tears, grieve in your mind, take a blessing from that tomb. Let it assist you in your prayers; make the account of his fight your constant reading; embrace the coffin; nail yourself to the shrine. Not only the bones of the martyrs, but their tombs also and their coffins, produce an abundant blessing. Take holy oil and sign your whole body with it, your tongue, your lips, your throat and eyes, and you will avoid the abyss of drunkenness.

. . . . . .

The Bodies of the Martyrs.

(*Homily on the Martyrs, Benedictine Edition,* t. ii., p. 650.)

. . . .

Yesterday was the martyrs' feast, and so is to-day. Would that we could be always keeping the feast of the martyrs! For if those who are mad after theatres, and who gape open-mouthed at horses racing, cannot have enough of those foolish spectacles, how much more should we be insatiable for the feasts of the saints. In the one place there is a diabolical pomp, in the other a Christian feast: in the one place devils are revelling, in the other angelic choirs are singing: in the one place souls are lost, in the other there is salvation for all who are gathered together. Do not theatres offer any pleasure at all? If they do, not such as the other. What pleasure, indeed, is there in seeing horses running senselessly to and fro? In the other case, you see, not brute animals yoked together, but countless chariots of martyrs, and God as charioteer in the midst of them, leading the way to heaven. Listen to the prophet saying that the souls of the saints are God's chariot: *God's chariots are ten thousand fold, and thousands those who rejoice.* That which He has made a gift to the powers above, He has granted to our nature also. He sits upon the cherubim, as the psalm says: *He ascended upon the cherubim, and He flew;* and again: *He who sitteth upon the cherubim and looketh into the abysses.* This He has given to us also. He sits on them, He dwells in us. *I will abide in you and will walk in you,* He says. They have become His chariot, let us become His temple. See you how these honours are akin? See you how He has reconciled the things above and the things below? Therefore, if we choose, we are in nothing removed from the angels! As I began by saying, yesterday was the martyrs' feast, and to-day is the martyrs' feast: not the martyrs who are amongst us here, but those who are in the country, or rather, they also are with us. Town and country, in the business of this life, are distinct from each other, but as far as piety is concerned, they meet on the same ground. Tell me not, then, that they have the tongue of barbarians: look rather at their mortified minds. How does unity of language serve me where the spirit is not one? How does a different speech hurt me where there is harmony in the things of faith? According to this reasoning, the country is in no sort of way worse off than the town: they enjoy equality of privileges in the head and chief of good things. So it was that Our Lord Jesus Christ did not confine Himself to cities, and leave country places empty and deserted, but He went about through cities and villages, preaching the Gospel, and curing every sickness and disease. . . . This is why God sowed martyrs not in cities alone, but in the country too, so that we may use their feasts as a necessary opportunity of meeting each other, and oftener in the country than in the city. For God gave the greater honour to the inferior, as this member is weaker, and therefore enjoyed more attention. Dwellers in towns always have the benefit of teaching at their command, but not so those who live in remote places. God, therefore, comforting the poverty of the teachers in the fruitfulness of the martyrs, has ordained that the greater number should be buried in the country. They have not always the voice of teachers, but the voice of the martyr speaking to them from his tomb, and with more force. And that you may know that the martyrs speak more powerfully in their silence than we by our voice, it has often happened that many have discoursed to multitudes concerning goodness, and have effected nothing; whilst others, who said no word, have done wonders through the shining example of their life. Much more have the martyrs effected this, not raising the voice of their body, but the voice of their deeds, which is far louder than the voice of the mouth. Through this voice they speak to everyone of the human race in these words: 'Look at us, and see what evils we have endured. What have we suffered in being condemned to death, and finding eternal life? We have been made worthy to lay down our bodies for Christ. If we had not offered them up then for Christ, in a little while we should have been obliged to put off this temporary life of theirs in spite of ourselves.[1] If martyrdom had not come upon us, the common death of nature would have dissolved our bodies. On this account we give thanks to God without ceasing for making us worthy to use inevitable death for the salvation of our souls, and for receiving as a gift from us, and with the greatest honour, that which was a matter of necessity. Are the torments oppressive and painful? If they are, they pass away in a moment of time, whilst the refreshment lasts during eternal ages. Nor are the torments painful even for one moment to those who have their eyes on what is to come, and who gaze intently upon the Judge. Because blessed Stephen saw Christ with the eyes of faith, he was not conscious of the volley of stones, but instead of the stones he was counting the rewards and crowns. So do you rise above present things to the contemplation of the future, and you will be insensible to even a brief consciousness of pain. This and much more is what the martyrs say, and they are far more persuasive than we are. For if I tell you that torment is not torment, my words are not to be trusted, for there is no difficulty about talking

---

[1] Blessed Thomas More's words to his wife will here occur to many: 'How long, thinkest thou, I might still live?' and when she replied, 'Full twenty years, if it so pleases God,' answered, 'Should I give up eternity for twenty years?'

wisely. But the martyr, who speaks by his deeds, cannot be gainsaid. And, as with ordinary baths, when they are bubbling over with hot water, no one has the courage to jump in, as long as those who are sitting by the bath invite each other to enter by word only, they induce nobody to try. But as soon as one of them puts in either his hand or his foot, and, encouraged by the attempt, plunges in his whole body, by his silence he persuades those outside, more than the others by all they say, to try the bath; and so it is with the martyrs. In their case we have the stake instead of the bath. Those outside, by all their talk, do not carry much weight; yet, if a single martyr plunge in, not his foot nor his hand alone, but his whole body, he offers by his action something more forcible than any advice or preaching, and he stops the anxiety of those standing round. See you how the voice of the martyr is more powerful even in its silence? This is why God has left us their bodies. This is why, victorious of old, they have not yet risen. Combats, indeed, they endured not long ago, but they have not yet enjoyed the resurrection, and this for your greater benefit, that you, pondering that fight of theirs, may be incited to carry out your own race. They do not suffer in the least from the delay, whilst *your* profit is immense. After these things they will receive their reward, even if they do not now. If God were to take them away from us at this present time, He would cut off much strength and consolation; because true strength and consolation come to all men from the tombs of the saints, and you are witnesses of what I say. For often when we have used threats, kindness, tears, and exhortations, you were not moved to fervour in prayer, but going to the shrine, without any sermon, and merely seeing the tombs of the saints, you shed a fountain of tears, and warmed to your prayer although the martyr is lying there voiceless in a deep silence. Whence, then, comes the good to the conscience, which opens, as it were, the floodgates of tears? It is the sight of the martyr and the remembrance of all his good deeds. Just as when the poor see other men who are rich and in high offices attended by body-guards, and enjoying great honour from the king, learn to feel their poverty more keenly in the prosperity of others, so is it with us when we call to mind the fortitude which the martyrs showed towards God, the King of all their shining example and their glory, and remember our own sins. Their abundance makes our grief and sorrow at our poverty more poignant, and this consciousness shows us how far we are left behind them: hence come our tears. Again, God left us their bodies, so that whenever the pressure of earthly business and cares should shroud our minds in darkness,—for private and public affairs are full of this,—we should leave our house, go out of the city, bid farewell to these harassing thoughts, and seek out the shrine. We may enjoy the spiritual atmosphere there, forget our business, feed on peace, have the companionship of the saints, pray to Him Who is their judge for our own salvation, pour forth many supplications, and through all these means, lightening our conscience, may return home in much sweetness of spirit. The biers of the martyrs are nothing else than secure harbours, the sources of spiritual streams, inexhaustible treasures of wealth which are never consumed. And just as harbours receive vessels which have been much tossed by the waves, and place them in safety, so the biers of the martyrs receiving these spirits of ours, which are absorbed by the cares of life, establish them in great peace and security. Just as streams of cold water revive failing and scorched bodies, so do those resting-places calm souls which are burnt up with foul passions. The mere sight of them quenches evil cupidity, and wasting envy, and burning desires, and any other trouble of the same kind, and they are superior to treasures of great wealth. For treasures of money present many dangers to those who find them, and when divided into many parts become less in the distribution. Here there is nothing of this sort, for the attainment is without dangers. Contrary to what happens in material treasures, this division does not diminish *this* treasure. The former, as I said, are lessened by being divided. Now, when these are distributed amongst many, then it is that they most of all show what their riches are. For such is the nature of spiritual things that they are increased by distribution, and become greater by division. Meadows with their sight of roses and violets are not so delightful as the tombs of the martyrs which offer to souls who gaze upon them an indestructible and undying delight.

. . . .

The Tombs of the Servants.
(Οἱ τάφοι τῶν δούλων.)

(Homilies on Second Epistle to Corinthians, xxvi., vol. iii., p. 273.)

. . . .

Thus God has led all the saints through tribulation and distress, helping them on the one hand whilst securing the rest against conceiving an unduly high opinion of their merits. Thus it was in the beginning that idolatries prevailed by the excessive admiration lavished upon men, and in this way the Roman Senate decreed Alexander to be the thirteenth god. For it had this authority of electing and making gods. When the whole work of Christ became known the provincial ruler sent to enquire whether they thought He too should be a god. They would not agree to that, and were impatient and angry that the power of the Crucified, bursting forth before their vote and decree, had attracted the whole world to its own majesty. This was ordained even against their will, so that the divinity of Christ might not be preached by vote of man, and that He should not be looked upon as one of the many decreed by them to be divine. For they made pugilists gods, and the creatures of Hadrian's infamous lust, whence, too, the city of Antinoos derives its name. For, since death bears witness against mortal nature, the devil lighted upon another way—the immortality of the soul, to which he joined gross flattery, and led many into impiety. What malice! Whenever *we* bring forward this argument in its proper place, he destroys it; but when he wishes to make an injurious use of it himself, he sets it up most zealously. If anyone should ask, 'How is Alexander a god? Did he not die and die miserably?' He answers, 'But his spirit is immortal'. Then you think over in your mind the argument for immortality, and play the philosopher in order that you may turn men away from the God of all; but when *we* say that this is the greatest gift of God, you persuade those whom you cheat that we are low-minded and cringing, and nothing better than unreasoning animals. And if we were to say that the Crucified lives, they would indulge in great laughter at us, although the whole universe is crying out that He does live, and did cry out of old, then by signs, now by converts, for these successes do not belong to a dead man; but if some one declares that Alexander lives, you believe him, although he has no wonder whatever to bring forward in proof of it. 'Yes, he has,' you reply; 'in his lifetime Alexander did many and great deeds, for he subdued peoples and cities, and made many victorious wars, and set up trophies.' Now, if I am able to show you things which neither Alexander nor any other man of his day contemplated in his lifetime, what further proof of the resurrection do you require? That a living man, being a king, and having an army, should carry out wars and victories is neither astonishing nor wonderful; but to do things so great after crucifixion and the tomb, to do them over land and sea, this is truly awe-inspiring, and proclaims divine and infinite power. After his death Alexander did not hinder his empire from dissolution, and when it had disappeared did not bring it back again. How should a dead man do this? Now, Christ set up His kingdom in dying. And why do I speak of Christ, since He gave to His disciples also to become famous after death? Tell me, where is Alexander's tomb? Show it to me and say what day he died. But the tombs of Christ's servants are famous; they have taken possession of the most royal city, and their days are solemnly kept as a feast for the world. Whilst the one is unknown amongst his own countrymen, even barbarians are familiar with the other. And the tombs of the servants of the Crucified are more splendid than the courts of kings, not in the greatness and beauty of the monument, though in this, too, they are remarkable, but, what is far more, through the devotion of those who frequent them. And he who is clothed in the royal purple leaves his throne to embrace those tombs, and, putting off the garb of vanity, stands as a suppliant of the saints in order to make them his intercessors with God, and the crowned king has need of a dead tent-maker and a fisherman as patrons. I ask you, would you dare to call the Lord of these a dead man, Whose servants, though no longer here, are the protectors of the kings of the earth? And you may see this happening not in Rome alone, but also in Constantinople. For here, too, the son thought his father, Constantine the Great, most highly honoured if he might be buried in the vestibule of the Fisherman. What door-keepers in palaces are to kings, this kings are at the tombs of fishermen. The fishermen, like lords of the spot, have taken possession of what is within; the kings, like sojourners and neighbours, have been contented to have a separate place in the doorway, thus proving to unbelievers that pre-eminence in the resurrection will belong to fishermen. For if it be so here in the matter of tombs, how much more in the resurrection. And the order is reversed: kings become servants and subjects, whilst subjects are invested with regal dignity, or rather with something even greater. The truth itself shows that there is no flattery in the matter, for kings have become famous through these subjects of theirs. Their tombs are far more awe-inspiring than those of all kings put together; there is great solitude in the one and a great crowd at the other. If you wish to compare these tombs with royal courts, here again they carry off the palm. Many are the bustling people at the court, but at the tomb many are they who call and attract rich and poor, men and women, slaves and freemen. There is great fear at the one, and an unspeakable delight at the other. But it is a pleasant sight to look upon the king with his golden sceptre and his crown on his head, his guards standing near, and princes, and generals, and commanders, and officers high and low. Yet the spectacle presented by the other is so much more magnificent and ineffable, that, compared to it, the court would seem to be a puppet show and child's play. You have hardly crossed the threshold when the place carries your mind up to heaven, to the King above, to the army of the angels, to the throne of the Most High, to glory unspeakable. At court it falls to the ruler's part to release one man and to put another in chains; now, the bones of the saints have not this poor and miserable authority, but a power far greater. For they call forth demons and torture them, and release from their sharpest chains those who are bound. What is more awful than this tribunal? Whilst no one is seen and no one appears by the devil's side, there are voices and convulsions, and blows and torments, and angry tongues, the devil not bearing that wonderful power. And they who carry those bodies have dominion over bodiless spirits: dust, and bones, and ashes, tear those invisible beings into pieces. So it is that no man would ever go a long journey to see royal palaces, whilst many kings have often travelled far for this spectacle. For the testimony of the saints furnishes a likeness and a symbol of the judgment to come, devils are punished, men are chastised and set free. See you the power of the saints even when they are dead, and the weakness of sinners even whilst living? Fly therefore from evil, that you may have dominion over these, and pursue goodness with all zeal. For, if things so wonderful take place here, judge what it will be like hereafter.

. . . .

PART III.

PERSONAL.

To Innocent, Bishop of Rome.[1]

To my most reverend Lord, and the most religious Bishop Innocent, John sends greeting in the Lord.

I think that before the reception of our letters your Piety will have heard of the iniquitous deed which has been attempted here; for the enormity of the evil has allowed scarcely a part of the world to be in ignorance of this direful tragedy. Report, carrying news of what has taken place to the farthest extremities of the earth, has everywhere called forth much wailing and lamentation. Since, however, it is not a question of tears alone, but of setting things straight and trying to find out how this most cruel tempest inflicted on the Church is to be stayed, I deem it necessary to urge my most

---

[1] Benedictine Edition, tom. iii., p. 515. St. Chrysostom wrote this letter, A.D. 404, before his second exile, from which he never returned. Copies of it were sent to the Archbishops of Milan and Aquileia.

honoured and reverend lords and bishops Demetrius, Pansophius, Pappo, and Eugenius to give up their own affairs, to brave the seas, and to set out on a long journey, and to hasten to your Charity, so that, when you have been clearly informed of all things, a remedy may be more speedily applied. With these we shall send the most esteemed and beloved of the deacons, Paul and Cyriacus. And I myself in the shape of a letter will inform your Charity briefly of what has taken place. Theophilus, being bishop of Alexandria, and certain men setting our most religious emperor against him, he was ordered to come here alone. Accompanied by not a few Egyptian bishops, he makes his appearance, as if wishing from the first to show that he comes to war and to fight us. Then, when he had arrived at great and heaven-favoured Constantinople, he did not come to the cathedral according to custom and old-established usage, nor did he visit us, nor did he take part in sermon, prayer, or communion, but on disembarking he passed by the vestibule of the church and established himself at a distance from the city, although we repeatedly invited him and those with him to stay with us, for lodgings and everything else needful for him were in readiness; neither they nor he would hear of it. Seeing this, I was much perplexed, not being able to imagine the cause of this unjust enmity. Still, we did our part and what was incumbent on us for them, and continually invited him to meet us and to say why he had thus made a quarrel with us from the very first and brought discord into so great a city. As he would not explain the reason, and as his accusers were urgent, our most religious emperor summoned us. He ordered me forthwith to go to the place where Theophilus was, and to hear the case against him. His accusers were urging assaults, and slaughterings, and numberless other things. We, however, who know the laws of our fathers, and reverence and honour the man, and having his own letters, too, to show that causes should not be carried out of their proper jurisdiction, but that matters concerning the province should be concluded in the province, did not accept the task of judging him, but declined with much firmness. He, on the contrary, adding to his previous conduct, summoned our archdeacon most peremptorily, as if the church were already widowed and without a bishop, and through him gained all the clergy to his side. So the churches became deserted, abandoned in each case by the clergy, who were preparing to take action against us and to accuse us. This done, he sent to summon us into court, though he had not cleared himself from the charges made against him, which was manifestly against every canon and every law. Now, we, knowing perfectly well that we were invited, not to a court of justice, or we would have gone a thousand times over, but to a foe and an enemy, as subsequent events, no less than what had already taken place, have proved, sent to him Demetrius, bishop of Pessinus, Eulysius, bishop of Apamea, and Lupicinus, bishop of Appiaria, and the priests Germanus and Severus, who made careful answer as befitting us, saying that we refused not judgment, but an outspoken enemy and a declared foe. For how is the man who, without receiving a charge against me, has so acted from the first, and held himself aloof from church communion and prayers, and incited accusers, who has gained the clergy to himself and emptied the cathedral, how is he fit to mount the judge's throne which is not his in any sort of way? For it does not belong to Egypt to sit in judgment on Thrace, when, too, he of Egypt is under accusation and a declared enemy. Yet he showed no regard to us, being bent on carrying out his own purposes, though we showed that we were equal to defend ourself before a hundred or a thousand bishops, and to prove ourself innocent, as we are; but he would not abide it. Now, in our absence, while we were demanding a synod and seeking judgment, not avoiding a hearing but open enmity, he received accusers, absolved those excommunicated by me, and took information from those very men who had not cleared themselves of charges, and had it written down officially, all which acts are against the ordinary course of custom and canon law. Why need I go on? He left nothing untried until he had cast us out with a high hand both from the city and the Church, and this late in the evening, all the people pressing after us. I was taken and carried off by the *curiosus*[1] in the midst of the city, thrown into a ship, and I sailed through the night, all this because I had demanded a synod for my just hearing. Who could listen to all this with dry eyes, however stony his heart? But, as I said, we need not only to grieve for the evil accomplished, we must also remedy it, and therefore I appeal to your Charity to stand by us and sorrow with us, and to do everything you can that it may go no further. For their illegal proceedings did not stop here, but were aggravated by others besides their former ones. When our most religious emperor turned them out of the church which they had shamefully usurped, and many bishops present seeing their iniquity, and flying from their approach as from a fire consuming everything, retired into their own dioceses, we at last were recalled to the city, and to the church from which we had been impiously cast out: more than thirty bishops brought us back, our most religious emperor sending a notary for the purpose, but he (Theophilus) took immediate flight. For what reason? Because, when we came back, we entreated our most religious emperor to call a synod to avenge what had taken place. Conscious, therefore, of his deeds, and fearing to be convicted, the imperial letters having been sent to all parts, calling all together, he threw himself in the dead of the night

---

[1] The *Curiosi* were officers whose business it was to pursue crime and treason of all kinds, and to summon and denounce the guilty to the emperor.—*Benedictine's note.*

into a little boat, and thus escaped, taking all his party with him. But we in the security of our conscience did not desist from entreating our most religious emperor as before, who with a kindness worthy of him sent for him again from Egypt, and for those with him, that they might give an account of what had taken place, and that he might not suppose the iniquitous attempt made by a party in our absence, in the face of all canon law, should be a sufficient excuse for himself. Yet he did not heed the imperial letters, but stayed at home, alleging the sedition of the people, and the untimely zeal of some who, forsooth, were opposing him, although before the imperial letters this same people had rained down accusations against him. However, we will not now enter into these things, but we have said this much, wishing to show that he was caught in the act of plotting. Moreover, after this, we did not rest, but demanded a judgment founded on enquiry and answer, for I said we were prepared to show ourself free from blame, and them most guilty. For certain Syrians who had been with him at that time were left here, and they had taken part in all his proceedings. These we approached in our readiness for judgment, and often repeated our demand, asking for the documents or heads of accusation, or to be told the nature of the grievance against us, or who the accusers are. We could obtain none of these things, and again we were thrust out of the see. How shall I narrate what then happened—an unequalled tragedy? What words will suffice? What ear will listen untroubled? Whilst we made the same offer, as I was saying, a great military force collected on the great Sabbath [1] itself, and we going into the church as the evening was drawing on, they tore by force all our clergy from our side, and surrounded the sanctuary with armed men. The women in the sacred building, who had undressed for baptism at that very time, fled away without their clothes in fear at this terrible invasion. Nor were they allowed to cover themselves as much as womanly decency would require, but many of them were wounded and thrust outside, the fonts were filled with blood, and the sacred waters polluted. Yet the evil did not stop even here. Proceeding to where the holy elements were reserved, the soldiers, amongst whom some were known to me as not Christians,[2] looked at everything within the veil (τὰ ἔνδον), and as it happens in a great tumult, the most sacred Blood of Christ was spilt upon those soldiers, and as in a barbarian captivity, everything was dared. The people fled into solitude, and the multitude passed their time outside the city, and the churches at so great a feast became empty, and more than forty bishops, our companions, with people and clergy, went into hiding

---

[1] Holy Saturday.

[2] Uninitiated (ἀμύητοι ἦσαν), to speak the language of that day.

for no cause. The sighs and groans and bitter tears called forth by these misfortunes filled marketplaces, and houses, and deserts, and every part of the city. Through the extreme wickedness of the deed, not the sufferers alone, but also those who were not sufferers in this way, sympathised with us: not the orthodox alone, but heretics, and Jews, and heathens. There was everywhere trouble, and agitation, and grief, as if the city had been taken by storm. And these things were attempted against the intention of our most religious emperor, at nightfall, by the machinations of bishops, who, in many instances, led the troops, and were not ashamed to have the attendance of civil officers instead of deacons. When day came the whole city was transported beyond the walls, under trees, and in valleys, finishing the feast like straying sheep.

You will be able to surmise the rest, for, as I said, it is impossible to repeat word for word what has taken place in each case. What is so grievous is that evils so great and crying have not yet come to an end, and that there is no hope of liberation. On the contrary, they increase day by day, and we have become a laughing-stock to many. Or rather, no man laughs, however unrighteous he may be, for all men are in tears, as I have said, at this recent iniquity, which is the climax of misfortune. What if we were to speak of the troubles of the other churches? —for the evil was not restricted to Constantinople, but spread to the East. For just as inflammation which begins in the head corrupts all the members, so now iniquities arising from the fountainhead, as it were, of this great city, have opened the door to a general agitation. Everywhere priests are against bishops, bishops against bishops, and people divided against themselves, whilst others are brooding sedition: badness is growing apace, and the whole world is overturned. When you learn all this, my most honoured and religious Lord, show forth a courage and zeal befitting you, that so great a flood of iniquity against the churches may be stemmed. For if this custom should obtain, and anyone who wishes it should be allowed free ingress into the dioceses of others at so great a distance, to thrust out those whom he chooses, to act on his own authority, as it pleases himself, understand that all things will be dissolved, that the whole world will be involved in irremediable war, every man fighting everyone else. Now, in order that so great a destruction should not overwhelm all things under the sun, I beseech you to enjoin by letter that what has been iniquitously perpetrated against us in our absence, and by one party, whilst we did not refuse judgment, may have no force, as indeed it has none by its very nature, and that those who are thus convicted may be subjected to the penalty of ecclesiastical laws. With regard to ourself, who have been neither condemned nor convicted, we ask you for the continued benefit of your letters and of your charity, and of everything else which we previously enjoyed. If they who have been so guilty would even now allege charges by reason of which they iniquitously cast us out, not telling us of the accusations nor making charges against us, the accusers not appearing, let us have an impartial judge, and we will submit ourselves to his sentence and prove ourself guiltless of what is brought against us, as indeed we are. Their recent deeds are against all propriety and every law and ecclesiastical canon. And why do I speak of ecclesiastical canon? Not even in secular tribunals have such things been ever attempted, nay, not amongst barbarians: neither Scythians nor Sauromites have ever given sentence for one party alone, in the absence of the accused, who was refusing, not judgment, but hatred, demanding a thousand judges, declaring himself innocent, ready to clear himself from charges in the face of the world, and showing that he is blameless in everything. Considering all this, and learning things more clearly from my lords and most religious brethren, the bishops, I beseech you show us that zeal which becomes your office. Thus you will rejoice not us alone, but all churches in general, and you will be rewarded by God, Who does all things for their peace. Farewell, and pray for me, most honoured and holy Lord.

Letter addressed to some Imprisoned Bishops and Priests, a.d. 404.

(Benedictine Edition, cxviii., t. iii., p. 689.)

You are dwelling in a prison and are in chains, and are shut up with unclean and filthy men: who could be more blessed than you on this account? Who wears on his head so noble a golden crown as he whose right hand is fettered for God? What dwelling-place so vast and splendid as a prison full of gloom, and dirt, and ill smells, and tribulation for the same cause? Rejoice, therefore, exult, you are crowned, be glad that these sad occurrences are the means of procuring you immense riches. This is the seed full of unspeakable promise; this is the combat which is secure of victory and reward; this is the voyage productive of a rich return. With these things in your minds, my most honoured and religious lords, rejoice and be of good cheer, cease not to give praise to God in all circumstances. You are inflicting severe blows on the devil, and laying up to yourselves a great reward in heaven. *For the sufferings of this time are not worthy to be compared to the glory to come which shall be revealed in you.* Pray write to me often. I desire most earnestly to receive letters from men who are in chains for God's sake, telling me of your sufferings, and even in a strange land I shall be greatly consoled by their perusal.

To the Priests and Monks Theodotus, Nicholas, and Cherea. Written from his Exile at Kucusus, a.d. 405.

(Benedictine Edition, cxlvi., t. iii., p. 685.)

You allege the incursion of the Isaurians as the cause of your absence, but I look upon you as present and myself as with you, and see no obstacle in this against your arrival. For such are the wings of charity that they fly swiftly and with great alacrity in every direction, in spite of a thousand impediments. But if I am deprived of your bodily presence, cease not from prayer, and our merciful God will grant it us. Since I too, bearing you constantly in my mind, long for a sight of you in the flesh, and I know that I shall have this too, as you are earnestly beseeching Him Who can do all things to break up the winter and to establish peace everywhere. Now, to gladden you with news of myself, I am enjoying much quiet and leisure. And although many things disturb my health, as, for instance, the absence of physicians and the want of necessaries (for there are no shops here and no drugs), a bad climate (for the summer tries me no less than the winter, by its excessive heat as opposed to the cold), a siege severe and constant, with perpetual fears of incursions from the Isaurians,—in spite, I say, of all this and much more which is undermining my strength whilst recovering from that great danger and severe illness, I am fairly well. Do not fail to write to me often, and to tell me how you yourselves are. For I view your affection as a great consolation and encouragement, as a treasure producing a multitude of good things. And whenever I think about your own state, your steadfast heart, your strong and enduring love, I cannot put it out of my mind. I take refuge in the thought as in a spacious and calm harbour away from the surging waves of tribulation.

To some Priests and Monks in Phœnicia, who were Instructing Heathens.

(From Kucusus, A.D. 405. cxxiii., t. iii., p. 663.)

Pilots, when they see the ocean stirred up from its depths, and a heavy storm and disturbance, not only do not desert the vessel, but show greater industry and more willingness by watching themselves and rousing the others. And physicians, too, when they see that the fever is active and very high, not only do not leave the sick man to himself, but then especially do all they can, and show a greater diligence and readiness both through others and through themselves so as to overcome the disease. Why do I say this? That no one of you through the disturbance which has taken place should desire to leave Phœnicia and to come here for quiet. The more the trials, the angrier the waves, the heavier the trouble, the greater the reason for your staying in readiness, and watchfulness, and diligence, showing forth more eagerness, so that your fine house may not fall, nor your labour be in vain, nor the fruits of your agriculture disappear. For God is able to quell the disturbance and to reward your patience. When things run smoothly our reward is not so great as it is for you now when there is much difficulty, great agitation, and when many are scandalised. Considering, therefore, the work done, and the labour surmounted, and the good works which you have accomplished, and that by the grace of God you have conquered impiety to a certain extent, that things in Phœnicia had come to improve, that your reward and crown are now greater, that God will remove obstacles before long and give you many compensations for your patience, stand fast and endure. Even now you should not want for anything, but it was my command that you should have the same plenty and abundance, whether in clothes, or shoes, or food, as the brethren. If I, who am in so much tribulation and affliction in a solitude of Kucusus, take your good deeds so much to heart, how much should you, who are enjoying great plenty, do your part, as far as necessity allows you. I repeat, then, let no one frighten you, for things gave good promise, and this you may ascertain from the answers sent by his Reverence the priest Constantine. If you remain, be there a thousand obstacles, you will overcome them all. There is nothing equal to patience and endurance; it is like a rock. In truth, those disturbances and plottings against Churches are like waves beating against a rock, dissolving in their own foam. Consider what the blessed Apostles suffered, both from their own people and from strangers; how during all their time of preaching they passed through temptations, and dangers, and plottings, and were consumed by prisons, and chains, and stripes, and hunger, and nakedness. Still, dwelling in those very prisons, they did not relinquish the stewardship entrusted to them. Blessed Paul, in his prison, scourged, covered with blood, fastened to the wood, in the midst of all this suffering. gave instruction, baptised his jailor, and left nothing unturned. Pondering on all this, according to my counsel, stand bravely and without flinching, with your hope on God and on His help, which is before everything, and be careful to let me have a detailed answer. On this account I have sent the priest John, that he may quiet your minds, and not suffer you to be disturbed by anyone. I have done my part, encouraging you by words, exhorting you by advice, and offering you plenty of necessaries, so that you may want for nothing.

. . . .

To Studius, the Prefect of the City, on the Death of his Brother.

(From Kucusus, A.D. 404. Benedictine Edition, cxcvii., t. iii., p. 710.)

I know that you have understanding and can reason, and that before my letter reaches you you will have heard in meekness of your happy brother's departure, for I would not call it death. Now, since we, too, must do our part, I invite you, my most honoured Lord, to show yourself as you are at this time; not that you should not grieve, for this is impossible, being a man clothed in flesh and looking in vain for such a brother, but that you should restrain your sorrow. You know the perishableness of human things, how worldly business is like flowing rivers, and how we should call blessed only those who depart this life with good hope. They go not to death, but from combat to rewards, from wrestlings to crowns, from a storm-tossed sea to a calm harbour. Pondering on these things, be consoled, since my own grief is not small, and we have a sovereign consolation in it—his goodness, which, I think, must offer you true solace. If the departed had been bad and full of evil, we ought to weep and mourn for him; but being what he was, after a life of mildness and goodness, as all the city knew it to be, fearing what was just, showing a fitting courage, independence, and fortitude, despising present things, a stranger to worldly cares, we should rejoice with him and with you that you have sent before you *this* brother, who may place the treasure which was his on his departure in a sure and safe place. Do not, then, my most honoured Lord, have any thoughts unworthy of yourself, or be broken by grief, but show now what you are, and let me see for my comfort that even *my* letter has done something for you. So, at our great distance from each other, I shall be proud to have overcome much of your sadness by a mere letter.

To Malchus on the Death of his Daughter.

(Μαλχῳ, lxxi., t. iii., p. 632.)

Do not be sad; do not put down the beautiful death of your happy daughter to your sins. She has reached the waveless shore and come to everlasting life. Removed from the troubled waters of this present life, she stands upon the rock, and whatever good things she has gathered together, those she holds as a most secure treasure. You should rejoice and exult and be glad that, like an intelligent gardener gathering the ripe fruit, you have offered her soul to the common Lord of all. Applying the remedy of such thoughts as these to yourself and to my most honoured lady, her mother, increase the reward reserved to you under these circumstances, so that not only on account of her excellent early training, but also for humbly and thankfully bearing her happy departure hence, you may receive a great crown from our merciful God.

To Olympias, a.d. 404.

(*On the Virginal Life*, ii., t. iii., p. 542.)

. . . . . .

Virginity is so great a thing, and requires so much labour, that when Christ had come down from heaven in order to make men angels, and to sow the heavenly life on earth, He did not venture even then to enjoin it or to make a law of it, but He *did* teach death to self, than which there is nothing harder. He taught men to crucify themselves, always to do good to their enemies, yet He did not make a law of virginity. He left it to the free-will of His hearers, saying, *Let him who can, take it.* It is a weighty undertaking : it has arduous wrestlings with the sweat of combat, and its path is rugged and precipitous. This is plainly shown by those in the Old Law, who were full of good deeds. For Moses, that great man who summed up the prophets in his person, the intimate friend of God, who enjoyed so much favour with Him as to be able to snatch six hundred thousand from the chastisement of a divine stroke, and was so great as to command the sea, who parted the ocean, drew water from the rock, and transformed the atmosphere, who changed the Nile's waters into blood, who opposed Pharaoh with an army of frogs and locusts, and changed the whole face of creation, and worked a thousand other wonders, and many virtuous deeds,—for he was remarkable in every way,—yet he could not even look at *these* wrestlings, but needed marriage and the society of his wife, with its security. He dared not launch himself on the ocean of virginity fearing its waves. Then there was the patriarch who immolated his son and was strong enough to tread upon the most tyrannical of nature's feelings. He had courage to sacrifice his son, that son being Isaac, in the bloom of his age, in the very flower of his youth, his own and only-begotten son, vouchsafed to him contrary to all hope, and full of righteousness, his one stay in his old age. He it was who led this son forth to the mountain for that consummation, and prepared the altar and laid the wood upon it, who placed the victim in readiness, and drew the sword and held it to his son's neck. For he who was of adamant, or rather harder than adamant, both held him for slaughter and drew the knife. He who was thus firm by nature increased his natural fortitude by the mortification of his will, and gave proof of angelical calmness in his deeds. Yet the man who could encounter so great a battle, and go beyond nature itself, dared not face the combats of virginity. He also dreaded its wrestlings, and took to himself the comfort of marriage.

. . . .

THE BLESSEDNESS OF SUFFERING.

(*To Olympias*, A.D. 404 or 405. Ὀλυμπιάδι, xvii., t. iii., p. 604.)

Nothing strange or out of the way is happening to you, but it is extremely fitting and proper that the strength of your spirit should be increased by constant temptations, and your fervour and power in combat become greater, and that you should reap therefrom much sweetness. It is the nature of tribulation, when it encounters a brave and ardent soul, to bring about these results. And as the fire refines gold by its action, so does tribulation purify and refine golden souls. Therefore Paul says, *Tribulation worketh patience and patience probation.* Hence, I too am in joy and gladness, and in this vast solitude am consoled by this fortitude of yours. Therefore, even if thousands of wolves hem you in and endless evil plottings, I have no fear; but it is my prayer that present temptation may pass away and that you may not encounter others, thus fulfilling the divine law, which bids us pray not to fall into temptation. And if, perchance, it should happen again, I have confidence in your soul of gold, and in the great riches which you would gain for yourself. With what threat will they who act against their own interests be able to frighten you? By loss of money? But this, I know well, is like smoke in your eyes, and is accounted more worthless than mud by the way. Is it by exile from home and country? But you are able to live in great and populous cities as well as in deserts, and to pass your time in peace and quiet, and to put away worldly visions. Or do they threaten you with death? This, too, has been always in your thoughts, and if they should drag you to execution they will find a dead body in their hands. Why need I say more? No one will be able to do anything to you which you have not already borne with much patience. You, who have ever walked on a steep and thorny path, have accustomed yourself to all these things; you, who have shown consummate skill under training, now appear more radiant in the combat: not only are you not troubled by what has taken place, but you are soaring above the earth and rejoicing. You are glad to have a part now in those combats for which you had prepared yourself, and this in your woman's body, which is weaker than a spider's web. Whilst men are raging and gnashing their teeth, you are treading their madness under foot in much cheerfulness, and you would be ready to suffer many more things than they could prepare against you. Blessed and thrice-blessed are you by reason of the crowns to come, or rather by those very wrestlings. For these struggles, even before the reward, and in the oppression of the fight, have their present rewards, and compensations, and sweetness; they have contentedness, and fortitude, and steadfastness, and patience in making you invincible, unconquerable, far above all; they so exercise you that you can suffer no evil from anyone, and make you stand upon the rock in spite of angry waves, and bear a furious ocean with great peacefulness. These are the rewards of tribulation, even before the kingdom of heaven. I know that, already, you account yourself divested of the body, on the wings of sweetness, but that if called upon you would put it off more easily than others do the clothes which they wear. Rejoice, then, and be glad both over yourself and over those who die the blessed death, who die not in their bed, not in their houses, but in prisons, and chains, and torments. Grieve only for the doers of these things, and weep for them: this is worthy of your virtue. Since you wish to hear about my bodily health, I have so far got rid of the illness which troubled me and am better now, if only winter when it comes does not affect my weakness of stomach. We are also in perfect security from Isaurian invasions.

To Olympias.

(From Arabissus, A.D. 406. Ὀλυμπιάδι, xv., t. iii., p. 601.)

Would you, who have given proof of so much mortification from your youth upwards, and have trodden human pride under foot, expect to live a quiet life without combat? How should this be? For if men who are fighting other men receive a thousand wounds in combats and wars, you who have been armed against principalities, and powers, and the lords of darkness in this world, against spiritual forces of wickedness, who have fought thus valiantly, and set up victorious trophies, and thus vexed the devil,—how should you hope to lead a peaceful and untroubled life? Therefore you should not be disquieted because battles, and agitation, and fears assail you on every side. You should wonder, on the contrary, if none of these things came to pass. Labour and peril are the lot of goodness. You knew this well enough before my letter, and do not need to learn it from others. I write this, then, since I am not instructing one who is ignorant. For we know that neither banishment from our country nor the loss of money, though insupportable to most men—neither contempt nor any other suffering of the kind, will be able to disturb you. For if the companions of those who have suffered these things have become enviable, how much more those who are actually suffering them? Therefore, on both accounts, Paul proclaims believers amongst the Hebrews, saying: *Call to mind the former days, wherein, being illuminated, you endured a great fight of afflictions, and on the one hand, indeed, by reproaches and tribulations, were made a gazing-stock, and on the other became companions of them that were used in such sort.* Therefore, there is no need for *me* to write a long letter. No man, indeed, goes to offer assistance to a conqueror who holds a splendid trophy of victory in his hands, but only praise. I, too, know how much interior spirit you have shown in what has befallen you. I account you blessed, and admire you for your patience in the present, as well as for the rewards which it will bring to you. I am well aware, however, that you wish to hear how I am getting on, for I have been silent for a very long time. I have thrown off the violence of my illness, but still feel its effects. I have had excellent physicians, yet the want of necessaries destroys the good of my cure. For not only are there no remedies here, and no one of the things required for a suffering body, but both famine and pestilence are imminent.

. . . .

To Pœanius. 'Glory be to God in all things.'

(A.D. 404. Παιανίῳ, cxciii., tom. iii., p. 708.)

You greatly refreshed me and made me rejoice, when, in telling me of your misfortunes, you added the word, which we should always say in everything befalling us: 'Glory be to God in all things'. This is a stroke which hits the devil in the right place; this is great security and happiness in every danger to the man who utters it. In giving voice to it, dark despondency vanishes. Cease not, then, from saying it and from teaching it to others. Thus a destructive storm, even should it increase in fury, will be changed into peace; thus the storm-tossed will reap a greater reward, whilst they are also removed from evils. This it was which crowned Job; this word overthrew the devil, and made him retire in confusion; this removes all anxiety. Continue, therefore, to use it on all occasions. Let no one be in trouble about this place. For if Kucusus be indeed a solitude, I enjoy much quiet there, and I have been able to cure a large part of the no small infirmity contracted through weakness on my journey, by sitting constantly in the house.

. . . .

Vanity of Vanities.

(Homily on Eutropius,[1] Benedictine Edition, tom. iii., p. 381.)

At all times, but especially now, it is pertinent to say, *Vanity of vanities, and all is vanity.* Where is now that splendid consulship, those magnificent torches and applauding assemblies, those balls and banquets and stately feasts? Where are those crowns and curtains, those gatherings of a whole city, the cheerings of amphitheatres, the flatteries of crowded houses? All these things have vanished: a mighty gale has blown down the leaves, and shown us a naked tree, one shaken from its foundations. Such has been the force of the wind that, after sapping the tree's life, it threatens to tear it up by the roots. Where are now those false friends, and those drinking parties and banquets? Where are those swarms of parasites, that wine which never ceased flowing all day long, those wonderful dishes produced by the cooks, those servants of the consulate,—all those who spoke and acted to curry favour? They were a night's dream, and they vanished with the daylight; they were spring blossoms scorched by summer heat: they were passing shadows, dissolving smoke, bubbles which have burst, a cobweb torn away.

---

[1] Eutropius, the eunuch, the unworthy minister of the emperor, who had attempted to take away the right of asylum from the Church, fell suddenly, and fled for refuge to the altar of the cathedral. On this occasion Chrysostom defended him from the angry people and the soldiers sent to apprehend him.

Therefore I would put before you the frequent use of those spiritual words: *Vanity of vanities, all is vanity.*

These are words which should be engraved on walls, on clothes, on the market-place, in dwelling-houses, by the wayside, on doors and thresholds, and, most of all, in the conscience of each one of us, which we should regard through everything, since trickery and masks and hypocrisy seem to be truth amongst the majority of men. These are words which every man should speak to his neighbour both at the morning and the evening meal, and at meetings, and which he should hear from others: *Vanity of vanities, and all is vanity.* Was I not always telling you that riches are fleeting? You would not believe me. Did I not tell you that wealth is an arrogant companion? You would not be persuaded. Now, a personal experience has shown you that it is not only fleeting, not only arrogant, but also murderous, for it has caused your fear and trembling at this hour. Did I not tell you, when you so often reproached me for speaking the truth to your face, that I loved you better than your flatterers? Am not I, your reprover, in greater trouble about you than those who fawned upon you? Did I not add to these words that the wounds inflicted by a friend are more to be trusted than the kisses of enemies? If you had borne my wounds those kisses of theirs would not now have brought forth death, for *my* wounds work health, whereas their kisses prepared a fatal disease! Where are now your cup-bearers?

Where are those who cleared the market-place before you, and who were full of your praises in the crowd? They have fled, and given up your friendship; they provide for their own safety at the cost of your agony. It is not so with us, but we would not be rebuffed even when you did not want us, and now that you have fallen we stand by you and protect you. That Church, which was warred upon by you, has opened her heart to receive you; whereas those fostered theatres, which you often fought us about, have delivered you up to destruction. Still we ceased not to say, 'Why do you act thus? You rage against the Church and are walking towards a precipice,' and you heeded nothing. Yet the races, those squanderers of your wealth, have sharpened their sword against you, whilst the Church, the object of your unseemly wrath, hastens to meet you, wishing to rescue you from their wiles.

I say these things now, not desiring to insult the fallen, but in order to increase the security of those who have not fallen: not to tear open the sores of the wounded, but to maintain in sound health those who are not wounded: not to shipwreck the man tossed by the waves, but to warn those who are sailing in calm seas so that they may avoid sinking. How can this be done? By taking to heart the vicissitudes of human things. For if *this* man had feared a change of fortune, it would not have come upon him, but neither his own lot nor that of others improved him: now do you who are nursing your riches gather your lesson from this man's misfortune, for nothing is more insecure than human things. Consequently, if a man were to call them neediness itself, he would say less than the truth, whether he liken them to smoke or mire, or a dream, or spring blossoms, or anything else, so perishable are they, and so less than nothing. That nothingness has indeed much that is insecure is evident from this: who was ever a mightier man than he? Did he not surpass the whole world by his wealth? Did he not rise to the height of honours? Did not all men hold him in fear and awe? Yet see, he is more miserable than slaves, and more to be pitied than menials, in greater want than the poor who are pinched with hunger, having before his eyes day by day swords pointed at him, and dungeons and executioners, and the road leading to death. Nor does he enjoy the memory of his past pleasure, nor is he conscious even of the light; but in the midst of day, as if in darkest night, encompassed by anguish, he is deprived of his sight. Try as I will, however, I cannot measure that suffering by words, which delivers him up to an hourly expectation of death. But what need is there of our words since he bears them distinctly written on himself for us, as if engraven on a statue? For yesterday men came to him from the imperial court, wishing to drag him away by force, and he took refuge amongst the sacred vessels: he looked already nothing better than a dead man, his teeth were chattering, his whole body shivering and trembling, his voice was broken, his tongue faltering, and he himself as if the life in him had turned to stone.

I say these things, not in scorn nor in reproach at his misfortune, but in the wish to soften your judgment, and to enkindle your pity, and to persuade you to be satisfied with the chastisement already inflicted. For there are amongst you many inhuman men who would even reproach me for receiving him at the sanctuary. I should desire to soften their cruelty by dwelling on the sufferings of this man. Why do you reproach me, beloved brethren? Because, you say, he who warred incessantly against the Church has found shelter in it. For this very reason you should have praised God the more for allowing him to fall into a need so great as to learn both the power and the kindness of the Church: the power, on the one hand, to outlive so overwhelming a reverse inflicted by his enemies, and the kindness with which she who was persecuted extends her shield, and covers him with her own wings, putting him in perfect security, and bearing no memory of former things, but opening her heart to him with the most tender love. This is more wonderful than any trophy, this is a magnificent victory: by this the heathen is converted and even the Jew put to shame: this it is which shows forth the brightness of her countenance; that, taking her foe captive, she spares him; that whereas all men forsake him, she alone, as a tender mother, hides him in her own sanctuary curtains, and encounters imperial wrath, an angry populace, a boundless hatred, on his account. This is the altar's adornment. What adornment is it, you ask, that the man who is abominable, and avaricious, and cursed, should touch the altar? Speak not thus, since the harlot too touched the feet of Christ, and she was indeed full of sin and impurity, yet it was no reproach to Jesus, but a great wonder and song of praise, for she who was unclean did not defile the Holy One; on the contrary, He, the Good and the Pure, made that abandoned harlot clean through His touch. Do not bear malice, O man. We are servants of Him Who was crucified, and Who said, *Forgive them, for they know not what they do.* 'But,' you say, 'it was he who, by various laws and regulations, cut off flight to the altar.' Consider, then, that experience has taught him the value of his own action, and he himself has been the first to break the law which he made. He has become a spectacle to the world, and in his silence he raises a voice of warning to all men, 'Do not likewise, that you may not suffer in like manner'. Through his misfortune he has become a teacher, and through it the altar sends forth a great radiance. It is now especially terrible, and evident to all men, because it holds the lion in chains. The royal statue would be greatly adorned, not so much by depicting the king as he sits on the throne, clothed in purple, and wearing his crown, as by barbarians under the royal feet, with their hands tied behind them and their faces to the ground. You yourselves, in your eagerness to come here, can testify that he has spoken no word, for indeed the spectacle before us to-day is noteworthy, and I see here as many people collected together as in the holy Easter festival. He in his silence has called them; his deeds have spoken louder than the voice of a trumpet. You have come here, virgins from your chambers, women from your drawing-rooms, men leaving the marketplace deserted, that you may contemplate human nature convicted, and see the perishableness of earthly things laid bare, the shameful spectacle of that which was yesterday, and but lately so brilliant. So much for the success born of avarice, which is more shamefaced than any old woman's blotches: the change of fortune has passed over it like a sponge, and wiped away both paint and titles.

Such is the power of this catastrophe: it has made him who was conspicuous and illustrious now appear more miserable than all. If the rich man come in, he will be taught much, for, contemplating him, who had the whole world at his command, thrown down from so mighty a height, trodden under foot, fallen lower than a hare or a frog, fastened without chains to this pillar, and done to death by fear in his anguish though unfettered, he restrains his wrath, humbles his pride, and draws that lesson of wisdom which it behoves him to draw, from human things, and so goes away, learning by facts what the Scripture speaks of in the words, *All flesh is grass, and all human glory as the flower of the field,* that the grass has been burnt up and the flower thrown away: that man shall be burnt up as swiftly as grass, and trodden under foot as quickly as the flower of the field: that our days are like smoke, and so on. In his turn, the poor man comes in, and, gazing at this spectacle, he does not despair of himself, nor is he afflicted at his own poverty, but he is thankful to his neediness for providing him with a place of refuge, and a calm harbour, and a wall of strength. And often, seeing these things, he would prefer to remain where he is, rather than to have all things for a short time, and then to be in danger of his life. See you how this man's flight hither is no small advantage to the rich and poor alike, to small people and great people, to bondsmen and freemen? See how each one has gone away with his own lesson drawn from the sight alone? Now, have I succeeded in softening your passion and putting an end to your anger? Have I extinguished your inhumanity and enkindled sympathy within you? Indeed, I think so, for your faces show it, and your tears. If, then, your stony hearts have been softened and mellowed, put forth also the fruit of alms-giving, and, showing the ear of sympathy, let us solicit the emperor, or rather let us call upon our merciful God to mitigate the emperor's wrath, and to make him kind, so that he may grant us a full pardon. Already, indeed, since the day of his flight, there has been no small change; for when the emperor learnt that he had taken refuge in this place, in the presence of the soldiers who were incited against his crimes and preparing to put him to death, he made a long speech. In it he quieted their anger, alleging not only this man's delinquencies, but giving him credit for whatever good he had done, and calling upon them to show him mercy in the one case, and in the other to pardon him as a man. Upon their again urging him to avenge the insulter of the emperor, crying out, stamping with their feet, threatening him with death, and brandishing their spears, he drew floods of tears from the driest eyes, and, reminding them of the sacred table to which he had fled, he put an end to their anger.

Let us, then, do our part also, for what excuse would you have if the emperor, when insulted, bears no malice, and you who are not insulted should be thus angry? How, when this spectacle is removed, would you approach the mysteries and recite that prayer in which we are commanded to say, 'Forgive us our trespasses as we forgive those who have trespassed against us,' whilst you are calling for revenge against *your* trespassers? Did he commit great injustice and look down upon all? I do not deny it, but this is no time for judgment, this is the time for mercy; not for chastisement, but for kindness; not for examination, but for concession; not for strict justice, but for pity and kindness. Therefore, let no man be wrathful nor discontented; rather let us supplicate our merciful God to grant him a period of life, and to snatch him from impending death, so that he may redeem his transgressions. Let us go together to our merciful emperor, entreating him, by the Church and by the altar, to release that one man who is seeking refuge at the sacred table. If we do this, the emperor too will approve, and God will ratify the emperor's decision, and He will give us a great reward for our mercy. For in proportion as He turns away from the hard and inhuman man, and hates him, so does He protect and cherish the kind and merciful man. If he be a just man also, God holds brighter crowns in reserve for him: if he has sinned, He overlooks his iniquities, and gives him this great reward for his kindness to his fellow-man. *I desire mercy and not sacrifice*, He says. And everywhere in the Scripture you find Him seeking for this and saying that it is the remission of sins. So, then, we shall make Him merciful to ourselves, and atone for our own sins. Thus we shall adorn the Church, and win the applause of our merciful emperor, as I was saying, and all the people will rejoice: the ends of the earth will be in admiration at the kind and gentle spirit of our city, and throughout the whole world those who hear what has taken place will sing our praises. In order that we may enjoy these goods, let us fall down on our knees in supplication, entreat, beseech; let us shield the captive from danger, from flight, from death, so that we ourselves may enjoy lasting goods by the grace and mercy of our Lord Jesus Christ, to Whom be glory and might, now and for ever and ever. Amen.

THE END.

INDEX.

A.

Abraham, sacrifice of, 290.
Alexander, thirteenth god, 266 ; his tomb obscure, 268.
Altar, radiance of, 301 ; fruitfulness of, 233.
Almsgiving, by words, 65 ; value of, 70 ; interest of, 71.
Angels of the mysteries, 211.
Antioch, John of, 1 ; surnamed Golden Mouth, 2.
Anthusa, St., mother of St. Chrysostom, 1.
Apostles, condition of, 102 ; victory of, 103 ; mines of, 109 ; glory of, 96.
Arcadius, emperor, 6 ; death of, 14.
Argument, an irrefutable, 98.
Arsacius, intruded into see of Constantinople, 12.

B.

Basil, friend of Chrysostom, 3.
Bond of new Covenant, 219, 220.
Blood of Our Lord, 242 ; drunk by Himself, 221.
Bread, one for all, 244.

C.

Charity not consumed, 31.
Chastisement here, 123, 124.
Children, witness of, 50.
Christ, our High Priest, 214 ; His Pasch, 229.
Christians, responsibility of, 62.
Chrysostom, government of, 8 ; expulsion of, 11 ; appeal to Pope, 12 ; at Comana, 13 ; death of, 14 ; his body translated to Constantinople—to Rome, 15 ; character of his works, 17 ; summary of, 18, 19, 20 ; his letter to Pope Innocent, 272 ; unjustly summoned into court, 275 ; thrust out of his see, 277 ; in exile, 283.

Church, invincible, 90, 190; brighter than sun, 190; heaven made for it, 192; soul's remedies in, 194; olives of, 240; vengeance of, 298; generosity of, 300.
Cities, strong walls of, 151.
Clothing Christ, 69.
Conquering by contraries, 141, 142.
Community life, 149.
Conscience, tribunal of, 122.
Constantine the Great, where buried, 269.
Crucified ever living, 267; power of, 144.

D.

Departed at the mysteries, 250, 254.
Diodorus, bishop of Tarsus, 3.
Dispositions for the mysteries, 215, 216, 238, 247.

E.

Eucharist, union of, 243; makes earth heaven, 246.
Eternity, proved by suffering, 131.
Eudoxia, empress, 9; statue to, 11; death of, 14.
Eusebius, bishop of Nicomedia, 5.
Eutropius, fall of, 296; anguish of, 299; spectacle to all men, 302.

F.

Feast of the martyrs, what, 259.
Flavian, bishop of Antioch, 4; election of, 7.
Forgiveness as we forgive, 304.
Friendships, spiritual, 48; worldly, 47.

G.

Gallic Rufinus, 8.
Gifts of God through senses, 237.
Gladness in tribulation, 126, 127.
God, good by essence, 42; His instruments, 146; His kindness, 179; His paradoxes, 32; in visible things, 120; not to be encompassed, 166.
Golden heart, 68.
Goodness, a beacon, 58, 60; voice of, 56, 57; peace of, 81.
Gospel, propagation of, 89; announcement of, 101, 104.
Gregory Nazienzen, St., 6.

H.

Heathen, argument with, 97.
Holiness everywhere possible, 78, 80.
Holy Spirit, gifts of, 34.
Holy tears, 249.
Human glory, vanity of, 296, 297.
Humble, abode of, 148.
Humility in labour, 150.

I.

In chains for Christ, 153, 154.

J.

Jews, dispersion of, 181.
Jewish sacrifice ceased, 231.
Jona, son of, 183.
Joy for faithful departed, 287.
Judas, communion of, 218.
Judgment, proved by suffering, 25.
Jurisdiction, each province its own, 274.

K.

Kindness, reward of, 305.

L.

Loss of a daughter, 288.
Love, true, 46, 140.

M.

Magi, faith of, 245.
Man made for eternity, 168; the man not the state, 79, 82.
Marriages of old, 106; money marriages, 107.
Martyrs, voice of, 261, 263; shrines of, 264, 265.
Martyrdom, the blessed death, 293.
Matthias, election of, 189.
Meletius, bishop of Antioch, 3; death of, 7.
Ministering to Christ, 75.
Miracles, spiritual, 86, 88, 175.
Mites, spiritual, 100.
Money, tyranny of, 41, 43.
More, Blessed Thomas, 262.
Mortification, happiness of, 121.

N.

Nature, good, 28.
Nova Roma, see of, 9.

O.

Oak, Synod of the, 10.
Olympias, 293; fortitude of, 294.

P.

Paschal Lamb, a figure, 230.
Patience, more than alms-giving, 135; a rock of strength, 285.
Paul and Plato, 95.
Paul, humility of, 115; chains of, 155; voice of, 223; heart of, 224, 225; Peter's companion, 227; apostolate in prison, 286.
Persecution for justice, 282.
Peter's prerogatives, 27, 184, 185; Peter scandalised, 186; before and after Resurrection, 176, 178, 187; temptation of, 196; sin of, 197; at Jerusalem, 188.
Pilots, necessity of, in storm, 284.
Plato, achievements of, 143.
Pope Innocent, protest of, 12.
Poverty, 40; voluntary, 44, 45.
Power of holy bodies, 270.
Priesthood, 202.
Priests, 195; sinners not angels, 198; spiritual generators, 201, 203; responsibility of, 205; purity required of, 206; snares of, 207, 208; rulers of the world, 209.
Priscilla and Persis, 105.
Privilege of servant, 156.
Probation, 133, 137.
Prosperity, vanity of, 303.

R.

Resurrection, proved in nature, 159, 160; by creation, 163; by human things, 165; confirmed by signs, 169, 170, 174; by faith of world, 177; same body in, 161, 162.
Riches and poverty, whence, 35, 39.
Rome, why blessed, 222.

S.

Sacrifice of new law, 199, 200, 210; for the dead, 251, 255.
Salt and light, 55.

Signs of Apostles, a testimony, 173 ; greatest of, 52, 53.
Socrates, end of, 145.
Sojourners, 72.
Sorrow, false, 253.
Soul, worth of, 99.
Stilicho, 8.
Strength in weakness, 83.
Sufferings of just, 134, 137 ; suffering its own reward, 292.

T.

Table of peace, 235, 236.
Teacher's example followed, 92.
Teaching by life, 77, 91, 93.
Temple, buyers and sellers in, 49.
Thanksgiving, 128, 129, 136, 138, 295.
The truth and the figure, 213.
Theodosius, death of, 4 ; reign of, 6.
Theophilus, patriarch of Alexandria, 5, 273, 276 ; enmity of, 9 ; summoned to Constantinople, 10 ; instigator of sacrilege, 278, 279.
Time and eternity, 33.
Timothy, 110 ; infirmities of, 111 ; advice to, 112, 113 ; diligent in fasting, 114 ; his zeal, 116.
Tongue, a hand, 64.
Touch of faith, 66.

U.

Unleavened bread, 256.

V.

Vespasian and Titus, 180.
Virginity not commanded, 289.

W.

Way, truth, and life, 23.
Wickedness, way to unbelief, 167.
Why Our Lord ate after Resurrection, 172.
Wine, gift of God, 258 ; drinking, 117, 118.
Working for eternity, 139.

Z.

Zebedee, sons of, 26.

www.ingramcontent.com/pod-product-compliance
Lightning Source LLC
Chambersburg PA
CBHW030811230426
43667CB00008B/1165